REVELATION

Revelation

Towards a Christian Interpretation of God's Self-revelation in Jesus Christ

GERALD O'COLLINS, SJ

UNIVERSITY PRESS

OXFORD
UNIVERSITY PRESS

Great Clarendon Street, Oxford, OX2 6DP,
United Kingdom

Oxford University Press is a department of the University of Oxford.
It furthers the University's objective of excellence in research, scholarship,
and education by publishing worldwide. Oxford is a registered trade mark of
Oxford University Press in the UK and in certain other countries

First Edition published in 2016
Impression: 1

Published in the United States of America by Oxford University Press
198 Madison Avenue, New York, NY 10016, United States of America

British Library Cataloguing in Publication Data
Data available

Library of Congress Control Number: 2016935482

ISBN 978–0–19–878420–3

Printed in Great Britain by
Clays Ltd, St Ives plc

Preface

Since faith is the human response to divine revelation, the classical account of theology as 'faith seeking understanding' should be expanded. Theology is 'faith in the divine self-revelation in Christ seeking understanding'. This makes it clear how revelation is a central question for Christian theologians. A well considered theology of God's self-revelation in Christ should prove a force of gravity holding together everything that follows in such particular sections as Christology, the doctrine of the Trinity, and ecclesiology.

Without an adequate view of revelation as an organizing principle, specific areas of theology will fly off uncontrollably or else collapse into each other. Witness, for example, the endemic tendency to identify divine revelation with biblical inspiration and what it produces, the Sacred Scriptures. We return below to the need to distinguish firmly between revelation, on the one hand, and biblical inspiration and the canonical Scriptures, on the other.

Up to the late 1980s, many notable contributions to a Christian theology of revelation had come from such scholars as Hans Urs von Balthasar, Karl Barth, Rudolf Bultmann, Avery Dulles, Romano Guardini, René Latourelle, H. Richard Niebuhr, Wolfhart Pannenberg, Karl Rahner, Paul Ricoeur, and Paul Tillich. Even early in the twentieth century Ernst Troeltsch could speak of an 'inflation' in theories of revelation. Since 1988, the year von Balthasar died, the more interesting reflections on revelation have been largely confined to such collections of essays as those edited by Paul Avis (1997) and by Ingolf Dalferth with Michael Rodgers (2014), and to entries in dictionaries and handbooks, like the *Dictionary of Fundamental Theology* (ed. Latourelle and Rino Fisichella, 1994) and the (five-part) entry on revelation in volume 25 of the *Theologische Realenzylopädie* (1995).

Sometimes the theme of revelation is simply left out in the cold. *The Oxford Handbook of Theology and Modern European Thought* of 2013 (ed. Nicholas Adams, George Pattison, and Graham Ward) runs to over 700 pages, includes chapters on atonement, the Bible, incarnation, and tradition, but no chapter on divine revelation, and makes only a few passing references to revelation. *The Routledge Handbook of Contemporary Philosophy of Religion* of 2015 (ed. Graham Oppy), a work of nearly 500 pages, contains no chapter on revelation and makes only four, brief references to it. Even more startling is the silence about revelation in Henry Bettenson's *Documents of the Christian Church* (4th edn, 2011). Surely the doctrine and practice of the Church should be anchored in God's self-revelation in Jesus Christ? But, while quoting ten pages from seven documents of the Second Vatican Council (1962–65), the new editor of Bettenson's work, Chris Maunder, draws nothing from *Dei Verbum*, the Dogmatic Constitution on Divine Revelation.

Some theologians fondly imagine that we are now in the age of post-foundationalism. That involves neglecting the study of revelation. It is an eminently foundational issue. Other theologians, preferring the somewhat equivalent language of 'the Word of God', have quietly dropped 'revelation'. Thus in *Beloved Community: Critical Dogmatics after Christendom* (Grand Rapids, Mich.: Eerdmans), a 2015 work of nearly 1,000 pages, Paul Hinlicky attends to 'the Word of God'. His index contains not a single reference to 'revelation'.

Those (relatively few) authors, like William Abraham, David Brown, Colin Gunton, John Haught, and Richard Swinburne, who, since the late 1980s, have set themselves to interpret divine revelation within the story of Judaism and Christianity, despite their helpful insights and judgements, have sometimes left me dissatisfied, as we will see later in this book. Matthew Levering's *Engaging the Doctrine of Revelation* (Grand Rapids, Mich.: Baker Academic, 2014) has been a happy exception. But he focuses not so much on the divine self-revelation in Jesus Christ and its essential characteristics, but on the Church's faithful mediation of the revelation and, in that context, on the inspiration and truth of Scripture.

Let me mention three questions that the limited recent literature on revelation throws open.

First, should we describe Jesus Christ as the final access to the truth about God? Surely, if we follow the lead of John's Gospel, he is not merely the final access to the truth, but is the Truth (upper case) of God in person? Secondly, the self-revelation of Christ in God comes in the course of history. Can we agree with those who maintain that historical research will never lead beyond an account of possibilities and probabilities? This background view ignores the way historians reach genuine certainties about ancient matters such as the achievements of Julius Caesar and his death in 44 BC. As regards the historical origins of Christianity, convergent evidence often supplies not only high probabilities but also genuine certainties. Thus I judge it historically certain that Jesus of Nazareth died by crucifixion around AD 30. Thirdly, contemporary authors sometimes tolerate a certain fuzziness that would, more or less, identify revelation with biblical inspiration. To be sure, they are related, but identifying them, as we shall see, is a false move that creates confusion.

My dissatisfaction with contemporary writing on revelation extends also to a notable gap. Many scholars who have written on the theology of religions have dedicated much attention to the *salvation* for those who follow 'other' religious faiths or none at all. But they have engaged themselves far less with the question of divine *revelation* reaching these others. Yet can salvation ever be available for anyone or any group without a prior or a concomitant revelation? If Christ is the Life of the world, he is also the Light of the world.

All this dissatisfaction made me ask: how would I express the divine self-revelation in and through Jesus Christ (and also the revelation available for 'the others')? What questions should be posed and answered in constructing a coherent theology of revelation?

To begin with, such a theology needs to clarify what revelation means personally (or primarily) and propositionally (or secondarily), thus enabling faith *in* Christ to be expressed in ways that correspond to the articles of the Nicene-Constantinopolitan Creed and the Apostles' Creed (Chapter 1). Secondly, the self-revelation of God is a free act of love, and hence 'supernatural' as an unmerited gift from God. Yet, far from taking away the mystery of God, revelation enhances it (Chapter 2). Thirdly, accepted revelation brings salvation, and without or 'outside' revelation there can be no salvation (or 'extra revelationem nulla salus') (Chapter 3). Then we need to examine the 'sacramental' character of God's self-revelation as communicated through deeds and words (Chapter 4) and the endlessly various means and mediators of revelation (Chapter 5).

Chapter 6 develops the theme of divine revelation happening only when it is received in human faith. An inner working of the Holy Spirit and their own graced predisposition enable human beings to accept in faith the divine self-revelation. Yet there is no self-revelation of God without some concomitant revelation of those receiving it in faith.

Chapter 7 takes up the question: is there evidence that can make the recognition of divine revelation a reasonable decision? Does revelation jeopardize human freedom? Chapter 8 will distinguish foundational revelation (as it happened to the close of the apostolic age), dependent revelation (as it continues today), and final revelation (as it will come at the end of time).

A ninth chapter will discuss the relationship between revelation and tradition. A reality that remains wider than the Bible, tradition also preceded the writing of the inspired texts. Chapter 10 will explore the relationship between revelation and the inspiration of the Sacred Scriptures, leaving for Chapter 11 the question of their 'canonization' and truth.

A twelfth chapter turns to those who follow 'other' living faiths or none at all. It argues that the divine revelation which prompts real faith must in some way be also available to them. This revelation depends universally on the risen Christ and his Holy Spirit. The book closes with an epilogue that draws together the conclusions of the whole study of revelation.

The outline indicates how this book examines themes for a Christian theology of revelation, rather than the history of reflection on revelation. The history of the doctrine of revelation has already been capably expounded by others: above all, by Hans Waldenfels, *Die Offenbarung: von der Reformation bis zur Gegenwart, Handbuch der Dogmengeschichte* 1/1b (Freiburg: Herder, 1977), and by Eilert Herms, in *Theologische Realenzylopädie*, xxv (Berlin: De Gruyter, 1995), 146–210. I will not ignore what my predecessors and contemporaries have written, at times entering into grateful and critical dialogue with them. But this book sets itself to articulate a theology of revelation, not to tell the story of how theologians have interpreted the divine self-revelation. It is written out of the conviction that an adequate account of the divine self-revelation in Christ is the basic glue which holds together all that follows in specific areas of theology. It aims to present a self-consistent theological vision of this revelation.

My PhD thesis presented at the University of Cambridge (1968) examined 'The Theology of Revelation in Some Recent Discussion'. Although remaining as such unpublished, the dissertation yielded several articles in academic journals. My first book in theology, *Theology and Revelation* (Cork: Mercier, 1968), took up squarely the divine self-revelation in Christ. That theme was subsequently treated at length in *Foundations of Theology* (Chicago: Loyola University Press, 1971), *Fundamental Theology* (Ramsey, NJ: Paulist Press, 1981), *Retrieving Fundamental Theology* (Mahwah, NJ: Paulist

Press, 1993), and *Rethinking Fundamental Theology* (Oxford: Oxford University Press, 2011). I have also discussed God's self-revelation in numerous places—in journal articles, chapters in books, and entries in encyclopaedias. I now want to revise some positions, pull matters together, and enlarge into a coherent whole various conclusions I have reached about revelation.

New material will appear (e.g. evidential considerations in favour of revelation and a discussion of the paradox of God being simultaneously revealed and hidden). Some helpful philosophical language will be borrowed from Gilbert Ryle and Jean-Luc Marion, and I engage with new 'debating partners' (e.g. William Abraham, Lieven Boeve, Matthew Levering, and Richard Swinburne). More support for positions on revelation will be drawn from recent biblical scholarship. Some previous positions will be modified or dropped: for example, too much insistence on the distinction between 'general' (better called 'universal') and 'special' revelation.

I dedicate this work to those who, in particular ways, have helped to shape my thought on revelation: Karl Barth, David Braithwaite, David Brown, Rudolf Bultmann, Caroline Walker Bynum, Sarah Coakley, Stephen Davis, Avery Dulles, Jacques Dupuis, Gerhard Ebeling, Rino Fisichella, Hans-Georg Gadamer, Eberhardt Jüngel, Daniel Kendall, Robin Koning, René Latourelle, Philip Moller, Jürgen Moltmann, Christiaan Mostert, H. Richard Niebuhr, Wolfhart Pannenberg, Pheme Perkins, Karl Rahner, Alfred Singer, Janet Martin Soskice, Marguerite Shuster, Eleonore Stump, Denis White, Jared Wicks, N. T. Wright, and Norman Young. When quoting the Bible, I normally follow the NRSV; the translations from the Latin texts of the Second Vatican Council (1962–5) are my own. As a Christian I use the terminology of the Old Testament and New Testament. Here 'old' is understood as good and does not imply 'supersessionism', or the view that the NT has rendered obsolete and so superseded the OT.

Australian Catholic University
and University of Divinity,
Gerald O'Collins, SJ, AC.

Melbourne
New Year's Day 2016

Contents

Contents

List of Abbreviations

ABD	D. N. Freedman (ed.), *Anchor Bible Dictionary*, 6 vols (New York: Doubleday, 1992).
Bettenson	H. Bettenson and C. Maunder, *Documents of the Christian Church*, 4th edn (Oxford: Oxford University Press, 2011).
DzH	H. Denzinger and P. Hünermann (eds), *Enchiridion symbolorum, definitionum et declarationum*, English trans., 43rd edn (San Francisco: Ignatius Press, 2012).
DV	The Second Vatican Council, *Dei Verbum* (Constitution on Divine Revelation).
HFTh	W. Kern, H. J. Pottmeyer, and M. Seckler (eds), *Handbuch der Fundamentaltheologie*, 4 vols (Freiburg im Breisgau: Herder, 1985–8).
ND	J. Neuner and J. Dupuis (eds), *The Christian Faith*, 7th edn (Bangalore: Theological Publications in India, 2001).
par(r)	parallel(s) in other Gospels.
ST	Thomas Aquinas, *Summa theologiae*, trans. T. Gilby et al., 61 vols (London: Eyre & Spottiswoode, 1964–6).
TDNT	G. Kittel and G. Friedrich (eds), *Theological Dictionary of the New Testament*, trans. G. W. Bromiley, 10 vols (Grand Rapids, Mich.: Eerdmans, 1964–76).
TRE	G. Krause and G. Müller (eds.), *Theologische Realenzylopädie*, 36 vols (Berlin: Walter de Gruyter, 1977–2004).

1

Revelation as Self-revelation and Communication of Truth

When writing this chapter, I picked up two daily newspapers to be confronted with the headlines: in one 'Chief justice reveals intention to resign', and in the other 'Sex abuse revelations at prestigious college'. Here the vocabulary used by the press partially overlaps with the way in which many Christian theologians have traditionally employed the language of 'reveal' and 'revelation'.[1]

Journalists converge with theological usage by understanding 'reveal' to mean 'disclose', 'divulge', or 'make known' something previously hidden to the general public, often something that is both mysterious and important, and that, without the revelation(s), would otherwise have remained unknown. The meaning is suggested by the Latin *re-velare*, 'to remove the veil (*velum*)'. For journalists and theologians, 'revelation' can be seen as *both* the (sometimes startling) act of making something known *and* the new (sometimes sensational) knowledge now made available to us.

Contemporary television and marketing also embrace similar terminology of 'revelation'. While I was writing this chapter, Channel 7 was reaching the end of a soap that featured six couples across Australia. After being given the keys of another house, each team had the task of transforming every room in that house. When the owners returned, the renovations were 'unveiled' in what was called a 'whole house reveal'. As regards marketing, a quick google for health and beauty fragrances disclosed a similar affinity to theology: Pierre Cardin sells products named 'Revelation Perfume' and 'Revelation Aftershave'.

[1] On revelation see the bibliography at the end of this book.

But, as was pointed out in the preface, since the late 1980s many Christian theologians have not followed their predecessors by attending to the theme of the divine self-revelation in Christ. It has been partly left to journalists, the TV, and advertisers to keep alive the language of 'reveal' and 'revelation'. Theological thinking about revelation could have been stimulated by the philosophy of Jean-Luc Marion. Merold Westphal, when commenting on Marion's contribution to phenomenology, remarks that 'he argues that only such phenomenology [Marion's own phenomenology] can do descriptive justice to the experiences that faith takes to be revelation'.[2] Marion, remaining faithful to his philosophical task, will not, however, pronounce on the veridical status of such experiences. In the words of Westphal, 'whereas faith and theology affirm that revelation has occurred, that God has spoken, that God has appeared, phenomenology only describes the form of givenness such events would have to have, whether illusory or veridical. It neither affirms nor denies what faith and theology affirm'.[3]

After paying tribute to journalists and to Marion for keeping alive, respectively, the language of revelation and a possible philosophical approach to the divine self-revelation, what should I say about revelation? In particular, where do I want to start my theological reflections on revelation?

Before replying to these questions, let me once again warn against a false move that will be discussed more fully below, that of identifying divine revelation, more or less, with biblical inspiration. Years ago Stanley Hauerwas envisaged that possibility, only to distance himself from it: 'the very idea that the Bible is revealed (or inspired) is a claim that creates more trouble than it is worth'.[4] But why not say clearly and firmly that it is false to claim that the Bible is revealed? More recently Nicholas Adams has summarized F. D. E. Schleiermacher's view that, since the Bible was 'written in human languages and we have only one method of interpreting human languages, regardless of what is written', there is no 'special hermeneutics' for '*revelation*'.[5]

[2] M. Westphal, 'Phenomenology', in N. Adams, G. Pattison, and G. Ward (eds.), *The Oxford Handbook of Theology and Modern European Thought* (Oxford: Oxford University Press, 2013), 523–41, at 539.

[3] Ibid. 538.

[4] S. Hauerwas, *A Community of Character: Toward a Constructive Christian Ethic* (Notre Dame, Ind.: University of Notre Dame Press, 1981), 57.

[5] N. Adams, 'The Bible', in Adams et al. (eds.), *The Oxford Handbook of Theology and Modern European Thought*, 567–87, at 572; italics mine.

Such language, despite Adams's best intentions, runs perilously close to identifying the Bible *tout court* with revelation. Why does he not simply say that there is no special hermeneutics for the Bible? After this warning let me begin by examining *who* and *what* are revealed through God's revelation in Jesus Christ.

REVELATION AS PRIMARILY PERSONAL SELF-REVELATION

Well into the twentieth century much theology and official teaching more or less identified revelation with content: that is to say, with a set of divinely authenticated truths otherwise inaccessible to human reason and now accepted on God's authority. This 'propositional' view represented revelation as primarily the supernatural disclosure of new truths which significantly enriched our knowledge about God. The First Vatican Council (1869–70), for instance, although it did speak of God as being 'pleased to *reveal himself* and his eternal decrees' (DzH 3004; ND 113; italics mine), placed its emphasis on a propositional approach rather than on the divine self-revelation. This approach interpreted revelation as the *revelata* (things revealed) rather than as the divine action of self-revelation, and closely associated revelation with doctrine and creed. Logically Vatican I explained the act of faith as assent to truths (plural) or believing 'the things' to be true that God has revealed (DzH 3008; ND 118).

This propositional version of divine revelation has its partial counterpart in the language that the media continues to use. Every now and then headlines may announce: 'Startling Revelations Shock Prime Minister'. Two investigative journalists have uncovered a sordid episode involving the bribing of a cabinet minister. Their newspaper dramatically unveils for the public some new and explosive items of information that may significantly change the prevailing attitude towards the government in power. We are asked to accept as accurate what the journalists report about facts that would have remained unknown to us unless they had discovered them.[6] At least

[6] When writing this chapter, I came across the headline, 'Labour Puppet Master Revealed'. A journalist had tracked down the way a trade union leader was manipulating members of the state parliament.

some of the public believe that the report is true. If no one at all accepts the findings of the two journalists, their alleged revelation would not take place. We return to this point in Chapter 6.

Sometimes the propositional view of revelation is presented as characteristic of Roman Catholicism and even as the faulty view of one theologian who widely influenced his successors. Thus Tracey Rowland reports that Francisco de Suárez (1548–1617) 'fostered a propositional account of revelation by which revelation does not disclose God himself as much as pieces of information about God', which 'top up' what reason knows about God. Rowland adds that 'this Suárezian account of revelation' was 'widely taught in Catholic academies up until the Second Vatican Council' and then *rejected* by *Dei Verbum* (*DV*), its 1965 document on revelation.[7]

Beyond question, a propositional view of revelation characterized much Roman Catholic theology prior to Vatican II. Yet we should not forget other, somewhat different, Catholic approaches such as those of the Tübingen School (e.g. Johann Sebastian Drey, Johann Adam Möhler, and Johann Evangelist Kuhn). Furthermore, it caricatures Suárez's account of revelation to speak of 'pieces of information about God' that 'top up' what reason knows. His view centred on divine witness, 'the divine word witnessing (*locutio Dei attestans*)' to the '*revelata*' or things/truths revealed. The very influential Johann Baptist Franzelin (1816–86) drew on Suárez *and* Juan de Lugo (1583–1660) in holding revelation to be 'a divine locution, made up of words stating a truth and of facts proving that these words are a divine locution'.[8] In the years leading up to Vatican II, the equally influential Réginald Garrigou-Lagrange (1877–1964) held a similar view of revelation, but this Neo-Thomist Dominican would have been surprised to be named Suárezian for his propositional view of revelation. In any case, such a theological view was persistently more sophisticated than Rowland allows.

Moreover, far from being a Catholic monopoly, the view was widely shared, even if not always named as a 'propositional' view of revelation. Thus a Calvinist theologian, Archibald Alexander Hodge (1823–86), wrote in a work published in 1863, *Outlines of Theology*:

[7] T. Rowland, 'Tradition', in Adams et al. (eds.), *The Oxford Handbook of Theology and Modern European Thought*, 277–300, at 278–9.

[8] J. B. Franzelin, *Tractatus de divina Traditione et Scriptura* (Rome: Typographia Polyglotta, S.C. de Propaganda Fide, 1896), 618.

'we define faith . . . to be the assent of the mind to truth, upon the testimony of God, conveying knowledge to us though supernatural channels . . . when we know what He [God] says, we believe it because he says it'.[9] Another Princeton theologian is also remembered for his propositional view of revelation: Benjamin Breckenridge Warfield (1851–1921). He would have been astonished to be classified as Suárezian, and so too would the Canadian evangelical scholar, Clark H. Pinnock (1937–2010). He stated: 'the biblical pattern of revelation includes propositional communication as well as personal communion'.[10] Add too all the evangelicals who espouse a verbal-inerrancy view of biblical inspiration. Those who, more or less, identify inspiration with revelation or even continue to maintain a mechanical dictation of the Scriptures, endorse in effect the propositional view of revelation.[11]

Finally, an Anglican scholar who switched to being Russian Orthodox, Richard Swinburne continues to endorse clearly 'a propositional revelation'. In his view revelation provides reliable information about God, 'a message from God' that lets us know the truth about God and the way to be saved. The 'point of a revelation is to provide honest and diligent enquirers with some *information* quite likely to be true about the way to salvation, on which those who seek salvation can rely'. Such 'real revelation' from God should be tested in a way that resembles our methods for testing letters to establish their 'genuineness'.[12] In Swinburne's view, miracles become God's 'authenticating signature' which shows that some prophetic teaching truly 'comes from God'.[13] Such a view of revelation was and, to some extent, still is shared by many Christians of different denominations.

From the late nineteenth century more and more theologians and, eventually, such official documents as the Constitution on Divine Revelation of Vatican II developed as the primary model of revelation

[9] Quoted by J. Baillie, *The Idea of Revelation in Recent Thought* (London: Oxford University Press, 1956), 5.

[10] C. H. Pinnock, *The Scripture Principle: A Systematic Defence of the Full Authority of the Bible* (London: Hodder & Stoughton, 1985), 27.

[11] See H. Harris, 'Fundamentalist Approaches to Religion', in G. Oppy (ed.), *The Routledge Companion to Contemporary Philosophy of Religion* (London and New York: Routledge, 2015), 74–89, at 87–9.

[12] R. Swinburne, *Revelation: From Analogy to Metaphor*, 2nd edn. (Oxford: Oxford University Press, 2007), 105, 107, 125.

[13] Ibid. 120–1.

the notion of interpersonal encounter or dialogue.[14] Thus we find Wilhelm Herrmann (1846–1922), a German Lutheran, firmly stating in his 1887 work, *Der Begriff der Offenbarung*: '*all revelation* is the self-revelation of God'.[15] Instead of highlighting God revealing hitherto unknown truths (lower case and in the plural), many theologians came to understand revelation to be primarily the self-revelation of God who is Truth itself (upper case and in the singular). They expounded revelation as first and foremost the gratuitous and redemptive self-manifestation of God who calls and empowers human beings to enter by faith into a new personal relationship. Over and over again the Scriptures witness to revelatory events, in which God personally encountered such figures as Abraham, Sarah, Moses, Isaiah, Peter, Mary Magdalene, and Paul, and in unexpected ways called them to rethink their worldview and turn to a new faith commitment.

Jesus himself at times delivered teaching in propositional form. But he also questioned his hearers with parables, healed the sick, forgave sinners, delivered the possessed, called disciples, and in other ways established new relationships with many men and women. We can sum up what he did as a saving revelation (of himself and of the God whom he called 'Abba'), which could then be expressed and reported in true statements. Thus during his lifetime three disciples saw and heard what transpired at his transfiguration on the mountain; subsequently they reported this experience to others (Mark 9: 2–10 parr). Likewise, 1 Corinthians 15: 3–5 embodies four propositions of revealed truth, but these propositions derive from personal encounters with Jesus in his death and after his resurrection.

Thus revelation is not primarily a matter of revealing truths (plural) about God or even the truth (singular) about God. It involves

[14] At the start of the nineteenth century, Friedrich Schleiermacher in *The Christian Faith* (II. 10) brought up the notion of divine self-revelation but distanced himself from it: 'complete truth would mean that God made Himself known as He is in and for Himself' (trans. ed. H. R. Mackintosh and J. S. Stewart (Edinburgh: T. & T. Clark, 1928), 52). W. Pannenberg names Friedrich Schelling (1775–1854) as the scholar who introduced the expression 'self-revelation (Selbstoffenbarung)', but traces the notion back to Philo and Plotinus and cites Aquinas, Bonaventure, Cajetan, and Hegel as proposing a divine self-revelation even if not using the precise term. See Pannenberg, 'Offenbarung und "Offenbarungen" im Zeugnis der Geschichte', in *HFTh*, ii, 63–82, at 78–81.

[15] Quoted by Baillie, *The Idea of Revelation*, 34. The idea of divine revelation as God's self-revelation was to flourish in the writing of Barth, Rahner, and many others.

God disclosing the Truth or Reality that is God. Primarily, it reveals a person, or rather three divine Persons, rather than information about a person or about three divine Persons. We can summarize revelation as X reveals Y to Z, and Z believes/accepts this disclosure, adding at once that not only X (God) and Z (human beings) but also Y (the divine Selves) are, primarily, personal. Chapter 6 will explain how, for revelation to occur, it is necessary that Z accepts the revelation.

Hence I consider inadequate William Abraham's statement: 'He [Jesus Christ] operates as the final, definitive access to the truth about God'.[16] Rather Christ is in person the revelation of the Truth that is God. In a later chapter, the use of 'definitive' will be questioned and qualified. But here the issue is rather this: the language of 'access to the truth about God' waters down the startling Christian claim, made, for instance, in John's Gospel that Jesus, even (or especially?) on the cross, is the self-disclosure of God in *person*. Echoing Exodus 3: 14, Jesus says, 'when you have lifted up the Son of Man, then you will realize that I AM' (John 8: 28), and not, 'when you have lifted up the Son of Man, then you will have access to the truth of I AM'.

THE GOSPEL OF JOHN ON REVELATION

Rudolf Bultmann, who took up the notion of self-revelation from his teacher Wilhelm Herrmann, pointed to the strong emphasis on the divine self-disclosure found in the Fourth Gospel. When expounding 'the Theology of the Gospel of John and the Johannine Epistles', he presented Christ as 'the Revealer whom God has sent', whose 'distinguishing characteristic is the "I am..." of the Revealer'.[17] In *The Gospel of John: A Commentary*,[18] Bultmann made the theme of revelation central to his two major divisions of the Gospel: 'The Revelation of the *Doxa* to the World' (chs 1–12), which contains subsections ('The Encounter with the Revealer', 'The Revelation as *Krisis*', 'The Revealer's Struggle with the World', and 'The Revealer's

[16] W. J. Abraham, 'Revelation and Reason', in I. U. Dalferth and M. Ch. Rodgers (eds), *Revelation* (Tübingen: Mohr Siebeck, 2014), 29–46, at 31.

[17] R. Bultmann, *Theology of the New Testament*, ii, trans. K. Grobel (London: SCM Press, 1955), 4.

[18] Trans. G. R. Beasley-Murray (Oxford: Basil Blackwell, 1971).

Secret Victory over the World'); and 'The Revelation of the Doxa before the Community' (chs 13–20). While some major features of this commentary (e.g. Bultmann's theory about Gnosticism and speculations about sources) have been generally and widely questioned, he rightly read the Fourth Gospel in the key of revelation—or better, in the key of the divine self-revelation.

Even if the Fourth Gospel never explicitly gives Christ the title of 'Revealer', it applies to him a rich and variegated language of revelation: 'glory' (and 'glorify'), 'light', 'signs', 'truth', 'witness' (as both noun and verb), the 'I am' sayings, 'disclose', and so forth. The Johannine vocabulary concerned with Christ's identity and activity is heavily revelatory.

Key words constantly recur for expressing the divine self-revelation that Christ has brought in his own person. Through the incarnation, believers have been enabled to contemplate the 'glory (*doxa*)' of the Word of God (1: 14). His 'sign' at the marriage feast in Cana discloses his divine 'glory' (2: 11); at the end he prays that the Father would 'glorify (*doxazein*)' him (17:5; see 17: 22, 24). He is the 'light (*phōs*)' of the world (8: 12; see 3: 19–21; 12: 35, 46), the 'light that shines in the darkness' (1: 5; see 1: 7). He is 'the truth (*alētheia*)' (14: 6; see 1: 17). He bears 'witness (*marturia*)' (8: 13–14, 18) to what he has seen (3: 11).

Where the other Gospels call Jesus' miracles 'acts of power (*dunameis*)', John turns towards their revealing function and speaks of 'signs (*sēmeia*)'. Right from their first occurrence these signs 'disclose (*phaneroun*)' the 'glory' of Jesus (2: 1), which is not something reserved for his future, eschatological condition (as in the Synoptic Gospels).[19] According to John, Jesus will enter into his definitive glorification by dying and rising (17: 1, 4–5). But that divine glory has been disclosed in advance through the earthly ministry, and this theme of his glory already manifested serves to sum up the whole ministry (12: 37–43).

The 'I am' sayings reveal various aspects of Jesus' person and work ('I am the true bread; I am the light of the world; I am the good/beautiful shepherd; I am the way, the truth, and the life'; and so forth).

[19] See Mark 13: 26 about 'the Son of Man coming with great power and glory'; Matt. 25: 31 about the Son of Man at the future judgement 'sitting on the throne of his glory'; and Luke 24: 26 about the risen Christ 'entering into his glory'. By way of exception, Luke applies the language of 'glory' (9: 31–2) to the episode of the Transfiguration which, like Mark and Matthew, he situates in the earthly ministry of Jesus.

These sayings culminate in the absolute 'I AM' (8: 58; see 18: 5, 6. 8), which recalls the divine self-presentation of Exodus 3: 14. Jesus is the epiphany of God.

From its opening verses, John makes it clear that the coming of Christ reveals One who has been eternally 'with God' (the Father). Very quickly the Holy Spirit enters the divine 'equation'. While not directly narrating the baptism of Jesus, the evangelist implies it, and twice adds the detail that the Spirit not only descended on Jesus but also 'remained on him' (1: 32–3). What of the revelation of the Holy Spirit in the Johannine testimony?

According to John, the Spirit comes from Jesus, is sent by Jesus, and is bestowed by Jesus (7: 39; 15: 26; 19: 30, 33; 20: 22). At the same time, the sending of the Spirit, so it is disclosed, does not involve Jesus alone. This sending depends on the Father, as does the inner-trinitarian 'proceeding': 'When the Spirit comes whom I will send you from (*para*) the Father, the Spirit of truth who proceeds (*ekporeuetai*) from (*para*) the Father, that One will bear witness to me' (15: 26). John also talks about the Father 'giving' the Spirit (14: 16–17) or 'sending' the Spirit (14: 26), albeit in response to Jesus' prayer and in the name of Jesus.

John's teaching on the self-revelation of the tripersonal God is located firmly in the immediate context of Jesus' death and resurrection (13: 1–21: 25). The evangelist also witnesses to that revelation being communicated through the incarnation (1: 1–18) and the public ministry (1: 19–12: 50). As the Revealer (or Self-Revealer) right from the start (1: 14), Jesus has also manifested the glory of God the Father (17: 4). But the narrative of the Last Supper, passion, death, and resurrection articulates the trinitarian revelation even more clearly, above all as regards the manifestation of the Holy Spirit.

In the last couple of pages we have been translating the first-order, witnessing language of the Fourth Gospel into the second-order language of theology. The divine self-revelation proclaimed by John is nothing less than the tripersonal God being revealed through the incarnation of the Son of God and the mission/coming of the Holy Spirit. This divine disclosure calls people to 'abide' lovingly in Jesus 'the true vine' (15: 1–11) and so share in the trinitarian life of God.

In these terms, revelation is primarily an interpersonal encounter, event, or dialogue that takes place between the tripersonal God and those who experience and in faith 'receive' the presence of the self-revealing God. Three terms, (a) presence, (b) experience, and (c) faith, prove significant here, and can each be illuminated by John's Gospel.

(a) A majestic statement forms a highpoint in John's opening chapter: 'The Word became flesh and pitched his tent among us, and we have seen his glory, the glory of the Father's only Son' (1: 14; see 11: 40). Through the incarnation, the Word fully took on the human condition, and came to be present, dwell, or live among us, so that 'we' (initially the Johannine community and then other Christians) could through faith contemplate his divine glory, or the visible manifestation in him of God's presence and power. Thus the Fourth Gospel highlights 'the Word's "enfleshed" *presence* in the world', a revealed presence that enables believers to 'see' and acknowledge the divine presence and power.[20]

Later we will see how the revealing (and saving) presence of Christ is persistently mediated in many ways and by many persons—above all, by the community of the Church and the person of the Holy Spirit.

(b) The Fourth Gospel constantly talks of people seeing Jesus (or his glory), hearing him, coming to him, finding him, and knowing him. These verbs express, with different nuances, how people *experienced* and continue to *experience* him as revealed to them. Jesus invites Andrew and his anonymous companion to 'come and see' (1: 39)—an invitation that Philip repeats to Nathanael when, in response to the claim that 'we have found him about whom Moses in the law and also the prophets wrote' (1: 45; see 1: 41), the latter at first sceptically asks: 'can anything good come out of Nazareth?' (1: 46). Then Nathanael acknowledges the identity of Jesus: 'Rabbi, you are the Son of God! You are the King of Israel' (1: 49), Jesus indicates where this experience of faith will take him: 'you will see heaven opened and the angels of God ascending and descending upon the Son of Man' (1: 51).

A little later in John's Gospel, many Samaritans set aside the testimony of the woman who had met Jesus at Jacob's well: 'it is no longer because of what you said that we believe, for we have heard [Jesus] for ourselves and we know that this is truly the Saviour of the

[20] On John 1: 14, see Brendan Byrne, *Life Abounding: A Reading of John's Gospel* (Collegeville, Minn.: Liturgical Press, 2014), 30–3. For what the language of 'presence' involves, see G. O'Collins, *Salvation for All: God's Other Peoples* (Oxford: Oxford University Press, 2008), 208–14, and for what should be said about the universal presence of Christ and his Holy Spirit, see ibid. 214–29.

world' (John 4: 42). Through coming to Jesus, and then seeing and hearing him, they 'know'—that is to say, they have experienced in faith—Someone whom they call by a remarkable title found nowhere else in the New Testament, 'the Saviour of the world'. Elsewhere I have spelled out at length what I understand by 'experience'.[21] The most experiential of the four Gospels, John repeatedly sets before us how the personal self-revelation of God reaches people when they come to Jesus, see him, hear him, and find him. They too can 'know' or experience him in faith, as many Samaritans do.

For the most part, the Gospel of John remains discreetly restrained in describing how the experiential knowing, which shapes the revealing (and saving) encounters with the person of Jesus, engages the affections of Andrew (1: 35–42), the royal official (4: 46–54), a Samaritan woman (4: 7–30), the man born blind (9: 1–41), Mary Magdalene (20: 11–18), and the others who respond with faith to the revelation of Jesus. John does, however, underscore the 'joy' brought by a relationship with Jesus (15: 11; 16: 20–4). Here John Henry Newman was second to none in suggesting how the heart and its 'affections' are reached in experiences of divine self-revelation: 'persons influence us, voices melt us, looks subdue us, deeds inflame us'.[22]

What comes through loud and clear from John's Gospel is that the self-revelation of God in and through Jesus must be experienced if it is to 'be there'. The notion of a non-experienced revelation is an oxymoron. Either the revelation is experienced, to be accepted or rejected (as is apparently the case of a lame man healed by Jesus on the Sabbath (John 5: 1–15)), or revelation is not there at all. It is axiomatic for the theology of revelation: outside human experience there is no revelation (*extra experientiam nulla revelatio*). Non-experienced revelation does not exist. There can be no revelation that is not experienced.[23]

(c) John's Gospel proves a gold mine for those searching for a narrative theology of God's self-revelation in Christ. Over and over again, Christ presents himself to individuals or groups of people as the Revealer and the Revelation of God. Those encounters call for the

[21] G. O'Collins, *Rethinking Fundamental Theology* (Oxford: Oxford University Press, 2011), 42–55.

[22] J. H. Newman, *An Essay in Aid of a Grammar of Assent* (London; Longman & Green, 1903), 92–3.

[23] See Jan-Olav Henriksen, *Life, Love and Hope: God and Human Experience* (Grand Rapids, Mich.: Eerdmans, 2014).

response of *faith*. A later chapter will explore the human faith that should respond to divine revelation and so make divine revelation possible as a reciprocal event. To those who in faith accept this revelation, God is revealed.

REVELATION AS COMMUNICATION OF TRUTH

With its obviously Christocentric view of divine revelation, John's Gospel is primarily concerned with the question: *Who* is revealed? But that question also essentially involves, albeit secondarily, the question: *What* is revealed? Revelation is an experience of Someone, an experience that underpins and leads to statements about who and what were revealed.

When Jesus encounters and reveals himself to Nathanael, the latter at once blurts out a confession of faith: 'you are the Son of God! You are the King of Israel' (1: 41). Believing *in* Jesus means believing *that* about him. At the end of the Fourth Gospel, the evangelist sums up the purpose of his project: he has written what he has written, so that 'you may come [or continue] to believe that Jesus is the Messiah, the Son of God and through believing you may have life in his name' (20: 31). Later we will return to the, distinguishable but inseparable, salvific dimension of revelation ('having life' in Christ's name). Here the point is rather: believing in Jesus necessarily entails believing that certain things are true about him: his identity as Messiah and Son of God.

Hence, when noting above the shift that has taken place from a propositional to a personal view of revelation, I do not want to represent these two views as mutually exclusive. In fact they imply each other. The experience of a revealing (and redemptive) dialogue with God does not remain private, incommunicable, and locked away within an inarticulate subjectivity. The faith that responds to the self-revealing God announces what it now knows of God. As Paul put matters, 'since we have the same spirit of faith as he had who wrote, "I believed, and so I spoke", so we too believe, and so we speak' (2 Cor. 4: 13). In addressing human beings, God says something that they can formulate and pass on. We may call revelation 'proposition-able', since it can be expressed in true propositions derived from the divine dialogue with human beings.

Thus revelation as a person-to-person, I–Thou encounter between God and human beings gives rise to true propositions. In their turn they can prompt divine revelation, as when human beings are addressed by the Scripture, preaching (supremely Jesus' own proclamation of the kingdom), the classic creeds and other doctrinal statements, the words and actions which constitute the conferring of the sacraments, various icons and further works of sacred art and music, and other 'accounts' drawn from previous revelatory encounters with God. Thus the formulations of faith not only issue from such encounters but also provoke them. A narrative or other versions of prior revelatory events and 'the things' disclosed through them can bring about fresh revelatory situations and initiate (or confirm) the faith of later believers.[24]

To sum up: even if the personal question ('*Who* is revealed?') is the primary one, the propositional content of revelation (the answer to the question '*What* is revealed?') maintains its proper, albeit secondary place. The personal view highlights the *knowledge of* God (a knowledge by acquaintance) which the event of revelation embodies. Yet this implies, secondarily but necessarily, that believers enjoy a *knowledge about* God. The communication of truth or truths *about* God belongs to revelation, even if always at the service of the personal experience *of* God or encounter *with* God.

Hence, *pace* Tracey Rowland, the Second Vatican Council did not endorse a 'rejection' of the earlier propositional view of revelation advanced by Suárez, de Lugo, Franzelin, Garrigou-Lagrange, and others (including many non-Catholic Christians).[25] Yes, the opening chapter of the Constitution on Divine Revelation, *Dei Verbum*, makes it abundantly clear that revelation means *primarily* God's personal self-revelation (*DV* 1–4). But that carries with it the conviction that, *secondarily*, the divine revelation discloses something *about* God and human beings. The pre-Vatican account of revelation is not rejected, as Rowland claims, but rather moved into second place.[26] *Dei Verbum*

[24] For the texts of the two classic creeds of Christianity, see Bettenson, 25–6 (the Apostles' Creed), and 26–8 (the Nicene-Constantinopolitan Creed).

[25] Rowland, 'Tradition', 279.

[26] Matthew Levering's *Engaging the Doctrine of Revelation* (Grand Rapids, Mich.: Baker Academic, 2014) explores above all the mediation of divine revelation through the Church and Scripture: that is to say, concentrating on revelation in the secondary sense, the book engages with the doctrine of propositional revelation and with the faithful mediation of true propositions that have emerged from God's self-revelation in Christ.

accepts a propositional view of revelation, but only as coming after the primary, personal view.

Thus the second chapter of *Dei Verbum* opens: 'God graciously arranged that *the things he had revealed* for the salvation of all nations should remain in their entirety forever, and be transmitted to all generations' (*DV* 7; italics mine). Since it deals with the transmission of revelation, that same chapter naturally speaks of 'all revealed things' (*DV* 9) and goes on to use a classic term for the full revelation communicated through Christ and his apostles: 'all that it [the magisterium] proposes for belief as being divinely revealed (divinitus revelata) is drawn from this one *deposit of faith*' (*DV* 10; italics mine). At the end, *Dei Verbum* uses an equivalent term when it talks of 'the *treasure of revelation* entrusted to the church', which is to be faithfully preserved and proclaimed (*DV* 26; italics mine).

After treating the transmission of divine revelation in chapter 2, *Dei Verbum* begins its very next chapter by speaking of 'the divinely revealed *things* (divinitus revelata), which are *contained* and presented in the text of Sacred Scripture' (*DV* 11; italics mine). Here we come up against the limits of the verb 'contain'. In its primary sense, revelation, inasmuch as it is an interpersonal event of God's self-communication, cannot be 'contained' in or by anything, not even the inspired Scripture. Primarily, revelation does not consist in 'things' that might be contained by some vessel, but in God's own self-manifestation. It is only secondarily that we can speak of revelation's content, to be found recorded in the Bible and elsewhere (e.g. in liturgical texts).

At first glance, it may not seem necessary to keep insisting (a) that, while secondarily being a disclosure *about* God, revelation is primarily the self-disclosure *of* God; and (b) that, while being distinguishable, these two dimensions of revelation belong inseparably together. I do so, because the need for more clarity shows up in many places.

In the course of an essay on 'Biblical Concepts of Revelation', for instance, James D. G. Dunn puts the question about Christianity: 'can a prophetic religion survive unless it is open to the Spirit of prophecy, to inspire afresh *and reveal new things*?'[27] Later we will have occasion to take up this close association of prophetic inspiration and revelation, a view that also affected St Thomas Aquinas's understanding of

[27] Dunn, in P. D. L. Avis (ed.), *Revelation* (London: Darton, Longman & Todd, 1997), 1–22, at 14; italics mine.

revelation. Here I simply want to note the ambiguity in speaking of 'revealing new things'. Surely Dunn does not expect Christian prophets, under divine inspiration, to disclose new propositional truths (revelation in the secondary sense) which would add substantially fresh content to the Nicene Creed? Does he rather envisage such prophets helping believers, through new insights, to experience freshly what they already know through revelation and to put this experience into new forms of practice?

More recently Joshua Kira draws the needed distinction between the primary and secondary meanings of revelation:

> Revelation, in the primary sense, is the revelation of God in Godself. It is God's self-presentation and is an *inherently relational idea.* Revelation can also be used in a . . . secondary sense as revelation of something about God, which is a cognitive idea . . . knowing God in Godself *appears to require* knowing something about the divine self.[28]

My main proposal here concerns stating more emphatically that knowing God in the primary sense of revelation always requires (and not merely 'appears to require') or at least always implies knowing something about the divine self. A completely non-cognitive revelation, in which nothing is known either before, or during, or after the revelatory event would be an oxymoron. I am not talking about an elaborately understood and interpreted cognitive content. But a revelation that evades any understanding and interpretation whatsoever should be ruled out. That would be revelation in the primary sense, without any revelation at all in the secondary sense—a blatant impossibility.

Writing to the Galatian Christians, St Paul insisted: 'the gospel that was proclaimed by me is not of human origin; for I did not receive it from a human source, nor was I taught it, but I received it through a *revelation* of Jesus Christ' (Gal. 1: 11–12). Through encountering the risen Jesus (revelation in the primary sense), Paul received the good news he proclaimed (revelation in the secondary sense). The personal self-revelation of Christ to Paul communicated the content of the gospel which the apostle proceeded to announce.

[28] J. Kira, 'A Response to Stephen T. Davis', in I. U. Dalferth and M. Ch. Rodgers (eds.), *Revelation* (Tübingen: Mohr Siebeck, 2014), 65–72, at 71; italics mine. 'Inherently reciprocal' (rather than merely 'relational') clarifies better the interplay between divine revelation and human faith.

Beyond question, God always remains the 'absolute mystery', the 'ineffable One',[29] that is to say, far too great and mysterious ever to be comprehensively described. Nevertheless, even if only a minimal description is possible, something can be known and said about the human experience of the divine self-revelation—what led up to it, what it was like, and what it led to afterwards.

Below we will come to views of revelation that understand it as God speaking and the word of God. This interpretation of revelation involves the consequence: if God has spoken or speaks to human beings, they can, in some sense and in some degree, know and speak of God. Naming revelation as *locutio Dei* or *Dei Verbum* necessarily entails acknowledging some cognitive dimension in revelation.

KNOWING AND KNOWING ABOUT THE TRINITY

The Hebrew Scriptures narrate many specific episodes in which the self-revelation of God brings human beings to know something new about God: for instance, the divine encounters with Moses which revealed that God wished to enter a special, covenant-relationship with the people of Israel. Then the whole story of the Son of God's incarnation, life, passion, death, resurrection, and ascension, together with the outpouring of the Holy Spirit, disclosed the tripersonal God.[30] Of course, one should avoid being anachronistic by reading too clearly and fully the revelation of the Trinity out of the whole story of Jesus. Nevertheless, we find there the starting-point for what would be deployed in later church teaching. The self-manifestation *of the truth that is God* necessarily entailed revealing *truths about God*: above all, the truth that the one God is Father, Son, and Holy Spirit. The 'law of revealing (*lex revelandi*)' would become the 'law of believing (*lex credendi*)', enshrined pre-eminently in the Apostles' Creed and the Nicene Creed, both with their trinitarian structure.

Thus the classical creeds supremely exemplify the importance of revelation in the secondary sense. They constitute the core confession (or 'believing that') of Christian faith. Under the guidance of the Holy

[29] Karl Rahner, *Foundations of Christian Faith: An Introduction to the Idea of Christianity*, trans. William V. Dych (New York: Seabury Press, 1978), 119–20.

[30] O'Collins, *Rethinking Fundamental Theology*, 120–8.

Spirit, believers made a journey from their original experience of God to a clearer grasp of what it communicated and more refined propositions in expressing its meaning.

For the first Christians encountering (or knowing) God revealed in the person of Jesus Christ (revelation in the primary sense) and so coming to know that God is triune (revelation in the secondary sense) involved a dramatic change in their knowledge of God and about God. Thus Paul split the Jewish confession in the *Shema* (Deut. 6: 4–5): 'Hear, O Israel: the Lord is our God, the Lord alone. You shall love the Lord your God will all your heart, and with all your soul, and with all your strength.' The apostle glossed 'God' with Father and 'Lord' with Jesus and so putting Jesus as Lord alongside God the Father: 'For us there is one God, the Father, from whom are all things and for whom we exist, and one Lord, Jesus Christ, through whom are all things and through whom we exist' (1 Cor. 8: 6). Here the title 'one Lord' and the explanation added to it ('through whom are all things and through whom we exist') expanded the *Shema* to include Jesus Christ. Drawing on what he had experienced through revelation and using the classic monotheistic text of Judaism, Paul recast his perception of God by introducing Jesus as 'Lord' and redefining Jewish monotheism to produce a new, Christological monotheism.[31]

When contemporary Christian believers recite the creed (revelation in the secondary sense), they may experience in a fresh way a sense of the Holy Trinity and feel the presence of the tripersonal God (revelation in the primary sense). God speaks to them and is disclosed to them. Such revelatory moments involve something cognitive, but not a total cognitive change. Experientially they are knowing once again what they have already known and confessed. While with Paul and others at the origins of Christianity, the cognitive change effected by the divine self-revelation was, in part, dramatically new, in the ongoing life of Christian faith the cognitive change will take the form of remembering and experiencing freshly what has already been known.

In both its (a) primary and (b) secondary sense, revelation remains strongly cognitive. If we attend to meaning (a) and speak of 'experienced knowledge of God', we continue, nevertheless, to speak of knowledge. Talking in sense (a) of God's self-disclosure and the

[31] See A. C. Thiselton, *The First Epistle to the Corinthians* (Grand Rapids, Mich.: Eerdmans, 2000), 631–8.

divine–human dialogue, such disclosure involves emerging from a mysterious hiddenness to make oneself 'known'. 'Dia-logue (*dialogos*)' implies a 'word (*logos*)' communicated, a meaning to be understood or—in other words—sense (b). The language of revelation retains a strongly cognitive sense.

Church teaching and much theology have shifted from talking primarily about the manifestation of meanings, truths, and mysteries (in the plural) to talking about the divine revelation in Christ, who is *the* Meaning, *the* Truth, and *the* Mystery (in the singular).[32] Yet cognitive overtones still hang around this updated language. There is a meaning to be understood, a truth to be known, and a mystery to be disclosed. Cognitive concerns inevitably attend the term 'revelation' and its normal synonyms.

This chapter has laid the basis for understanding revelation as meaning primarily the divine self-revelation and secondarily the truths that are revealed in, with, and through that self-disclosure of God. We can now press on to explore various characteristics of revelation—to be begin with, its utter gratuity.

[32] Thus the sixteen documents of Vatican II (1962–5) speak of 'mystery' in the singular 106 times but in the plural only 22 times.

2

The Love that Reveals and Conceals

Christians have valued the way in which the First Letter of John drew together the self-revelation of God in Jesus Christ: 'God is love'. To this, the letter added at once: 'God's love was revealed (*ephanerōthē*) among us in this way: God sent his only Son into the world, so that we might live through him' (1 John 4: 8–9).

Associating like this the divine love and God's self-revelation might easily lead us to think that the divine self-disclosure flowed inevitably from the identity of God as love. After all, human beings, more or less inevitably, reveal themselves to those whom they love. Loving others seems to involve the need to reveal oneself to them. Jesus' loving friendship leads him to disclose to his disciples himself and his life's greatest treasure, the Father from whom he came: 'I have called you friends, because I have made known to you everything that I have heard from my Father' (John 15: 15; see 14: 21).

Without questioning the utter centrality of divine love for any theology of revelation, let me give it a context by exploring four theses: revelation depends on God totally; God could have remained silent; the divine self-revelation is 'an act of the most free love';[1] far from taking away the divine mystery, God's loving self-revelation enhances it. Commenting on the theology of Karl Barth (1886–1968) and apropos of the fourth thesis, George Hunsinger remarks: 'the truth of God's identity remains hidden in the midst of revelation and revealed in the midst of hiddenness'.[2]

[1] K. Rahner, *Foundations of Christian Faith*, trans. W. V. Dych (New York: Seabury Press, 1978), 123.

[2] G. Hunsinger, *How to Read Karl Barth; The Shape of His Theology* (New York: Oxford University Press, 1991), 79. Hunsinger expresses the point also by saying: 'God as revealed in Jesus Christ remains revealed in the midst of hiddenness and hidden in the midst of revelation' (ibid. 81).

THE DIVINE INITIATIVE

Never to be reduced to human discovery, as if it were made up of insights achieved by spiritually sensitive persons or were, in general, the outcome of some human quest for ultimate knowledge, revelation is always freely initiated and carried through by God. Hence all revelation is genuinely 'supernatural', in the sense of being a free disclosure and unmerited gift coming from God. The Letter to the Hebrews opens by highlighting the prior initiative of God, who 'in these last days has spoken to us by a Son' (1: 2).

Right from New Testament times, Christian teachers have insisted that the divine self-revelation depends on the prior action of God. In the second century Irenaeus wrote: 'no one can know God, unless God teaches [him or her]; that is to say, without God, God cannot be known (Deum scire nemo potest, nisi Deo docente; hoc est, sine Deo non cognosci Deum)' (*Adversus Haereses*, 4. 6. 4). Centuries later Anselm of Canterbury prayed to God: 'teach me to seek You, and reveal Yourself [to me] when I seek [You], because I cannot seek You unless You teach [me], nor find [You] unless you reveal Yourself [to me] (doce me quaerere Te, et ostende Te quaerenti, quia nec quaerere Te possum nisi Tu doceas nec invenire nisi Te ostendas)' (*Proslogion*, 1). In the twentieth century Karl Rahner wrote: '[human beings] can never even begin to have anything to do with God or to approach God without being *already* borne by God's grace'.[3]

This conviction at times drew on Third Isaiah's words about the rebellious Jewish people: 'I was ready to be sought out by those who did not ask, to be found by those who did not seek me' (Isa. 65: 1). Explicitly referring to Isaiah, Paul took up this theme and applied it to the Gentiles: 'I have been found by those who did not seek me; I have shown myself to those who did not ask for me' (Rom. 10: 20).

From start to finish, love characterizes the divine initiative that brings about the self-revelation of God. It is a love that crosses the infinite distance between the creator and the creatures. What Jean-Luc Marion writes about erotic love also applies here:

> Loving requires an exteriority that is not provisional but effective, an exteriority that remains for long enough that one may cross it seriously. Love requires distance and the crossing of distance. Loving requires

[3] Rahner, *Foundations of Christian Faith*, 146.

> more than a feigned distance, or one that is not truly dug out or truly crossed. In the drama of love, actions must be accomplished effectively over distance.[4]

'Crossing' an infinite distance, our loving God is revealed to us and saves us. More specifically, we should speak here of the missions of the Son and the Holy Spirit. The two missions reveal the loving presence of the Trinity and communicate salvation.

However we express the gratuitous initiative of God that always characterizes revelation, from start to finish the divine self-disclosure depends totally on God and the divine love. Hence it can be misleading to speak of our 'possessing' revelation.[5] The disclosure of the self-revealing God—to put it personally—possesses us, not vice versa.

GOD COULD HAVE REMAINED SILENT

Karl Barth may have gone too far in flatly denying that we can in any way show it to be credible that there should be revelation. Richard Swinburne and others have made their case for a kind of antecedent probability or an a priori plausibility for divine revelation: after freely and lovingly creating human beings, God might be expected to emerge from the divine mystery and enter into a personal relationship with them.[6] The love disclosed in the free act of creation suggests that, especially after human beings have fallen into sin, creation would be followed up by some divine revelation. Human beings, to shape correctly the choices they should make and discern the path they should follow in life, need the instruction provided by a divine revelation. Prioritizing propositional revelation or knowing revealed truth, Swinburne explains reasons 'for expecting a revelation'. There are 'truths' which 'all humans need to know', if, for instance, they are 'to distinguish adequately between right and wrong'.[7]

[4] J.-L. Marion, *The Erotic Phenomenon*, trans. S. E. Lewis (Chicago: University of Chicago Press, 2007), 46–7.

[5] W. J. Abraham, *Crossing the Threshold of Divine Revelation* (Grand Rapids, Mich.: Eerdmans, 2006), 5; see Abraham, 'Revelation and Reason', in I. U. Dalferth and M. Ch. Rodgers (eds.), *Revelation* (Tübingen: Mohr Siebeck, 2014), 29–46, at 32, 37.

[6] R. Swinburne, 'The Need for Revelation', *Revelation: From Metaphor to Analogy*, 2nd edn. (Oxford: Oxford University Press, 2007), 79–106.

[7] Ibid. 95–8.

Through the Middle Ages, Anselm, Thomas Aquinas, Duns Scotus, and other theologians wrestled with a similar question: was the incarnation necessary? Would the incarnation not have taken place if human beings had not fallen into sin and so come to need the further divine help provided by the incarnation? Or, as an appropriate and even 'necessary' follow up to creation, would the incarnation have happened anyway?

In the theory of satisfaction for sin that he developed in *Cur Deus homo*, Anselm argued that God does not wish to punish sinful human beings but to see the good project of creation 'completed' (2. 5). Since human beings are incapable of offering the appropriate reparation, which would be something of infinite value, Anselm concluded to the 'necessity' of the incarnation. Only Christ, the God-man could offer the gift of his life as the needed work of reparation for the whole human race (2. 6–7, 11, 14, 18–19).

Thomas Aquinas took up the theory of satisfaction but did not endorse the 'absolute' necessity for the incarnation that it embodied. Rather he detailed reasons for a certain lesser 'necessity' or 'fittingness' of the incarnation. He mitigated Anselm's thesis by maintaining that God could pardon sin even though adequate satisfaction was not made and by stressing the way love makes satisfaction valid.[8] In the light of human sin, Aquinas characterized the incarnation as 'fitting' rather than strictly or absolutely 'necessary'.[9]

Much of that classical debate could be *transposed* in terms of a concept fully developed centuries later: revelation. Swinburne stresses the way sinful human beings need divine instruction to deliver them from sinful alienation and make them ready for heaven. Their situation makes divine revelation plausible. Curiously he does not seem to realize that his case for the antecedent probability of divine *revelation* has its earlier counterpart in the medieval debates over the 'necessity' of the *incarnation*.[10] Swinburne's own position about the revelation needed in the light of human sin recalls arguments from Anselm and Aquinas about the incarnation becoming 'necessary' or at least 'fitting' after human beings fell into sin.

[8] *ST* IIIa. 48. 3; 79. 5. [9] *ST* IIIa. 1. 1–3.

[10] In his pages on 'The Need for Revelation', Swinburne refers occasionally to Thomas Aquinas and Duns Scotus, but not to their treatment of the incarnation, a/the highpoint of divine revelation, as being 'fitting' or 'necessary' (Swinburne, *Revelation*, 79–106).

Personally I hesitate to speak of a certain 'necessity' for the divine self-revelation. God was under no obligation to reveal himself through an incarnation, and could have remained mysteriously silent. The divine self-revelation, which reached its fullness with the whole Christ-event, was not necessary, or at least not strictly necessary.

The next chapter will examine the essential link between revelation and salvation, as being distinguishable but inseparable. This dyad can also be expressed as divine revelation and the saving incarnation. God did not need to emerge from the divine hiddenness, just as the incarnation of the Son of God was not a necessary act but one of gratuitous love. 'God so loved the world that he sent his only Son' (John 3: 16).

AN ACT OF HIGHEST FREEDOM

Rahner wrote of the divine self-communication as 'absolutely gratuitous', an act of 'God's highest personal freedom', and 'an act of the most free love'.[11] In a later chapter we will return to the rich meaning of 'self-communication', which expresses not only the free self-disclosure of God but also the way in which the divine 'giver is, in his own being, the gift'. In and through 'his own being the giver gives himself to creatures as their own fulfilment'.[12] Here I want to stress only the divine freedom expressed in the act of self-revelation.

The simplicity of God means, of course, that, strictly speaking, it is misleading to speak either of the divine freedom being exercised in a 'higher' fashion or of acts coming from the most free, divine love. It is better not to follow Rahner's language about the divine self-communication being an act of 'God's highest personal freedom' or 'an act of the most free love'. Such a 'higher/lower' or 'most free/less free' scale in expressing freedom (and love) characterizes better the freedom (and love) exercised by human beings. In their case such actions as freely risking death for others can stand out and express freedom and love in the highest and most free way possible.

Nevertheless, Rahner was right in highlighting the unique loving freedom embodied in God's self-communication or self-revelation.

[11] Rahner, *Foundations of Christian Faith*, 123. [12] Ibid. 120.

Paul celebrated the freedom of God's love, which identifies with sinful human beings and wants to endow them through Christ with every blessing (Rom. 8: 31–9). The fullness of God's unforced love for human beings allowed the First Letter of John to identify God with love (4: 8, 16). The divine love embodied in the incarnation and the self-revelation that it involved are nothing if not free (1 John 3: 1; 4: 9–11).

THE REVEALED AND HIDDEN GOD

In his commentary on John's Gospel, Rudolf Bultmann wrote: 'the word of the revealer . . . at once reveals and conceals him'.[13] God is known as unknown, revealed as incomprehensible.[14] Here theologians have often spoken of God as the 'hidden and revealed mystery (mysterium absconditum et revelatum)'.[15]

The story of Moses meeting and being called by God remains paradigmatic (Exod. 2: 23–4: 17). When Moses asks who is commissioning him, God reveals the name which is not a name, providing it in three forms: 'I AM WHO I AM' (or 'I AM WHO I WILL BE'), 'I AM', and 'YHWH' (which could mean 'he who causes to be') (Exod. 3: 14–15). The ambiguity persists and enhances the mystery of Israel's God, who now emerges from a silent mystery to encounter Moses.

The self-revealing God is known in and through the religious experience of those who accept in faith the divine disclosure. But there remains an infinite difference between the experiences of finite human beings and the divine Reality that transcends the whole created world. The hidden God remains infinitely beyond what might be revealed and known through events of divine self-revelation. We can put this difference visibly by saying that, while God is revealed (lower case), God remains much more Hidden (upper case). Revelation makes the triune God more mysterious, not less.

[13] R. Bultmann, *The Gospel of John: A Commentary*, trans. G. R. Beasley-Murray (Oxford: Basil Blackwell, 1971), 161.

[14] R. Bultmann, 'Concerning the Hidden and Revealed God', *Existence and Faith*, trans. S. M. Ogden (London: Hodder and Stoughton, 1961), 23–34.

[15] See D. Howard-Snyder and P. K. Moser (eds.), *Divine Hiddenness* (New York: Cambridge University Press, 2002).

Christian theology, old and new, offers various attractive 'models' of God, revealed as Trinity. In book 15 of his *De Trinitate* Augustine highlighted the love analogy as a way of 'interpreting' the Trinity. The Holy Spirit is the Gift of mutual love between Father and Son—a theme already developed much earlier in the *De Trinitate*, 5. 11–12. Centuries later Richard of St Victor (d. 1173) argued that mutual love, to be perfect, must be love shared by a third person. In God we find not just an I–Thou relationship of reciprocal love but also the Holy Spirit as the 'Co-beloved (Condilectus)'. There is a 'movement' from self-love (the Father) to mutual love (the Father and Son) to shared love (Father, Son, and Holy Spirit). This view of God as absolute communion of love takes a little further Augustine's Trinitarian theology of love.[16]

In recent times a Barthian-style, more laconic model has been offered. The Trinity may be seen as the Revealer (the Father), the Revealed (the Son), and the Revelation (the Holy Spirit). But no model of the Trinity should be allowed to cloak its deep mystery.

The differentiated unity of the triune God means three co-equal, divine persons who are, however, not autonomous subjects. If we propose an interpersonal model of the Trinity, with the three persons totally related and transparent to the other two, we 'save' the divine Threeness but may seem to sacrifice the unity and lapse into tritheism. But if we stress the unity of God, we may 'save' the divine Oneness but lose the Threeness.[17] Millions of believers, not least Jews and Muslims, cherish a strict, mono-personal vision of God and find an 'alleged' revelation of the Trinity irreconcilable with true monotheism.

In 1 Corinthians, Paul attended to another aspect of the *Deus absconditus* and *revelatus*: the 'secret and hidden' wisdom of God (1 Cor. 2: 7–10) which has been revealed through the Holy Spirit and which made the crucifixion the key event in the divine plan for revelation and salvation. The image of God as a tortured criminal dying in terrible pain and utter disgrace subverts human expectation; this image remains totally scandalous and 'foolish'

[16] Richard of St Victor, *On the Trinity*, trans. A. Ruben (Eugene, Or.: Cascade Books, 2011).

[17] These challenges are well expounded by Sarah Coakley and other contributors to S. T. Davis, D. Kendall, and G. O'Collins (eds.), *The Trinity: An Interdisciplinary Symposium on the Trinity* (Oxford: Oxford University Press, 1999).

(1 Cor. 1: 18–23).[18] That Jesus' death on the cross disclosed a love that effectively saves the world seems mysteriously bizarre.

It is hard to bring the Trinity and the cross together. Atheists point to the senseless suffering of innocent people symbolized by the crucified Jesus as *the* proof that God does not exist. They view the cross as the place where God is absent and where any belief in an all-powerful, all-loving God should decently end. If there is a God, how can we explain such evil (*si Deus, unde malum*)? This radical difficulty brought up by theoretical and practical atheists serves to extend and illustrate the truth of Paul's words: 'we preach Christ crucified, a stumbling block to Jews and folly to Gentiles' (1 Cor. 1: 23).

Mark's Gospel joins Paul in portraying the Son of God as identified with sinful and suffering humanity and revealed in the degradation of the crucifixion (Mark 15: 39). A Roman centurion, in charge of the execution squad on Calvary, became the first human being to break through the divine incognito and recognize the divine identity of Jesus.

The 'secret and hidden' divine wisdom has also planned the deliverance of God's people: 'what no eye has seen, nor ear heard, nor the human heart conceived, what God has prepared for those who love him'. These things too 'God has revealed to us through the Spirit' (1 Cor. 2: 9–10). Paul, either directly or indirectly, drew this language from Third Isaiah: 'from ages past no one has heard, no ear has perceived, no eye has seen any God besides you, who works for those who wait for him' (Isa. 64: 4).

Thus the revealed and hidden wisdom of the triune God comprises both the past (the scandal of Christ's cross) and the future (the mysterious destiny that awaits those who love God). The paradox of a God who, while revealed, remains hidden, enfolds both the crucified Jesus and the coming destiny of his disciples.

From the early centuries of Christianity, many have struggled with the revealed truth expounded by the Council of Chalcedon (AD 451), Jesus Christ one divine person who enjoys two distinct but inseparable natures, divine and human. The persistent temptation has been either to jettison his full humanity and accept him as 'God in disguise'

[18] On these verses see J. A. Fitzmyer, *First Corinthians* (New Haven, Conn.: Yale University Press, 2008), 151–60; and A. C. Thiselton, *The First Epistle to the Corinthians* (Grand Rapids, Mich.: Eerdmans, 2000), 147–72. On revelation through the cross, see G. O'Collins, *Rethinking Fundamental Theology* (Oxford: Oxford University Press, 2011), 138–44.

who visited our earth, or to jettison his true divinity and accept him as the uniquely great but merely human teacher to be followed. Without belittling the challenge expressed by the truth of 'one person in two natures', I think there is a similar or even greater challenge in associating the cross with the revealed mystery of the Trinity. In the late second century and early third century, Melito of Sardis and then Tertullian appreciated what this association implied—confessing that the Son of God died on a cross.

THE SATURATED PHENOMENON

The Jewish and Christian Scriptures record and interpret much that bears directly on God's self-revelation. Jesus, the fullness of revelation, emerges as the highpoint in the whole story. Nevertheless, we have to be content to live 'in the presence' not only of 'Mystery' but also of 'Absolute Mystery'.[19] Revelation enhances rather than removes the absolute mysteriousness of God. The more one knows God, the more mysterious God becomes.

Marion has popularized the notion of 'the saturated phenomenon'—'the impossibility of attaining knowledge of an object, comprehension in the strict sense'. This happens not 'from a deficiency in the giving intuition, but from its surplus, which neither concept, signification, nor intention can foresee, organize or contain'.[20] Marion describes this 'overabundance' of the object as its remaining 'invisible, unreadable, not by lack, but indeed by an excess of light'.[21] In these terms, the self-revelation of God proves the 'saturated phenomenon' par excellence. The divine 'surplus', 'overabundance', and 'excess of light' means

[19] Rahner, *Foundations of Christian Faith*, 44–89.

[20] J.-L. Marion, 'In the Name: How to Avoid Speaking of "Negative Theology"', in J. D. Caputo and M. J. Scanlon (eds.), *God, the Gift, and Postmodernism* (Bloomington: Indiana University Press, 1999), 20–53, at 39–40. This essay is substantially reproduced as 'In the Name: How to Avoid Speaking of It', *In Excess: Studies in Saturated Phenomena*, trans. R. Horner and V. Berraud (New York: Fordham University Press, 2002), 128–62.

[21] J.-L. Marion, *Being Given: Toward a Phenomenology of Givenness*, trans. J. L. Kosky (Stanford, CA: Stanford University Press, 2000), 198. See also Marion, 'The Saturated Phenomenon', in *Phenomenology and the 'Theological Turn': The French Debate*, trans. B. G. Prusak (New York: Fordham University Press, 2000), 176–216.

'the impossibility of attaining knowledge of God, comprehension of God in the strict sense'. The divine mystery gives itself to us, but exceeds and overwhelms our capacity to receive it. The revealed God remains 'invisible, unreadable', and unknowable in what Pseudo-Dionysius the Areopagite called 'dazzling darkness'. 'Dazzling' and 'darkness' catch up the story of Moses.

On the one hand, 'the Lord used to speak to Moses *face to face*, as one speaks to a friend' (Exod. 33: 11; see Num. 12: 8; Deut. 24: 10). On the other hand, after God revealed the Ten Commandments, 'the people stood at a distance, while Moses drew near to *the thick darkness* where God was' (Exod. 20: 21). When God renewed the covenant by writing once again the commandments, Moses went up Mount Sinai: 'The Lord descended *in the cloud* and stood with him there and proclaimed the name, "The Lord"', and *disclosed himself* as 'The Lord, the Lord, a God merciful and gracious, slow to anger, and abounding in steadfast love and faithfulness' (Exod. 34: 4–6).

1 Kings provides another example of God being present and revealed by a cloud and even by 'thick darkness'. When the priests brought the ark of the covenant into Solomon's temple, 'a cloud filled the house of the Lord, so that the priests could not stand to minister because of the cloud. Then Solomon said, "The Lord has said that he would dwell in thick darkness"' (8: 10–12).

This striking sign of God being present and revealed in thick darkness and a cloud prompted Gregory of Nyssa into reflecting on God whose revelation does not take away his hiddenness:

> When, therefore, Moses grew in knowledge, he declared that he had seen God in the darkness, that is, that he had come to know that what is divine is beyond all knowledge and comprehension, for the text says, 'Moses approached the dark cloud where God was'. What God? He who 'made darkness his hiding place', as David says [Ps. 139: 12], who was also initiated into the mysteries in the same inner sanctuary.

Gregory envisaged here an experience of God that 'transcends all knowledge, being separated on all sides by incomprehensibility, as by a kind of darkness'.[22]

While Moses saw God disclosed to him, he was seeing God in darkness. God's self-revelation took nothing away from his hiddenness.

[22] Gregory of Nyssa, *Life of Moses*, II. 163, 164, trans. A. Malherbe, in *The Classics of Western Spirituality* (New York: Paulist Press, 1978), 95.

For Gregory of Nyssa, the first order language of Psalm 139: 12 hints at this truth by addressing God: 'even the darkness is not dark to you; the night is as bright as the day, for darkness is as light to you'.

Pseudo-Dionysius the Areopagite followed Gregory by accepting that all ends in a 'truly mysterious darkness of unknowing'. In the words with which his *Mystical Theology* begins, darkness is almost equated with light: 'the mysteries of God's Word lie . . . in the brilliant darkness of a hidden silence. Amid the deepest shadow they pour overwhelming light on what is most manifest.'[23] The coincidence of the 'truly mysterious darkness of unknowing' with the 'overwhelming light' parallels the theological paradox of the *Deus absconditus* being the *Deus revelatus*.

When referring above in passing to the rich meaning of the divine 'self-communication', we spoke of the intrinsic link between revelation and salvation. To that we now turn.

[23] Dionysius, *Mystical Theology*, 1. 1, 3; 997B, 1001A; in *Pseudo-Dionysius: The Complete Works, The Classics of Western Spirituality*, trans. C. Luibheid (London: SPCK, 1987), 135, 137.

3

Revelation Informs and Transforms

A German term reputedly coined by Rudolf Bultmann, *Heilsoffenbarung* (saving revelation), provides the theme for this chapter: the inseparable union between revelation and salvation. *Heilsoffenbarung* nicely suggests both salvation that is revealing and revelation that is intrinsically salvific.

We can explore the union between God's self-revelation and human salvation by examining (a) the effectiveness of the divine word, (b) the 'gospel' that saves, (c) the 'light' that brings 'life' in John, (d) the 'economy of revelation' and the 'history of salvation' as used by the Second Vatican Council, and (e) the possibilities offered by the term 'self-communication'.

THE WORD IS EFFECTIVE

The Scriptures constantly witness to ways in which the divine revelation, whether expressed as 'word', 'wisdom', 'truth', or in other terms, redemptively changes human beings. Thus the call to repentance which concludes Second Isaiah (40–55) draws its conviction from the firm assurance that the word of God is always effective and fruitful:

> As the rain and the snow come down from heaven and do not return there until they have watered the earth, making it bring forth and sprout, giving seed to the sower and bread to the eater, so shall my word be that comes out of my mouth. It shall not return to me empty, but it shall accomplish that which I purpose, and succeed in the thing for which I sent it (Isa. 55: 10–11).

These verses about the divine word which mark the end of Second Isaiah echo what was said at its beginning: 'The grass withers, the flower fades, but the word of our God will stand forever' (Isa. 40: 8). The image of withered vegetation may refer to the end of the Babylonian Empire. Whether or not that is the case, the divine word remains permanently valid, effective, and life-giving.

In the Old Testament 'the word of the Lord' occurs 241 times, and '225 occurrences are a *terminus technicus* for the prophetic revelation', with *dābār* meaning both 'word' and 'event'. Horst Dietrich Preuss explains: 'this word of YHWH, this *word event*, which was an *active power* as well as the means for conveying the divine message, was not only a "word" that imparted to the prophet what he or she was to say but also a power that he or she was to experience'.[1]

Where Second Isaiah compares the impact of the divine word with rain and snow, Jeremiah represents the message spoken by a prophet as fire and a devouring word of judgement. Since the people of God have spoken falsely of the Lord and not obeyed his message, the fiery divine judgement will be effected through a foreign nation whose language they cannot understand:

> Therefore thus says the Lord, the God of hosts: 'Because they have spoken this word, I am now making my words in your mouth a fire, and this people wood, and the fire shall devour them. I am going to bring upon you a nation from far away, O house of Israel,' says the Lord. 'It is an enduring nation, it is an ancient nation, a nation whose language you do not know, nor can you understand what they say' (Jer. 5: 14–15).

The prophet cannot refrain from proclaiming this burning word of judgement (Jer. 20: 9; 23: 29). The prophetic message of revelation can also prove powerful and effective in bringing to bear the grace of divine judgement.

In recent years Lieven Boeve has written of the way that God's revealing word is unsettling, even disruptive.[2] It can break open the 'certainties' with which believers seek to protect themselves in a hostile situation. What Boeve says about an impact that revelation has or should have today draws support from Isaiah's disrupting

[1] H. D. Preuss, *Old Testament Theology*, trans. L. G. Perdue, ii (Edinburgh: T. & T. Clark, 1996), 73, 75; italics mine.

[2] L. Boeve, *God Interrupts History: Theology in a Time of Upheaval* (New York: Continuum, 2007).

'oracles against the nations' (Isa. 13–23) and from Jeremiah's vivid language about God's 'cup of wrath' (Jer. 25: 15–38). In particular, the latter prophet adopts the unsettling images of 'roaring', 'treading grapes', courtroom indictment, and slashing with a sword to suggest the 'interrupting' power of the divine word in human history:

> The Lord will roar from on high, and from his holy habitation utter his voice; he will roar mightily against his fold, and shout, like those who tread the grapes, against all the inhabitants of the earth. The clamour will resound to the ends of the earth, for the Lord has an indictment against the nations; he is entering into judgement with all flesh, and the guilty he will put to the sword (Jer. 25: 30–1).

It is at our peril that we allow the life-giving, fruitful effect of God's word to distract us from its impact as unsettling and even disruptive.

THE GOOD NEWS OF SALVATION

Second Isaiah also expressed the union between revelation and salvation through the theme of good news or good tidings: the people will be freed from captivity and come home from exile.

> Get you up to a high mountain, O Zion, herald of *good tidings*; lift up your voice with strength, O Jerusalem, herald of *good tidings*, lift it up, do not fear; say to the cities of Judah, 'Here is your God!' See, the Lord God comes with might, and his arm rules for him.... He will feed his flock like a shepherd; he will gather the lambs in his arms, and carry them in his bosom, and gently lead the mother sheep (Isa. 40: 9–11).

Thus the prophet announces the good news of salvation and peace to the cities of Judah. The Lord will rule over them once more, like a loving shepherd. The revealing message of good news initiates the salvation that is under way.

A little further on in Second Isaiah the imagery associated with the 'good news' switches from shepherding to that of lookouts on the mountains and sentinels on the walls of Jerusalem:

> How beautiful upon the mountains are the feet of the messenger who announces peace, who brings good news (*euangelizomenos*), who announces salvation, who says to Zion, 'Your God reigns'. Listen! Your sentinels lift up their voices, together they sing for joy, for in

> plain sight they see the return of the Lord to Zion. Break forth together into singing, you ruins of Jerusalem; for the Lord has comforted his people; he has redeemed Jerusalem (Isa. 52: 7–9).

'Lookouts' and 'sentinels' are code words for the prophet who announces the good news: the divine Redeemer draws near and the people return from exile. The revealing announcement coincides with the salvation that has begun.

St Paul took up the language of the good news being a powerful message. He confessed his faith ('I am not ashamed') that the gospel (*euangelion*), as a message that reveals the divine power, leads to salvation, and, in particular, brings human beings into a right relationship with God: 'I am not ashamed of the gospel; it is the power of God for *salvation* to everyone who has faith, to the Jew first and also to the Greek. For in it [the gospel] the righteousness of God is *revealed* through faith for faith' (Rom. 1: 16–17).

Later in the same letter, Paul wrote of faith (in the revealing God) coming through the experience of hearing those who have been sent to proclaim. He recalled the words from Second Isaiah that we have quoted above: 'How beautiful are the feet of those who bring the good news' (Rom. 10: 15). Right from the start, Romans made it clear that the proclamation of this 'gospel' centred on Christ's resurrection from the dead (Rom. 1: 1–5).

Writing to the Christians of Corinth whom, unlike the Christians of Rome, he had personally evangelized, Paul took up the good news of Christ's resurrection from the dead that mediated salvation: 'I would remind you, brothers and sisters, of the *good news* that I proclaimed to you, which you in turn received, in which also you stand, through which also you are being saved' (1 Cor. 15: 1–2). The apostle pressed on to recall the early creed about Christ dying 'for our sins', being buried, being 'raised on the third day', and 'appearing to Cephas and then to the twelve' (1 Cor. 15: 3–5). At greater length he expounded the good news of believers sharing through resurrection in Christ's victory over death (1 Cor. 15: 12–34). The 'gospel', which had already worked upon them by delivering them from their sins, would make them 'alive in Christ' when everything will be subjected to God for ever (1 Cor. 15: 22, 27–8). In short, receiving the proclamation brings salvation. The first order language of 'good news', which Paul took over from early Christians, holds together what theology, in second order language, expresses as the union of revelation (received in faith) and salvation here and hereafter. This union is also suggested when the apostle associates 'the word of truth' with 'the power of God' (2 Cor. 6: 7).

The Gospel of Mark presents itself as 'the good news of Jesus Christ, the Son of God' (Mark 1: 1). Joel Marcus points out that 'of Jesus Christ' could 'be taken either as an objective genitive (the good news about Jesus Christ), or as a subjective genitive (the good news that Jesus Christ himself announces), or a combination of the two'. Marcus defends the combination: 'Mark's composition is not only the good news about Jesus but also the good news that Jesus himself proclaims through Mark'.[3] To this one might add as a further nuance a genitive of identity or 'epexegetical' genitive: the good news that is Jesus himself.

The use of 'gospel' in the prologue of Mark finds an 'inclusion' some verses later, in a double use of the term when Jesus opens his ministry by proclaiming 'the good news of God'. He reveals that 'the time is fulfilled' and 'the kingdom of God has come near'. Repenting and believing in this 'good news' will re-orient the lives of his hearers and renew Israel (Mark 1: 14–15). 'The old age of Satan's dominion' is 'at an end', and 'the new age of God's rule is about to begin'. Those who hear Jesus 'are called to turn in faith toward the new age that is dawning, in which God will reign as king'.[4]

In Mark, as in Paul, 'gospel' corresponds to the doublet, revelation/ salvation. We move now to John's Gospel, which, while never using the term '*euangelion*', in other ways suggests the coincidence of revelation and salvation.

THE GOSPEL OF JOHN

The Gospel of John links 'word' and 'truth' when Jesus promises liberation to those who believe in him and remain open to the divine revelation he communicates: 'if you continue in my word, you are truly my disciples; and you will know the truth [that is to say, know God as Jesus reveals God to be], and the truth will make you free'. Liberated from the slavery of sin, they will become sons and

[3] J. Marcus, *Mark 1–8* (New York: Doubleday, 1999), 146–7.
[4] Ibid. 175.

daughters of God enjoying eternal, divine life (John 8: 31–6). Thus appropriating the true self-revelation of God in and through the person and word of Jesus means being committed to the lasting, liberated relationship of believing in ('knowing') the one, true God and Jesus Christ whom God has sent (John 17: 3). In short, accepting revelation ('knowing the truth') inseparably brings salvation.[5]

The self-revelation of God always aims at saving and changing human beings. In the language of John's Gospel, the *light* of revelation is inseparable from the *life* of salvation. Where darkness has hitherto prevailed, Jesus brings light. He is 'the light' (John 1: 8–9) or 'the light of the world' (John 8: 5; 9: 5). 'Coming to the light', which is equivalent to coming to Jesus, means being exposed to the light and truth of God (John 3: 18–21), that light which not only exposes but also takes away the sinfulness of people. Those who follow Jesus will not live ('walk') in darkness but 'will have the light of life' (John 8: 12), the light that leads to 'eternal life', the enhanced life which is the very life of God shared with human beings.[6]

Sometimes the couplet, believing in (or coming to) the *light* and so finding *life*, becomes believing and finding life.[7] An early highpoint in John's Gospel announces: 'God so loved the world that he gave his only Son so that everyone who *believes* in him may not perish but may have eternal *life*' (John 3: 16). Thus believing in Jesus means believing in God who is revealed as love, reaches out to take away the sins of human beings ('of the world', John 1: 29, 36), rescues them from death, and brings them into the eternal life of God.

This message of *believing* in the light of revelation and receiving the salvation of eternal *life* turns up several times in John: 'the one who hears my word and believes him who sent me has eternal life' (John 5: 24). Speaking with Martha, Jesus assures her: 'those who believe in me, even if they die [a physical death], they will live [an eternal life]' (John 11: 26). The couplet, believing in the light of revelation and so receiving salvation, features in a closing statement about the purpose of the whole Gospel: all this has been written 'so that you may come

[5] Somewhat similarly Paul closely associates the 'word of truth' with the 'power of God' (2 Cor. 6: 7) when vividly presenting his ministry (2 Cor. 6: 1–13).

[6] The expression 'eternal life' is found seventeen times in John's Gospel, and six times in 1 John.

[7] John's Gospel uses the verb 'believe (*pisteuein*)' ninety-nine times but never uses the noun 'faith (*pistis*)'.

[or continue] to *believe* that Jesus is the Messiah, the Son of God, and that through believing you may have *life* in his name' (John 20: 31).

The First Letter of John calls revelation 'the word of life' (1 John 1: 1), a phrase which can be understood three ways: first, as the word or message that is life—an epexegetical genitive or genitive of identity that we find elsewhere: for instance, 'the feast of the Passover' (John 13: 1). Second, this could be a qualifying genitive as in 'the bread of life' (John 6: 35) and the 'light of life' (John 8: 12)—that is to say, the bread that brings life and the light that brings life. Third, a kind of objective genitive might point to the content of the message: the word or revelation about life. The ambiguity may be inherent in the text, with 'the word of life' displaying all three meanings.[8] Each interpretation points to the inseparable link between the word (revelation) and life. As we can put matters, without revelation (and the faith that responds to it), there can be no salvation. Or, more briefly, 'outside revelation, no salvation (extra revelationem nulla salus)'. Conversely, the life of salvation always entails some form of divine self-revelation (word) and hence some form of knowing God.

To sum up what we have seen so far: using different terms, Second Isaiah ('word'), Mark ('the good news'), John ('light' and 'truth'), and 1 John ('word') converge in witnessing that divine revelation, when accepted in faith, changes human beings and brings a new, redeemed and graced relationship with God. This change may entail a radical re-orientation of one's life that creates a bridge to a remarkably new future, as happened with those original disciples who responded positively to what Jesus disclosed. Or the change may be a quieter, less dramatic affair, as happens when Sunday homilies throw new light on a person's daily challenges. However it happens, the light of (received) revelation remains inseparable from the acceptance of salvation.

DEI VERBUM

This link justifies the Second Vatican Council's Constitution on Divine Revelation (*Dei Verbum* of November 1965) using, more or less interchangeably, revelation and salvation. The opening chapter of

[8] See R. E. Brown, *The Epistles of John* (New York: Doubleday, 1982), 164–6.

this document shuttles back and forth between the two terms: for example, in this passage from article 2:

> This economy of *revelation* takes place through deeds and words, which are intrinsically connected with each other. Thus the works performed by God in the history of *salvation* manifest and bear out the doctrine and realities signified by the words; the words, for their part, proclaim the works and elucidate the mystery they contain. The intimate truth, which this *revelation* gives us about God and the *salvation* of human beings, shines forth in Christ, who is both the mediator and the fullness of all *revelation*.

As far as Vatican II was concerned, the history of revelation is the history of salvation, and vice versa.

It may seem somewhat unnecessary for me to insist once again on the link between revelation and salvation. But recently Eduardo Echeverria has challenged my position that, when human beings accept God's revelation, they receive something which sets them on the way of salvation.[9] *Pace* Echeverria, revelation and salvation may be distinguishable but they are not separable. Years ago Juan Alfaro used to insist on this, citing the Johannine language of Christ being our Light (revelation) and hence simultaneously our Life (salvation). Joseph Ratzinger also prompted me into long ago taking up this position. His study of Bonaventure's concept of revelation allowed him to retrieve the notion that divine revelation is actualized in its outcome, human faith. God's self-revelation exists in living subjects, those who respond with faith. In a lecture given in 1963, Ratzinger insisted that 'revelation always and only becomes a reality where there is faith . . . revelation to some degree includes its recipient, without whom it does not exist'.[10] To this we should add: whenever revelation becomes a reality, revelation to some extent brings salvation.

SELF-COMMUNICATION OF GOD

One way of integrating linguistically the divine activity of revelation and salvation is to speak of God's 'self-communication'. Taken

[9] E. Echeverria, 'Vatican II and the Religions: A Review Essay', *Nova et Vetera* 13 (2015), 817–73, at 839–40.

[10] J. Ratzinger, 'Revelation and Tradition', in K. Rahner and J. Ratzinger, *Revelation and Tradition*, trans. W. J. O'Hara (London: Burns & Oates, 1966), 26–49, at 36.

together, divine revelation and salvation constitute the history of God's self-communication to human beings.

In their different ways, Barth, Bultmann, Romano Guardini, and Rahner helped to spread the language of divine self-communication (*die Selbstmitteilung Gottes*). That language turned up earlier, for instance, in what Hermann Schell wrote originally in 1900: 'The supernatural revelation of God means the free self-communication of God through word and deed to a personal and real community of life with the created spirit [of human beings].'[11]

The language of self-communication reaches back many centuries: for instance, to Thomas Aquinas who drew on Pseudo-Dionysius the Areopagite and wrote: 'goodness implies self-communication; it is appropriate for the highest good to communicate itself (se communicare) to the creature in the highest way possible'.[12]

In human history, this revealing and saving self-communication has shown a sacramental face as it comes through events (acts) and words. We turn next to examine the sacramental character of the divine self-revelation.

[11] H. Schell, *Katholische Dogmatik*, ed. J. Hasenfuss, H. Petri, and P.-W. Scheele, i (Munich: Schöningh, 1968), 28, n. 1; trans. mine.

[12] *ST* IIIa. 1. 1. resp.

4

The Sacramental Character of Divine Self-revelation

'One reveals oneself in, with, and through various acts one performs.'[1] As it stands, this statement from William Abraham needs an addition that he supplies elsewhere: one reveals oneself in, with, and through various acts one performs and various words that one utters. That is to say, one reveals oneself in, with, and through one's acts *and speech-acts*. God, as we will discuss below, reveals through acts and speech-acts the divine mind, will, and reality.

A key maxim in modern workshops for creative writing warns: 'Show, don't tell.' For all its value, however, this maxim does not apply to the means adopted for communicating the divine self-revelation. God both shows (at times in events of great symbolic power) *and* tells (through the words of prophets, Jesus, apostles, and others). Revelation exemplifies a sacramental principle. Like the sacraments where actions (e.g. in baptism the use of water) and words (e.g. the baptismal formula) work together to effect the sacrament, revelation comes about, above all, by means of *words* that proclaim and illuminate *events*, or by blending actions and words. Actions may 'speak louder than words', but we need the actions. The sacramental character of revelation provides the topic for this chapter.

After evoking the witness of the Scriptures, we will examine the relationship of 'event' and 'word', paying particular attention to special divine actions and divine discourse, and, in particular, to what it means to say that 'the Holy Spirit spoke through the prophets'. This will involve discerning the details of the prophetic experiences.

[1] W. J. Abraham, *Crossing the Threshold of Divine Revelation* (Grand Rapids, Mich.: Eerdmans, 2006), 59.

Finally, we will take up one example of the use of the doublet, 'words' and 'actions': the teaching of the Second Vatican Council's constitution on divine revelation.

THE WITNESS OF THE SCRIPTURES

This linking of word and deed to bring about the divine self-revelation has rich warrant in the Scriptures. God disclosed himself through word and deed. Words articulated what God was doing or had done. The Israelites remembered and interpreted the exodus, the return from the Babylonian captivity, and other crucial events as YHWH's deeds which manifested the divine intentions in their regard. Words glossed such events. After the deliverance from the Egyptians, Miriam and other women did not celebrate the courage of the Israelites or the leadership of Moses. Their song highlighted YHWH's act of salvation: 'Sing to the Lord, for he has triumphed gloriously; the horse and his rider he has thrown into the sea' (Exod. 15: 21; see 15: 1–18). They acknowledged God as the real agent of their victory: 'I am the Lord your God, who brought you out of the land of Egypt, out of the house of bondage' (Exod. 20: 2). The song of Moses at the end of Deuteronomy (31: 30–2: 43) associated word and deed to evoke and interpret centuries of Israel's history.

Christians inherited such convictions about the revelation of God's saving deeds, and attached what they themselves had experienced in the events of Jesus' life, death, and resurrection, along with the coming of the Holy Spirit. They added their own words when discerning and interpreting these events as the highpoint of the divine activity on behalf of the human race. Thus the discourse of Peter on the day of Pentecost elucidated the deeds of God:

> People of Israel, listen to what I have to say. Jesus of Nazareth, a man attested to you by God with mighty works, wonders, and signs which God did through him in your midst, as you yourselves know—this Jesus, delivered up according to the definite plan and foreknowledge of God, you crucified and killed by the hands of lawless men. But God raised him up, having freed him from death, because it was impossible for him to be held in its power (Acts 2: 22–4).

How are event (here the resurrection of Jesus) and word (here the discourse of Peter) correlated in terms of timing?

The revealing word may not only (a) precede some event (e.g. through a prophetic promise or prediction) or accompany the event (e.g. as was the case of Jesus' preaching accompanying his miraculous deeds), but also (b) follow the event (as happened with Peter's discourse on the day of Pentecost). Thus the meaning of the passion and death of Jesus was communicated more fully to the imagination and heart of early Christians when they came to associate the story of the crucifixion with the fourth 'Servant Song' of Second Isaiah (Isa. 52: 13–53: 12). Words about the Servant, whose cruel suffering brought blessings to innumerable others, clarified the meaning of a horrifying event, the savagely violent death of Jesus. A spectacular example of such words subsequently illuminating the event comes from the late first-century writer, Clement of Rome. He did not offer in his own words any explanation of the crucifixion but simply quoted the fourth 'Servant Song' (1 Clement 16).

EVENT AND WORD

Having said all that, we need to scrutinize further 'event' and 'word', which summarize the 'sacramental' means used for divine revelation. The series of collective experiences, in which God acted and which together made up the history of revelation and salvation, include events that undoubtedly took place (like the reign of King David, the later deportation to Babylon, the preaching of John the Baptist, the ministry of Jesus, and the destruction of Jerusalem) and episodes like the creation and fall of Adam and Eve that have a mythical rather than an historical character. The dissimilarities between the known factual status of, let us say, (a) the departure of Abraham and Sarah from Ur and Haran into Canaan and (b) the crucifixion of Jesus, are startling. Nevertheless, revelation and salvation encompass events which on any showing belong to human history. In the Roman Forum the images of Jewish captives and of the seven-branch candlestick from the Jerusalem temple carved inside the Arch of Titus still vividly assure viewers about the factuality of what, in their very different ways, Romans, Christians, and Jews experienced at the fall of Jerusalem in AD 70. At the heart of the biblical history of divine revelation and salvation there lies a set of events which certainly occurred—to be experienced then by believers and non-believers alike and accessible now to common historical investigation, even if the Christian discernment and interpretation of these events embodies a specifically theological understanding shared only by believers.

The *word* lights up the revealing and saving values of events, which in some cases might otherwise seem merely anonymous and meaningless blows of fate. Thus the message of Second Isaiah, Jeremiah, and Ezekiel discerns and interprets the Babylonian captivity—something that without the prophetic word could seem just another dreary case of a small nation overrun and deported by a major power. The divinely authorized word of interpretation shows such events of secular history to be, in some sense, 'acts of God' in the history of revelation and salvation. That word also authorized the message prompted by such simple, everyday sights in the life of Jeremiah as those of an almond branch, a pot on the boil, and a potter at work (Jer. 1: 11–12, 13–14; 18: 1–12). Whether the events were major or seemingly very minor, the revealing word opened up their revelatory meaning.

Such a stress on the perspective supplied by the revealing word leaves unanswered the question: why was a special, prophetic, and (later) apostolic, interpretation available for *these* historical experiences and events and not for *those*? Was there something about *these* historical experiences that prompted and even required that theological explanation? A one-sided stress on the word may rob of any special significance the events that it interprets.

But the truth about the history of revelation and salvation is surely the opposite. Ultimately the word remains subordinate to the events and, specifically, to those events concerned with the person who stands at the centre of that centuries-long history. God's supreme act in the history of Israel was to raise Jesus from the dead. Here action has priority over word, the effected reality over any interpretation of its import and impact.

SPECIAL DIVINE ACTIONS

Through the history of the Jewish people, God was made manifest in a network of divine actions that reached their highpoint with the life, death, and resurrection of Jesus. Often these actions occurred in, with, and through events in the 'natural' order. Take, for instance, the everyday examples just cited from Jeremiah or Jesus' parables of the kingdom that drew on the growth of mustard seeds (Matt. 13: 31–2) and on women mixing yeast in dough (Matt. 13: 33). Sometimes, however, these actions, as with the miracles of Jesus and his being raised from the dead, we need to recognize what should be called 'special divine actions'.[2] Whether we consider special divine actions or the 'ordinary' actions of God (who is the primary or first cause of everything that happens), a theology of revelation occurring through 'deeds and words' needs to explore what could and should be said about God as agent, significantly active in various events in history.[3] I suggest briefly characterizing such divine acts as follows.

First, to describe some act in that way is to recognize a special presence and significant activity of God, who is doing something qualitatively different from the 'ordinary' divine work of creating and sustaining the universe. There are various degrees of engagement on the part of God. Some events or series of events, as well as some persons, reveal more of the divine concerns and interests than others. To deny such different degrees of divine engagement with the world and its multiform history logically leads to deism, or the belief in a creator who leaves the laws of the universe to control everything with rigid uniformity.

Secondly, the particular divine activity to be qualified as 'a special act of God' remains in some measure recognizably independent of the world and created causality. Thus the resurrection of the crucified Jesus manifests in a unique way an autonomous divine causality. Other happenings designated 'special acts of God' may also be 'acts

[2] It is better to avoid talking of (special) divine 'interventions', which can too easily and falsely suggest an 'outsider' God coming actively on the scene for the first time. Some, Deist-inclined theologians doubt or deny any special divine actions. Thus Maurice Wiles wrote: 'We do not need to postulate any exceptional form of divine action to account for the occurrence of revelation in and through the central figures and events that have determined the distinctive shape of Christian faith and understanding' ('Revelation and Divine Action', in P. D. L. Avis (ed.), *Revelation* (London: Darton, Longman & Todd, 1997), 100–11, at 110). But, first, it is a question, not of *postulating*, but of recognizing forms of divine action. Secondly, Wiles rules out a priori the supreme event of Christ's resurrection, which gave a distinctive shape to Christian faith and understanding; it obviously called for an 'exceptional form of divine action'.

[3] See G. O'Collins, *Christology: A Biblical Historical, and Systematic Study of Jesus*, 2nd edn. (Oxford: Oxford University Press, 2009), 112–18.

of human beings' and entail an array of human causes and agents. Thus the events which brought about the Babylonian captivity or the execution of Jesus involve fairly elaborate interactions on the part of various human agents. Yet even in such cases a certain degree of autonomous divine causality remains, and authorizes Paul, for example, to say of what God allowed to happen: 'he gave up his only Son for all of us' (Rom. 8: 32).

Thirdly, special acts of God imply a religious claim and convey moral messages. Thus the ministry, death, and resurrection of Jesus challenged and continues to challenge men and women to rethink their worldview and way of life. On the day of Pentecost, Peter's proclamation of God's special activity in the history of Jesus concluded with a call to repent and be baptized (Acts 2: 38).

Fourthly, the freedom, unpredictability, and novelty of a special act of God involve an element of mystery. Such acts are never unambiguously so. They remain concealed to the extent that people may see or fail to see these events as acts of God. Recognition remains uncompelled. The factor of relative concealment allows cognitive freedom to persist. There are signs to be perceived but no overwhelming evidence; we have enough light to make us responsible but not enough to take away our freedom.[4]

DIVINE DISCOURSE

Proposing that God's self-revelation comes through deeds *and words* calls for some account of how God speaks, how human language can embody divine revelation, how the word of God can be present in the words of human beings, and how language can not only speak about revelation but also convey or 'speak' revelation.[5] Any such account could examine the prophetic claim to communicate 'the word of God' and Jesus' (implied) claim to teach and speak with divine authority, as well as reflecting on what happens today when the word of preaching

[4] This theme of sufficient but not overwhelming light characterizes the *Pensées* of Pascal; see the trans. by A. J. Krailsheimer (Harmondsworth: Penguin, 1982), nos. 394, 427, 429, and 461.

[5] See N. Wolterstorff, *Divine Discourse: Philosophical reflections on the claim that God speaks* (Cambridge: Cambridge University Press, 1993).

and the proclamation of the Scriptures are called 'the word of God'. Let me limit myself by taking a cue from the Nicene-Constantinopolitan Creed and explore the background for its confession that the Holy Spirit 'spoke through the prophets'.[6]

Even a cursory glance at Old Testament prophecy reveals its rich diversity: from the early prophets like Deborah (Judg. 4: 4–16; 5: 1, 12),[7] Elisha, and Elijah, through such classic prophets as Amos, Hosea, and Isaiah, down to the post-exilic prophets like Haggai, Zechariah, and Malachi. On occasion, Abraham (Gen. 20: 7; see Ps. 105: 15) and David (Acts 2: 29–31) were called prophets. Moses was deemed to be the founder of Israelite prophecy and even its pinnacle (Deut. 18: 15–20; 34: 10–12). The name of prophet belonged also to the non-Israelite Balaam (Num. 22–4), and to bands who used music and dancing to enter into a state of ecstatic exaltation and induce divine utterance (1 Sam. 10: 5–7; 19: 20–4; 1 Kgs. 22: 10, 12). Prophetic elements also showed up in the life and work of Nazirites like Samuel. The Old Testament record of prophets and prophetic experience exhibits a remarkable diversity.[8]

Yet in one way or another, prophets were all called to make known the divine mind and will. God was specially present to them, even to the point of identifying with what they said or did. Their personal judgement and human words became endowed with divine authority. In the Old Testament the expression 'the word of the Lord/God' occurs 241 times, and in 225 of these cases we deal with a prophetic

[6] Thomas Aquinas did not distinguish revelation clearly from prophetic inspiration and scriptural inspiration. Nevertheless, that 'failure' recognized the central importance of prophetic experience for an adequate account of revelation; see *ST* IIaIIae. 171–8.

[7] The Hebrew Bible names four other women as prophets or prophetesses: Miriam (Exod. 15: 20), Huldah (2 Kgs. 22: 14), and Noadiah (Neh. 6: 14), as well as an anonymous woman, the wife of Isaiah (Isa. 8: 9).

[8] On prophecy, see M. J. Boda and L. M. Wray Beal (eds.), *Prophets, Prophecy and Ancient Israelite Historiography* (Winona Lake, Ind.: Eisenbrauns, 2013); V. P. Branick, *Understanding the Prophets and their Books* (Mahwah, NJ: Paulist Press, 2012); R. E. Clements, *Old Testament Prophecy: From Oracles to Canon* (Louisville, Ky.: Westminster John Knox, 1996); S. L. Cook, 'Prophets and Prophecy', in S. E. Balentine (ed.), *The Oxford Encyclopedia of the Bible and Theology*, ii (New York: Oxford University Press, 2015), 201–11; H. B. Huffmon et al., 'Prophecy', *ABD*, v, 477–502; W. Klein et al., 'Propheten/Prophetie', *TRE*, xxvii, 473–517; H. D. Preuss, *Old Testament Theology*, trans. L. G. Perdue, ii (Edinburgh: T. & T. Clark, 1996), 67–96; M. A. Sweeney, *The Prophetic Literature* (Nashville: Abingdon, 2005); E. Zenger et al., *Einleitung in das Alte Testament* (Stuttgart: Kohlhammer Verlag, 1995), 293–436.

word. Let me dwell on *five points* that may elucidate what it means to say that the Holy Spirit 'spoke through the prophets'.

(1) First, Amos records the *intense immediacy* of his call; it was something that suddenly and directly came to him, even though he lacked any expected training and preparation. God abruptly swept Amos into a new existence. The shepherd turned prophet explained to the priest in Bethel: 'I am no prophet nor a prophet's son; but I am a herdsman and a dresser of sycamore trees, and the Lord took me from following the flock. The Lord said to me, "Go, prophesy to my people Israel"' (Amos 7: 14–15; see 3: 8). Amos and other classical prophets did not take the initiative in actively seeking a prophetic career. They experienced a call coming to them from God, who unexpectedly overwhelmed them. As Jeremiah's complaints vividly illustrate, at times prophets followed their call with deep reluctance (e.g. Jer. 20: 7–9). If the prophetic experiences exemplified the immediacy of a direct and deep encounter with God, the role of the prophets, at least initially, was passive rather than active. They reacted only after God had acted upon them.

(2) Secondly, the life of the prophet was revealed in their initial experience. It disclosed what their life was and was to be. If God's call took Amos' life in a new direction, this proved even more startlingly true of Jeremiah. His whole life, and not just some months of it, coincided with his prophetic vocation and experience.

(3) Thirdly, the prophetic experience comes across as a multi-levelled affair affecting *the entire existence of the subject* and involving a broad range of spiritual and physical powers. While frenzy characterized the early bands of prophets and admittedly could be, in principle, a medium for communicating genuine revelation, it was not a fully human form for conveying God's saving message and became less prominent as time went by. To be sure, we meet an unusual psychological intensity, even abnormality, in Ezekiel's visions, ecstasy, shaking, dumbness, and possible temporary paralysis (e.g. 3: 22–7; 4: 4–8; 24: 27; 33: 22). However, the classical prophets, both the three major and the twelve minor prophets, normally do not receive the divine message through ecstasy, dreams, or other such states, but by consciously using their various powers. They look, listen, answer, and deliver a message. Thus Isaiah's vision in the temple ends: 'I heard the voice of the Lord saying, "Whom shall I send, and who will go for me?" Then I said: "Here am I! Send

me." And he said, "Go and say to this people: 'Hear and hear, but do not understand'"' (Isa. 6: 8–9). Jeremiah provides another such case, when the Lord first questions him about the things he sees and then communicates the divine intentions (Jer 1: 11, 13; see Amos 8: 1–2). Here and elsewhere, prophecy presents itself as a complex experience involving the whole person and a full range of human powers.

(4) Fourthly, unlike other experiences, the prophetic experience does not exist in general. Usually the prophetic writings, even if their introductions or 'superscriptions' come from later editing, make this point by specifying the *particular* date and place of their origin. The opening words of Amos (1: 1) and the vision in the temple recounted by Isaiah (6: 1–13) both highlight the particularity of their experience. Jeremiah likewise indicates the specific setting, in which the word of the Lord came to him: 'in the days of Josiah the son of Amon, king of Judah, in the thirteenth year of his reign. It came also in the days of Jehoiakim the son of Josiah, king of Judah, and until the end of the eleventh year of Zedekiah the son of Josiah, king of Judah, until the captivity of Jerusalem in the fifth month' (Jer. 1: 2–3). For all his abnormality, Ezekiel also provides details as to the date and place of his prophetic experience (1: 1–3). Such experience is nothing if not concrete. It happens at particular times, in particular places, and to particular persons who must convey this or that message to a specific audience.

(5) Fifthly, human experience, or at least significant human experience, is characteristically discerned, interpreted, and *communicated.* The Creed ('the Holy Spirit spoke through the prophets') reminds us that the prophets were primarily speakers. Jeremiah, however, seems to have used Baruch as his secretary (Jer. 30: 1–32). But normally it was left to the followers of prophets and others to collect, edit, arrange, and expand the prophetic oracles before distributing them in written form.

The prophets themselves proclaimed the divine word, announcing God's saving intentions and denouncing human failure, and at times did so through dramatic, symbolic actions. Thus Isaiah acted out a threatening future by going around for three years naked and barefoot like a prisoner-of-war (Isa. 20: 2–4). Jeremiah carried a yoke on his shoulders (Jer. 27: 1–2) as a sign of the yoke of Babylon imposed by God on Judah and her neighbours (Jer. 21: 1–10; 32: 3–5). Jeremiah also remained unmarried and childless to suggest the grim prospects that awaited Jewish parents and their children (Jer. 16: 1–9). Hosea may have entered an unhappy marriage as a means for communicating his word from the Lord (Hos. 1: 2–9). As well as expressing some message, these symbolic gestures also mysteriously helped to bring about what they represented. The prophets shared in the dynamic role of God's revealing word, which effected what it signified.

A later chapter will examine biblical inspiration. To anticipate one issue, we can state that the divine self-communication to the prophets, right down to John the Baptist, meant that they were inspired to speak and act, but not—in general—to write. The God-given impulse to write down their prophetic utterances belonged rather to those who came after them. The same conclusion emerges from the picturesque descriptions that Isaiah, Jeremiah, and Ezekiel gave of their vocations: they were all called to speak. The lips of Isaiah were consecrated for that mission (Isa. 6: 6–7), while Jeremiah received the word of the Lord in his mouth (Jer. 1: 9). Ezekiel, admittedly, had to eat a scroll that was to fill his stomach (Ezek. 2: 8–3: 3). This detail may suggest writing. Yet even in his case the predominant task remained speaking (e.g. Ezek. 2: 4, 7; 3: 1, 4).

Much of what I have drawn from the classical prophets may have raised for some readers the bothersome question: do we really know what happened? Can we be sure, for instance, that the experiences of the prophets, now well over two thousand years ago, were authentically initiated by God and that they inwardly heard communications from God? Reflection on the prophetic experience offers at least seven reasons for being positive, if cautious, about our conclusions.

DISCERNING THE PROPHETIC EXPERIENCE

(1) For the Old Testament the prophetic message, conveyed through words and symbolic actions, remains primary. From the message we may be able to infer something about the personal experiences that prompted it, but precise and assured evaluations will be hard to come by.

(2) We also have to reckon with the chronological gap between the actual events in the lives of the prophets and the final form of the biblical text. Oral and written traditions stretching over several centuries normally intervened before that text became settled. This complex process reduces any hopes about reaching easy certainties.

(3) Third, the prophets repeatedly affirm the divine origin of their message. They do so by means of such traditional formulas as 'Thus says the Lord'. But they themselves normally show little interest in reflecting on and analysing their inner experiences as such.

(4) Fourth, such formulas remain so brief and stereotyped that they hardly describe the experiences that may lie behind them. Traditional expressions for introducing authoritative messages, they rarely seem to be sharply autobiographical statements about specific experiences of the prophets. 'The word of the Lord' and 'Thus says the Lord' do not necessarily involve the claim that the prophets literally heard an inner or an outer voice speaking to them. Such conventional categories of announcement may be just that, conventional and no more. Likewise 'to receive a vision' can serve as a technical term for a prophetic revelation, and by no means should always be taken literally.

(5) Another, fifth, aspect to the problem is this. On the one hand, we cannot expect prophets to deliver a message that in form and content strikingly diverges from earlier prophetic messages. It would be unreasonable to expect that kind of originality as one of the tests of authentic prophetic experience. On the other hand, however, the fact that later prophets draw on earlier messages and expressions, even if they introduce their own modifications, obviously leaves us with the questions: To what extent are they endorsing a religious tradition rather than witnessing to their personal experience? Where do the traditional elements end and where does their own experience begin? To require massive originality from the prophets would be to slide over the fact that they are human beings born into a society with its religious traditions and language. Yet the more their message resembles what has gone before, the less sure we will be about identifying the shape of their own personal experience.

(6) Further questions arise when we notice how the frontier between what a prophet sees and what a prophet hears often gets blurred. Take the case of Balaam. With 'open eyes' and seeing 'the vision of the Almighty', he delivers 'the oracle' of one 'who hears the words of God' (Num. 24: 15–16; see 24: 3–4). What we meet here is properly speaking no vision but a message, words that the Lord puts in the mouth of Balaam (Num 23: 5, 12, 16). Another example. The biblical text calls Samuel's experience as a boy at the sanctuary of Shiloh a 'vision' (1 Sam. 3: 15), but the vision consists in his hearing God's call. At times the Scriptures speak about prophets or others having 'visions' and 'seeing' something, or about God 'appearing' or

'showing' them this or that, when the reality of the visual experience is not the issue. Talk about a vision or an appearance may simply mean that a communication from God has taken place, a promise or some other message has been received.

It would, for example, be a mistake to insist on the visionary nature of Abraham's experience according to Genesis 12: 7. Even if the text speaks of an 'appearance', it focuses rather on the promise understood to have been communicated to Abraham: 'The Lord appeared to Abram and said: "To your descendants I will give this land."' Isaiah reports a 'stern vision', but it is a vision that has been 'told' to him, an 'oracle', something that he has 'heard from the Lord of hosts' (Isa. 21: 1–2, 10). The blurring of the frontier between what is seen and what is heard by the prophets belongs to a general tendency to play down the visual phenomena. What is heard predominates over what is seen.

(7) Finally, the *call* of the prophets not only essentially shapes their stories but also highlights the difficulty of discerning what happened. The prophets know themselves to be specially chosen by God. Amos simply states his call as a fact (7: 14–15), without elaborating on how it came about. But with others, like the three major prophets (Isaiah, Jeremiah, and Ezekiel), we have call narratives that use common motifs to express the individual experience of the prophet and the authority they have received from God.

Ronald Clements classifies the prophetic call-narratives into two groups.[9] The first group, which includes Jeremiah, evokes also the experience of Moses (Exod. 3: 1–4: 17), Gideon (Judg. 6: 21–32), and Saul (1 Sam. 9: 1–10: 16). Here God overcomes an inadequacy and reluctance on the part of the person called. Members of the second group are summoned, through some vision of God, to join the deliberations of the heavenly council (e.g. Isaiah, Ezekiel, and Micaiah-ben-Imlah (1 Kgs. 22: 5–28)). God may be represented as equipping the prophet for the task, as in the case of Isaiah where we find the cultic motif of ritual cleansing (Isa. 6: 6–8).[10]

Now in both groups the prophet is often warned that his message will be rejected and that he must endure opposition. But does such a warning truly belong to the original call-experience? Or has the subsequent experience of rejection been projected back into the

[9] R. E. Clements, *Prophecy and Tradition* (Oxford: Basil Blackwell, 1975), 33–9.

[10] Some scholars interpret Isa. 6: 1–13 not so much as the prophet being called but rather as introducing his interventions in Judean politics.

story of the original call-experience? Such a prior warning, narrated as part of the call-experience, also happily meets the objection: if the prophetic message were from God, the people would have accepted it. With such a warning inserted into the call-narrative, the people's refusal to listen confirms the authenticity of a given prophet. Or has the warning about the opposition and hostility to be faced become a traditional way of presenting a prophetic call? New prophets, while aware of being authentically called by God, stand then in a tradition that would prompt them to use traditional motifs to describe their call.

While not intended to cast doubts on the whole reality of prophets' experiencing the revealing word of God, these seven considerations aim at raising questions and encouraging an appropriate caution when interpreting the prophetic texts. They heard the voice of God, but we need to be modest and careful in our interpretation of the details. The questions I have just raised are not typically raised by the Old Testament itself. What we do find is a persistent awareness of the need to discriminate true prophets from false ones. Both in the history of Israel (1 Kgs. 22: 1–28; Jer. 28: 1–17) and elsewhere the possibility of falsehood looms over all prophecy (see Matt. 7: 22–3; 1 John 4: 1–3). Has God spoken through *this* prophet? Does the divine authority and a genuine (and genuinely interpreted) experience of God stand behind his or her message?[11] All in all, it seems enough to follow the Creed in maintaining in general the experience of divine self-communication mediated through the prophets ('the Holy Spirit spoke through the prophets'), while allowing that particular details may be hard to discern and interpret.

In the past some scholars have tried to press analogies between the prophets and the experiences of Christian and other mystics. Recently Stephen L. Cook has drawn on a best-selling account of a catastrophic illness that shut down a surgeon's brain for a week, Eben Alexander's *Proof of Heaven: A Neurosurgeon's Journey into the Afterlife*,[12] to illuminate the experiences of Old Testament (and other) prophets.[13] But does this modern account of God being experienced in a deep coma shed light on the story and function of Isaiah, Jeremiah, Ezekiel,

[11] On this and further issues about prophetic revelation, see G. O'Collins, *Rethinking Fundamental Theology* (Oxford: Oxford University Press, 2011), 90–5.

[12] New York: Simon and Schuster, 2012.

[13] Cook, 'Prophets and Prophecy', 202–3.

and the other classical prophets? Two major considerations suggest otherwise.

First, neither the three major prophets nor the twelve minor prophets are remembered as experiencing God and receiving some divine message when some catastrophic illness left them in a coma for some days. It is significant that Cook cannot introduce anything from the prophetic traditions that matches what Alexander suffered—the experience of going through a week-long, near-death experience. Secondly, Cook endorses the still useful language of prophets functioning as both 'foretellers' and 'forthtellers', which strikes 'a balance between prophecy [a] as anticipation (rich with profound revelations of God's coming reign, of the Messiah) and prophecy [b] as self-standing (intrinsically revelatory of Yahweh, true God)'.[14] Alexander's story has nothing to say (or at least add) about [a]. It does not foretell anything about God's coming reign. As regards [b] it does not reveal something that was not or was not yet known about God. At best, as the subtitle of Alexander's book suggests, it may 'prove' or confirm for many people the Christian and Jewish belief in God and afterlife. Alexander himself enlisted his experience to 'prove' here and now the reality of heaven, not to prove the trustworthiness of the historical prophets.

Cook introduces two minor pieces of witness in defence of his analogy, (a) the first dealing with heavenly visions and the second taken from unfolding meaning. At Dothan, the servant of Elisha, when faced with a mighty Syrian army, had a vision of a heavenly army (2 Kgs. 6: 17). Thus he is alleged to have long ago learned 'the self-same truth' that Alexander has recently described: the normally functioning human brain 'blocks out, or veils, [the] larger cosmic background, just as the sun's light blocks out the stars'.[15] What counts here as 'the self-same' in the 'self-same truth'? It is simply unbelievable that Elisha's servant came to accept anything like the conclusion Alexander reached: 'in its normal function my brain blocks out the heavenly realities and I am not seeing what is always truly there in front of me'. Are we supposed to accept that any similar, heavenly vision, like the host of angels appearing to the shepherds in Luke's infancy narrative (Luke 2: 8–14), teaches the 'self-same truth'? Moreover, prophets may have visions of the 'other'

[14] Ibid. 210. [15] Ibid. 202; he quotes from Alexander, *Proof of Heaven*, 72.

world, but not all those who have visions of the 'other' world are prophets, let alone reach the conclusion that Alexander did.

Furthermore, let us remember that prophetic visions include not only 'objects' in the heavenly world but also objects in *this* world. The visions that conclude Amos (7: 1–9: 15) include, to be sure, a vision of the Lord 'standing beside a wall with a plumb line in his hand' (7: 7–9). But these visions *also* involve seeing 'locusts' (7: 1–2) and 'a basket of summer fruit' (8: 1–3). Such visions of *this-worldly* objects also disclose divine messages.

(b) Cook also picks up what Alexander wrote about receiving a 'seed' of 'trans-earthly knowledge', that will take years 'to come to fruition', 'years to understand', and invokes 'the seedlike quality of prophecy'. He comments: 'any one application of a *revelation* will not necessarily exhaust its meaning'.[16] This alleged parallel between Alexander's experience and that of the prophets proves so general as to be uninformative. It is true of an enormous range of deep experiences, whether specifically religious or not, that we can need many years to grasp much of their meaning, let alone exhaust that meaning. The little that we may learn on the occasion of such experiences often has a 'seedlike quality', which leads much later to growth in understanding and applying what we learned at the time. Once again Cook's analogy limps badly.

This chapter has dealt with various ways in which word and deeds mediate the divine self-revelation, and possible ways of thinking about divine acts and discourse. Let me draw together this 'sacramental' mediation by presenting and discussing a recent example of God's self-disclosure being interpreted by an interplay between word and deed.

WORD AND ACTIONS

The previous chapter cited the sacramental language of words and actions used by Vatican II's Constitution on Divine Revelation and

[16] Cook, 'Prophets and Prophecy', 203; he cites Alexander, *Proof of Heaven*, 82; italics mine. Did Cook intend to mean 'any one application of a prophetic message'? Or does he think that all God-given, prophetic messages are truly revelations? What about prophetic messages that simply confirm and apply what has already become known through revelation?

applied both to the 'economy of revelation' and the 'history of salvation' (*Dei Verbum*, 2, 4). By a covenant with Abraham and then through Moses, the constitution declares, God 'revealed himself in *word and deeds* as the one, true, living God' (*DV* 14; italics mine). Then Christ 'himself established on earth the Kingdom of God [and] revealed (manifestavit) his Father and himself by *deeds and words*' (*DV* 17; italics mine).

Some have understood this 'sacramental' way of presenting God's saving and revealing self-revelation to have an ecumenical origin, as if it combined the language of such (a) word-of-God theologians as Karl Barth and Rudolf Bultmann with (b) that favoured by Oscar Cullmann, Wolfhart Pannenberg, and George Ernest Wright about God's saving and revealing acts in history. Without ruling out all such ecumenical motivation, we should recognize how the word/deed language enjoyed a different and older background.

A year before *Dei Verbum* was promulgated in November 1965, the Constitution on the Church (*Lumen Gentium*) of 21 November 1964 recalled Jesus' proclamation of the divine kingdom: 'this kingdom shone out before human beings in the *words*, in the *works*, and in the presence of Christ' (art. 5; italics mine). The first document promulgated by Vatican II on 4 December 1963, the Constitution on the Sacred Liturgy (*Sacrosanctum Concilium*), adopted similar, sacramental language: the Eucharistic 'mystery of faith' involves both 'sacred action' and 'instruction by God's word' (art. 48), while an act of 'celebration' and 'words' constitute the other sacraments (art. 59). This liturgical document prepared the way for the sacramental language of *Dei Verbum*, which applied to the whole reality of revelation what *Sacrosanctum Concilium* had already enunciated about the liturgy. The 'law of praying (lex orandi)' helped fashion the 'law of believing (lex credendi)'.[17]

But one needs to go further back: in November 1962, the terminology of 'words' and 'works' had already entered the making of *Dei Verbum* through Pieter Smulders, a Vatican II *peritus* or expert. One should also mention what Smulders communicated several months earlier to Archbishop Giuseppe Beltrami, the papal nuncio to the Hague: revelation embraces not only the '*locutio Dei*' (the revelatory

[17] See further G. O'Collins, '*Sacrosanctum Concilium* as a Hermeneutical Key for Vatican II', *The Second Vatican Council: Message and Meaning* (Collegeville, Minn.: Liturgical Press, 2014), 57–88, at 65–7.

word) but also the '*magnalia Dei*' (the great deeds of God).[18] One of the leading experts on Hilary of Poitiers (d. 367/8), Smulders, consciously or unconsciously, echoed him. In the opening article of *Tractatus Mysteriorum*, Hilary had written of the biblical 'words (*dicta*)' and 'facts (*facta*)' that 'announce (*nuntiare*)' and 'reveal (*exprimere*)' the coming of Christ.[19]

This 'sacramental' language about the divine self-revelation being communicated through 'word and deed' has turned up in modern times: for instance, in what Hermann Schell wrote in 1900.[20] A few years earlier a posthumous book by Johann Baptist Franzelin (d. 1886) used similar language, when explaining revelation to be 'a divine locution, made up of *words* stating a truth and of *facts* proving that these words are a divine locution'.[21]

Such 'deeds' and 'words' that mediate sacramentally the divine self-revelation can assume very many different forms. The next chapter explores the polymorphous nature of this mediation.

[18] On the contributions from Smulders (and others) to the making of *Dei Verbum*, see J. Wicks, 'Vatican II on Revelation—From Behind the Scenes', *Theological Studies* 71 (2010), 637–50. See also G. O'Collins, *Retrieving Fundamental Theology* (Mahwah, NJ: Paulist Press 1993), 57–62.

[19] See *Traité des Mystères*, ed. and trans. J.-P. Brisson, rev. edn. (Paris: Cerf, 2005).

[20] For details see n.11 in Chapter 3 above.

[21] J. B. Franzelin, *Tractatus de Divine Traditione et Scriptura* (Rome: S. C. de Propaganda Fide, 1896), 618; italics mine.

5

Means and Mediators of Revelation

William Abraham calls 'revelation' a 'polymorphous' activity like that of teaching: 'one teaches by giving lectures, holding tutorials, setting papers, and requiring set texts to be read'.[1] His analogy alerts us to the great diversity in the mediators and means of God's self-disclosure. This is a far cry from those who narrow down the possible avenues of revelation: for instance, Martin Luther who tended to limit the revelation of God to the preached word that elicits faith.[2] The present chapter takes a cue from Abraham and argues a different case. The means through which God conveys revelation and the mediators of the divine self-revelation can be indefinitely varied. But, before reflecting more broadly on the means and mediators of revelation, let me begin with one specific issue: the self-disclosure of God communicated by created reality.

REVELATION THROUGH CREATED REALITY

Immanuel Kant famously remarked that two things make human beings think of God: the 'starry skies' above and the 'moral law' within their hearts: 'Two things fill the mind with ever new and increasing admiration and reverence, the more often and more steadily one reflects on them, *the starry skies above me and the moral law within me*'.[3] Thus Kant pointed to (a) the way in which the order and

[1] W. J. Abraham, *Crossing the Threshold of Divine Revelation* (Grand Rapids, Mich.: Eerdmans, 2006), 59.

[2] E. Herms, 'Offenbarung V', *TRE*, xxv, 162–4.

[3] I. Kant, *Critique of Practical Reason*, trans. M. J. Gregor, rev. edn. (Cambridge: Cambridge University Press, 2015), 129; italics Kant's.

beauty of the created world display the wisdom and power of God, and so manifest God to human beings everywhere. Somewhat like John Henry Newman a century later (who understood the voice of conscience to manifest the moral character of God), Kant also recognized (b) how the divine law written on human hearts (see Rom. 2: 14–15; Jer. 31: 31–4) makes known the mind and will of God. Thus two basic features of the universe, 'out there' in visible, created reality and 'in here', within the moral conscience of human beings, disclose something of God and the divine nature, character, and purposes.[4] Since the principle 'God can be known only through God' applies here as well, it is God who reveals himself through creation and conscience.

All human beings are offered the revelation of God mediated through (a) the beautiful and orderly works of creation and through (b) their own, inner spiritual reality. The author of the Book of Wisdom concentrated on the former, when criticizing any nature worship that took 'the luminaries of heaven' or other natural forces to be 'the gods that rule the world'. Delighting 'in the beauty of these things, people assumed them to be gods'.[5] They should have known 'how much better than these is their Lord, for the author of beauty created them'. 'If the people were amazed at their power and working', Wisdom goes on to say, 'let them perceive from them how much more powerful is the One who formed them'. The argument reaches its climax with the statement: 'from the greatness and beauty of created things comes a corresponding perception of their Creator' (Wis. 13: 1–9).

Do we detect here an early intimation of the modern argument from the Principle of Sufficient Reason, which requires some adequate explanation for the existence and nature of the universe? Why is there a universe in the first place? Why is there something rather than nothing?[6] Is it convincing to claim that the universe is

[4] Psalm 51 dramatically pictures a sinful conscience expressing remorse to God, who is utterly holy and life-giving in his moral requirements. On the voice of God in the human conscience, see D. Fleming, 'Primordial Moral Awareness: Levinas, Conscience and the Unavoidable Call to Responsibility', *Heythrop Journal* 56 (2015), 604–18, esp. 610–11.

[5] Developing this argument, Paul interpreted idolatry as an utterly foolish attempt to deny the real God and so evade accountability for immoral actions. When human beings culpably refuse to know God from the world in which they live, they suffer severe moral consequences (Rom. 1: 18–32).

[6] See J. C. Lennox, *God's Undertaker: Has Science Buried God?* (Oxford: Lion Hudson, 2007), 62–4.

self-explanatory and answer: 'it's simply there'? Does the universe bring about its own existence, simply popping into existence, as a massive exception to the Principle of Sufficient Reason (and any universal causal principle)? It is widely agreed that whatever comes to be has a cause distinct from itself, or—in brief—that there are no uncaused events and no self-causation. If so, can the universe be the big exception to this principle? If it is such a uniquely exceptional case, how did/does it cause itself?[7]

Wisdom envisaged no such argument mounted by reason or 'logos', as if God were merely the conclusion of rational discussion. Rather God is revealed in and as 'Sophia', Lady Wisdom, who encouraged an experience of the created world through which human beings should acknowledge the divine presence and enter into a living contact with God. Centuries before the Book of Wisdom was written, the order and beauty of the cosmos which God has created and continues to sustain in existence inspired the vivid hymn that is Psalm 104. Other psalms also praised creation's beauty and harmony (e.g. Ps. 19: 1–6; see also Job 38–9) and poetically celebrated the Creator's power and intelligence that can be experienced and recognized in the created world. But, unlike sections of psalms and two other psalms that deal specifically with creation (Ps. 8; 104), Psalm 148 gave a voice to creatures (e.g. to the mountains, trees, and some animals). Echoed by an addition to Daniel, The Prayer of Azariah (vv. 35–59), it helped to inspire St Francis of Assisi's Song of Brother Sun (*Cantico di frate sole*), paraphrased hundreds of years later as 'All Creatures of Our God and King'. Francis, the first Christian known to have received the stigmata or bodily marks of Christ's passion, embodied in that way the climax of the history of salvific revelation, but he also felt at home with the revelation conveyed by God's creatures.

All human beings are faced with this cosmic revelation of God. Even before examining the particulars of their history, we should agree that they never find themselves 'outside revelation (*extra revelationem*)'. Hence we need to qualify what Matthew Levering writes about the evangelizing activity of the Church: 'by proclaiming and witnessing to the gospel, the Church *extends* to the nations the good

[7] See D. H. Mellor, *The Fact of Causation* (London: Routledge, 1995).

news of divine revelation'.[8] As it stands, this statement suggests that, before the Church proclaims the gospel, divine revelation is not yet extended to the nations. However we interpret the history of their specific religious beliefs and practices, the nations are all offered at least cosmic revelation (see Chapter 12 below), which includes its full 'macro-scene' and the 'micro-scene', or the divine intimations coming through the exercise of the human mind and will, as we argue later. Extending beyond the gospel, divine revelation is found everywhere and reaches all human beings before they hear the message of the Church. That evangelization *enriches* the offer of God's self-revelation. But this revelation is not *extended* to them for the first time when they are evangelized.

THREE OBSERVATIONS ON COSMIC REVELATION

(1) First of all, a healthy theological view of creation and a deep concern for the environmental crisis can sometimes overemphasize revelation mediated through creation at the expense of revelation through history. Thus, following Thomas Berry, John F. Haught writes: 'we must look at it [revelation] not simply as a set of historical events, but *even more fundamentally as a cosmic phenomenon*'.[9] Unquestionably, the divine self-revelation is *also* a cosmic phenomenon: 'the heavens are telling the glory of God, and the firmament proclaims his handiwork' (Ps. 19: 1). Modern scientific knowledge of the shaping of the universe towards the appearance of life and then consciousness has plausibly encouraged such a vision. But Jews and Christians believe that this cosmic form of revelation is surpassed by 'a set of historical events' and persons.

The Israelite experience of the created world remained subordinate to their experience of history. The historical perspective, exemplified in the ancient confession of faith that summarized the saving history they had experienced (e.g. Deut. 26: 5–9; Josh. 24: 1–13), prevailed

[8] M. Levering, *Engaging the Doctrine of Revelation* (Grand Rapids, Mich.: Eerdmans, 2014), 56; italics mine.

[9] J. F. Haught, *Mystery and Promise: A Theology of Revelation* (Collegeville, Minn.: Liturgical Press, 1993), 151, 164; italics mine. On nature as an expression of the mind and power of God, see M. Wahlberg, *Reshaping Natural Theology: Seeing nature as creation* (Basingstoke: Palgrave Macmillan, 2012).

over any divine self-manifestation through nature. The Psalms reflect the same privileging of history as the environment of God's revelation. A psalm that praises God as creator and redeemer spends only five verses recalling the creation (Ps. 136: 5–9) but sixteen verses praising God for delivering Israel from Egypt and helping in battles to possess the promised land (Ps. 136: 10–25). Even the early chapters of Genesis fit into the larger context of Israel's salvation history. Those chapters show us how the Israelites, on the basis of specific experiences of God in their history, thought about the beginning of the world and the human race. The stories in Genesis answered the question: what must the origin have been like for our past and present historical experience to be what they have been and are?

The subordination of everything to salvation history went so far that even the *feasts* which dealt with creation and nature—or, more specifically, with the harvest and the flock—were tied to Israel's history. The Feast of the Unleavened Bread (which took place at the beginning of the barley harvest) was linked to the exodus from Egypt (Exod. 23: 15; 34: 18).Originally the Passover feast seemed to have been an offering made by nomads when they began their New Year's migration from the desert into the agricultural land. This feast too was drawn into the story of the exodus from Egypt (Exod. 12–13), and linked with the Feast of the Unleavened Bread. The two feasts were 'historicized and served to simulate, commemorate, or remember the Exodus'. For the Israelites the experience of God through history took precedence over any divine self-manifestation through the seasonal events of nature.[10]

In general, the Old Testament Scriptures show the Israelites in continuing conversation with great events, in their history but not in the heavens, which disclosed pre-eminently 'the glory of God' who had 'triumphed' historically on their behalf (e.g. Exod. 15: 1–21). Israel came to know 'that I, the Lord, am your Saviour and your Redeemer' (Isa. 60: 16). The God already manifested in the Jewish story is the God of the history of Jesus, the continuation and climax of all Old Testament revelation. For Christians, the birth, life, and death of Jesus constituted nothing less than the human history of God, *the* unique act of God's personal, self-giving love in history. Jesus was not merely 'a' parable or even 'the' parable of God, showing us what God is like. As *the* (historical) revelation of God, he was more than that. To

[10] See B. M. Bokser, 'Unleavened Bread and Passover, Feasts of', *ABD* vi, 755–65, at 760.

disclose his own person and activity was to disclose God: 'who has seen me has seen the Father' (John 14: 9). Through the revelation in Jesus, God defined the divine identity for all time and for all peoples.

To be sure, God is actively and intimately present in all creation and in all human life. In the words of Augustine's *Confessions*, God is 'more inward than my innermost self (*interior intimo meo*)'—a sentiment often rendered as 'closer to us than we are to ourselves' (3. 6. 11). But, in a truly unique event that went, in kind and not merely degree, beyond any previous historical act of God, as well as beyond the divine presence in creation, the incarnation revealed God with us and for us, as being personally present among us.

There is much to be said for following Wolfhart Pannenberg (1928–2014) and centring matters, not on the cosmic revelation (mediated by the universe), but on *homo historicus* (my expression, not his), who, being embedded in history, is still incomplete but moves towards a final consummation. In a tour de force, Pannenberg brought together the religious implications of (human) biology, cultural anthropology, psychology, sociology, and history to construct a religious account of human beings as created in the image of God but marred by historical sin that distorts their true identity. Human persons are social beings, whose subjective identity is shaped by society, with its institutions, political order, and culture that language expresses and develops in particular ways. Pannenberg understands history to embrace all these elements and to embody the concrete reality of human life.[11] Such a vision of the human person as *homo historicus* coordinates well with the biblical view of revelation's major context, history developing towards its consummation at the end of time.

A later chapter will address the question of divine revelation coming to those peoples for whom the historical revelation recorded, interpreted, and applied by the Old Testament and the New Testament has not been available or, for various reasons, has not yet proved acceptable. Here let me point out that (a) sets of events (and persons) in their particular histories have, as a matter of fact mediated to them the divine self-revelation even more than (b) any 'cosmic' revelation available through the created universe. Unquestionably, as the Book of Wisdom, Paul, and other religious 'authorities' recognize, 'the heavens show forth the glory of God' to all human beings, and the

[11] W. Pannenberg, *Anthropology in Theological Perspective*, trans. M. J. O'Connell (Philadelphia: Fortress Press, 1983).

divine law written in their hearts lets them hear God in the voice of their conscience. Nevertheless, they too could acknowledge the action of God revealed in their history. The rule of God is universal and universally disclosed.

Here the prophet Amos deserves a hearing. He picks out three peoples: the Nubians or Ethiopians, the Philistines, and the Arameans. Through the prophet, God questions Israel: '"Are you not like the Ethiopians to me, O people of Israel", says the Lord. "Did I not bring Israel up from the land of Egypt, and the Philistines from Caphtor and the Arameans from Kir?"' (Amos 9: 7). The Nubians form a distant population who live 'at the end of the earth'; the Philistines (along the Mediterranean coast) are the traditional enemy of Israel to the West; their 'exodus' has also brought them into the Holy Land. The Arameans or Syrians, to the East, had been in conflict with Israel only a few decades before Amos begins his prophetic activity.

The prophet proclaims that the Nubians, even if distant and different, are not therefore inferior in the divine plan. God's saving actions and, by implication, a revealed knowledge of those actions reach everyone, including enemies of Israel (the Philistines and the Arameans). All peoples are blessed in their history by God's saving and revealing activity.

What God says here through Amos puts the story of the Philistines and the Arameans on a similar level with that of the Israelites. The Philistines entered Canaan shortly after the Israelites and competed with them for dominance of the region. Like Amos, Jeremiah identified Caphtor (probably Crete) as the place from which they came (Jer. 47: 4). Kir was understood to be the place from which some at least of the Syrians came and to which they would be exiled (Amos 1: 5; 2 Kgs. 16: 9).[12] Amos 9: 7 ranks together in the saving (and, by implication, revealing) activity of God (a) the invasions of the Philistines and Arameans and (b) the foundational religious event for the Israelites: their exodus from Egypt which saw them become the covenanted people of God at Mount Sinai. The deliverance from Egypt was not unique and affords them no special assurance. The divine involvement in the history of all peoples could hardly be expressed more clearly than this. Despite the fact that the saving revelation of YHWH has granted special status to Israel, it is not a

[12] See B. S. Hess, 'Caphthor', *ABD* i, 869–70; on the difficulties of locating Kir, see H. O. Thompson, 'Kir', *ABD* iv, 83–4.

superior status; the divine care and guidance, as well as God's sovereign rights, extend to all peoples and their history.[13] They may also be recognized as God's chosen peoples.[14] God's hand is also revealed in their history.

(2) Secondly, we need to add flesh and blood to any talk of 'cosmic' revelation. Jesus invoked the self-witness that God offers when dispensing sunlight and rain for all human beings, good and bad alike (Matt. 5: 44), and when providing for the birds of the air and the lilies of the field (Matt. 6: 25–31). The words of Jesus entice Australians to recognize the Creator in the beauty of their flora and fauna: in the wildflowers of the Western deserts and the quolls, bandicoots, kangaroos, and other animals of their bush—not to mention the eagles, finches, flycatchers, parrots, wrens, and other birds that make the southern continent a paradise for birdwatchers.

The Book of Acts points to the divine self-disclosure mediated when God 'gives rains from heaven' and 'fruitful seasons', and fills people with food (Acts 14: 17). We can go further than this by recognizing, for instance, how language about human beings created in the 'image and likeness' of God (Gen. 1: 26–7) can be charged with life and beauty.

At every stage of their existence, men and women show forth their Creator. In *Intimations of Immortality* William Wordsworth (1770–1850) expressed the divine splendour of childhood: 'trailing clouds of glory do we come / From God who is our home. / Heaven lies about us in our infancy.' Benedict XVI (pope 2005–13), in his first encyclical, *Deus caritas est* (25 January 2006), saw God reflected and revealed in the passionate love of man and woman (art. 2). Thomas Aquinas (d. 1274) thrilled to the greatest and most beautiful paradigm of God's unconditional love, that of a mother for her child (*ST* IIaIIae. 27. 1). In *Rabbi Ben Ezra*, Robert Browning (1812–89) hinted at the beauty God reserves for the second half of life: 'Grow old along with me! / The best is yet to be, / The last of life, for which the first was made. / Our times are in his hand / Who saith "A whole I planned".' Having visited over many years retirement homes in Australia,

[13] See F. I. Andersen and D. N. Freedman, *Amos* (New York: Doubleday, 1989), 867–85; S. M. Paul, *Amos* (Minneapolis: Fortress, 1991), 282–4.

[14] See M. G. Brett, *Decolonizing God: The Bible in the Tides of Empire* (Sheffield: Sheffield Phoenix Press, 2008), 30, 73–4.

England, and Germany, I have glimpsed over and over again the special beauty of the elderly and terminally ill. They too 'show forth the glory of God'.

Talk of 'cosmic revelation' can lead us to raise our eyes above the human scene to the 100,000 million galaxies in the universe, each containing about 100,000 million stars. They disclose the exuberant power and wisdom of their mysterious Creator. Emphasizing 'cosmic revelation' might suggest that astronomers have a head start in the business of recognizing the self-manifestation of God. That would mean forgetting how the Creator is eminently revealed in those creatures made in the divine 'image and likeness', 'Crowned with glory and honour' (Ps. 8: 5), human beings show the majesty of God—as artists, builders, dentists, doctors, engineers, factory workers, farmers, grandparents, musicians, nurses, parents, secretaries, singers, teachers, train drivers, and the rest. Thus a woman gasping and panting in child birth expresses the life-giving action of God who brings the people home once more through the wilderness (Isa. 42: 14). Let us not forget how those who suffer as asylum seekers, homeless, intellectually disabled, prisoners, refugees also have their special role in revealing the face of God (Matt. 25: 31–46).The full human scene, even more than the vast theatre of galaxies, tells forth something of the existence, nature, and mysterious presence of God.

We need to keep an eye open to the indefinitely many ways in which human beings, as well as 'subhuman' nature, are 'charged with the grandeur of God' (Gerard Manley Hopkins). In such poems as 'God's Grandeur' and 'Pied Beauty', Hopkins (1844–89) evoked the self-revelation of God that comes through nature, while his 'Wreck of the Deutschland' summoned up the human mediation of revelation—in this case by five Franciscan nuns who were expelled from Germany and off the English coast drowned between midnight and morning on 7 December 1875.

(3) Third, highlighting 'cosmic revelation' risks privileging the macro-scene, the way to God provided by the greatest show out there, the expanding and evolving universe. It is at our peril that we forget the micro-scene, the deepest hungers of human beings, classically expressed by Augustine of Hippo at the start of his *Confessions*: 'You have made us for yourself, O Lord, and our heart is restless until it rests in you' (1. 1. 1). Every human being reveals something of God in his or her dynamic self-questioning and openness to the infinite.

The micro-scene of each mind and heart constantly puts God on display. Ways of expressing this truth have proved far from uniform.

With their many questions, children embody a ceaseless drive towards meaning and truth which human beings are born with and which points to God. Sooner or later we question ourselves. Where do we come from? Who are we? What does our existence mean—in its sinful failures, apparent successes, and future destiny? Is there a supreme Being in whose presence we play out our lives and to whom we are finally responsible? Will we go to meet that Being beyond death?[15]

The psychiatrist Viktor Frankl (1905–97), the founder of logotherapy, understood the struggle to find meaning to be the principal driving force in human beings.[16] The transcendental therapy of Karl Friedrich Graf Dürckheim (1896–1988) took a larger view of this quest. He detected a triple shape in our quest for fulfilment. (a) Human beings can feel threatened by death in its various forms. (b) They can be overwhelmed by a sense of injustice and meaningless absurdity. (c) They can be abandoned, cruelly treated, and hated. Then they can be given life; they can experience a deeper order and meaning in things; and they can know themselves to be the objects of loving goodness. These experiences can make people long even more for some experience of life, meaning, and love that will change everything. These experiences and longings studied by Dürckheim and his school may be seen to point to a tripersonal God, who is total Life, Meaning, and Love (all in upper case).[17]

Philosophers and theologians, like Joseph Maréchal (1878–1944)[18] and Karl Rahner (1904–84),[19] have unfolded the dynamic thrust of the human intellect that constantly presses beyond the immediate data of sense experience towards the fullness of meaning and truth to

[15] Robert Coles, in *The Spiritual Life of Children* (Boston: Houghton Mifflin, 1990), shows how, often with surprising feeling and subtlety, children ponder the great questions about the human predicament: our origin, our nature, and our final destiny.

[16] V. Frankl, *Man's Search for Meaning: An Introduction to Logotherapy*, trans. I. Lasch (London: Hodder & Stoughton, 1964).

[17] Alfred Singer, who became the literary executor of Graf Dürckheim, passed on to me the triple form taken by his transcendental therapy.

[18] See his 'Le dynamisme intellectual', *Revue néoscolastique de Philosophie* 28 (1927), 137–65.

[19] See his *Spirit in the World*, trans. W. V. Dych (New York: Herder & Herder, 1968), 142–5, 179–83.

be found in the Absolute. God shows himself as the One towards whom the human intellect is irresistibly drawn.

In Rahner's vision of the human condition, human beings put everything into question and do so within an infinite horizon of questioning. Every particular answer prompts a new question. Human beings are, in fact, the question that they can never adequately settle and answer by themselves.[20]

Artists and writers find their place among those who have expressed strikingly the human questing that draws attention to the presence of God. Shortly before his death in Tahiti, the post-impressionist painter Paul Gauguin (1848–1903) wrote out three questions on a large triptych he had completed: 'Where do we come from? What are we? Where are we going?' Classical writers, like Leo Tolstoy (1828–1910), have constantly raised these eternal questions in their novels and dramas, questions fuelled by the restless hunger of the human heart that unveils something of the divine goal in all its desires.

THE MEANS OR 'HOW?' OF REVELATION

As we saw above, William Abraham has described revelation as a 'polymorphous' activity that takes place by a variety of means. Years ago at a wedding breakfast in Oxford, a guest seated next to me enquired what I was doing. 'At the moment', I replied, 'I am writing a book on revelation.'[21] Excitedly he asked: 'Have you had any revelations yourself?' Obviously he supposed that revelation always implied dramatic, intense experiences in which one sees a vision or hears a heavenly voice. This was to forget 'the many and diverse ways' (Heb. 1: 1) in which God has spoken and continues to speak. Any human experience can convey a self-communication of God. The means for revelation encompass both common and uncommon experiences and all manner of positive and negative experiences. These means include but go far beyond the inspired utterance of prophets.

[20] K. Rahner, *Foundations of Christian Faith: An Introduction to the Idea of Christianity*, trans. W. V. Dych (New York: Seabury Press, 1978), 31–3.

[21] G. O'Collins, *Theology and Revelation* (Cork: Mercier, 1968).

The Old Testament records an innumerable variety of experiences which conveyed some divine self-communication.[22] An extraordinary vision of the heavenly throne room mediates the call of the prophet Isaiah or perhaps, more specifically, his call to intervene in Judean politics (Isa. 6: 1–13). Ezekiel's ecstasies, the patriarch Joseph's dreams (Gen. 37: 5–10), his interpretation of dreams (Gen. 40: 1–23), and the theophanies experienced by Moses convey God's revealing and saving purposes. But God also speaks through ordinary, inner states of anxiety and joy, through current events, and through everyday sights. Thus the psalms of individual lamentation and thanksgiving repeatedly attend to such all-pervasive human troubles as sickness, false accusation, loneliness, and persecution. Various sufferers picture these situations and their experience of God's activity on their behalf (e.g. Ps. 3, 6–7, 12, and 22). The coming birth of a child—its mother was probably either the wife of Isaiah or the mother of Hezekiah—becomes a sign that witnesses to the truth of the prophet's prediction about coming political events (Isa. 7: 10–14). Jeremiah sees an almond branch (1: 11–12), a pot on the boil (1: 13–14), and a potter at work (18: 1–12), and such sights all bring him God's revealing word. The fall of Jerusalem in 587 BC, while in one sense a relatively minor political catastrophe that has happened over and over again in human history, also manifested the purposes of God. The Israelites came to know God and the meaning of life more profoundly both through exceptional moments and dramatic events like the return from their Babylonian captivity, through quietly pondering the everyday experience of death that says so much about the vanity of human wishes (Ecclesiastes), and through sharing in sacred music led by an ancient orchestra (Ps. 150).

The psalms testify to the ways the Israelites experienced God's presence and power in situations that regularly occurred or through activities in which they regularly engaged—like pilgrimages to Jerusalem and worship in the temple. Yet prophets called on the same people to be open to new and extraordinary divine acts. Thus Hosea proclaimed a renewal in which the people would experience a fresh start (2: 6–7, 14–15; 3: 4–5). Isaiah announced a new Davidic king (9: 1–7; 11: 1–10), Jeremiah a new covenant (31: 31–4), Ezekiel (in his vision of the valley of the dry bones) a new life for the people

[22] On God's self-revelation recorded by the Old Testament, see H.-D. Preuss, *Old Testament Theology*, trans. L. G. Perdue, i (Edinburgh: T. & T. Clark, 1995), 200–26.

(37: 1–14), and Second Isaiah a new exodus (40: 1–11). Nothing expressed more vividly the need to reckon with fresh, surprising experiences than the divine command in Second Isaiah: 'Remember not the former things, nor consider the things of old. Behold I am doing a new thing' (Isa. 43: 18–19).

H. W. Wolff sums up the way in which the prophets invited the people to face new events in which God's revealing and saving activity would be experienced: 'The breakthrough to what lies in the *future* is the heart of their mission and the essential element in their prophetic office.' To be sure, 'they are concerned with Israel's *traditions* and *history*, and even more with the *present*, but the accounts of their calls and of the missions entrusted to them make it clear that the absolutely decisive factor is the announcing and bringing in of what is *radically new*.'[23]

It seems incontestable. The experiences that carry divine revelation into human history can stretch from what is utterly common to what is stunningly novel and even truly unique. That conclusion emerges easily from the Old Testament with its rich variety of historical, prophetic, and sapiential books. The written record of Israel's experience is almost four times as long as the New Testament and took something like a thousand (as opposed to less than one hundred) years to come into existence.

At the same time, however, the briefer New Testament record establishes the same thesis: all manner of ordinary or extraordinary experiences mediated God's saving revelation. In his preaching Jesus introduced a wide range of everyday events which point to the divine mercy, presence, and power: a woman hunting through her house for some mislaid money; a boy who leaves home to enjoy the world; the growth of crops; sheep that stray; and many other items that belonged to daily life in ancient Galilee. The ministry of Jesus took place in the violent setting of a divided country occupied by a foreign power—a tragic situation that has turned up repeatedly in human history. In such a context the killing of a religious reformer like John the Baptist and the slaughter of those Galileans 'whose blood Pilate mingled with their sacrifices' (Luke 13: 1) came easily. At the end Jesus himself was executed as one of a batch, outside the walls of Jerusalem—a normal enough affair under the Roman administration. In that sense the

[23] H. W. Wolff, *The Old Testament. A Guide to its Writings*, trans. K. R. Crim (London: SPCK, 1974), 62; italics mine.

crucifixion belonged among the 'ordinary' experiences which conveyed saving revelation from God. Nevertheless, among the means by which that revelation came, one must also remember the miracles performed by Jesus and the unique event of the resurrection. Nothing could be more 'extraordinary' or 'uncommon' than his victory over death, the beginning of the new creation that anticipates the end of all history.

All in all, in the history of the Old and New Testament and in our situation today, God communicates his saving self-revelation through an indefinitely varied range of experiences: from the most dramatic and unusual to the most ordinary and commonplace. God's purposes can be served by all kinds of means—from the remarkable language of Second Isaiah to the dull words of some preacher in the twenty-first century. The birth of a child, family life, political episodes, religious worship, the teaching of bishops, aesthetic experiences, and other human realities can all shape the medium through which God's saving word comes to us. An endless variety of experiences conveys the divine revelation.

We must reckon also with 'primitive' means that can bring revelation, such as (1) dreams and (2) the casting of lots. (1) We noted above the dreams of the patriarch Joseph and his role as interpreter of dreams. The prophet Daniel was remembered not only for his own dreams (starting in Dan. 7: 1) but also for God, 'the revealer of mysteries', having given him the gift of interpreting dreams (Dan. 2: 28–30). The New Testament follows suit with the dreams of Joseph (Matt. 1: 20–4; 2: 13–15, 19–23), dreams that played a crucial part in guiding his actions at the birth of Jesus and in the face of threats from Herod the Great. Matthew likewise tells of a dream that prompted the wife of Pilate to send word to him when he was engaged in the trial of Jesus: 'have nothing to do with that innocent man, for today I have suffered a great deal because of a dream about him' (Matt. 27: 19). Carl Jung (1875–1961) and other psychologists encourage us to assign more importance to our dream-life. It need not be a mere concession to some 'primitive' instinct of human beings if God were to use dreams as a means of communicating revelation.

(2) But what of the casting of lots? In a key episode that involved his son Jonathan and the war against the Philistines, Saul used the *Urim* and *Thummim* to decide between two alternate courses of action (1 Sam. 14: 36–46). We find something similar in the Acts of the Apostles, when Peter presided at the choice between two possible

candidates to replace Judas Iscariot. Lots were cast to let Jesus the 'Lord' show his choice of the one who should complete the ranks of the twelve apostles (Acts 1: 15–26). Both the Old and the New Testament shared the belief that God's will could be shown through the casting of lots (e.g. Lev. 16: 8; 1 Chron. 25: 8–31). Chosen by lot for the once-in-a-lifetime privilege of offering incense in the temple, Zechariah was 'in place' to receive from an angel a message concerning the birth of John the Baptist (Luke 1: 8–20). The casting of lots, no less than dreams, could feature among the means for indicating God's purposes and for bringing about the divine will.

More serious doubt can flare up when we move beyond positive and 'peak' experiences of individuals and groups (e.g. visions, deliverance from death, and prophetic calls) and 'neutral' means like dreams and the casting of lots, and begin including such 'negative' experiences as episodes of suffering, sin, and further evil among the means through which God communicates saving revelation. Yet the witness of the Bible proves clear. If the Israelites knew their God through the peak experiences of liberation from Egypt and entry into the promised land, God also spoke to them through the tough experience of their deportation to Babylon. 1 John testifies to 'the word of life' that has been joyfully 'heard', 'seen', 'looked upon', and 'touched'. But the Johannine literature testifies as well to the experience of Christ's death and invites its readers to 'look upon him whom they have pierced' (John 19: 35–7). Paul recalls the dramatic meeting on the road to Damascus that turned his life around (1 Cor. 9: 1; 15: 8; Gal. 1: 11–15). Yet he also recognizes the divine power of salvation manifested in the utter vulnerability he constantly experiences on his apostolic mission (2 Cor. 4: 7–12; 6: 4–10; 11: 23–9; 12: 7–10).

In theory and even more in practice, many Christians prove slow to admit that episodes of ugliness rather than beauty, of hatred rather than love, and of sin rather than virtue can become the channels of God's saving revelation. Such experiences appear destructive rather than redemptive, confusing and threatening rather than illuminating, alienating from God rather than connecting with and disclosing God. Nevertheless, the Scriptures and Christian experience agree that evil, including sin, can become means by which divine revelation is communicated. The light of divine love can shine through the darkness of human suffering and sin. When King David committed adultery and murder, his sin occasioned some profound moments of truth about his state before God and future destiny (2 Sam. 11–12).

In this case the courageous intervention of the prophet Nathan prompted David into discerning the situation very quickly. Frequently, however, episodes of sin and evil do not reveal any meaning so readily. It may take years, even a lifetime, before some disorders and seemingly pointless atrocities are understood for what they disclose about revelation and salvation and the human need for God's initiatives. Sinful and tragic situations can leave us lastingly puzzled and appalled. While the first Christians rapidly appreciated and interpreted the unique and positive experience of Jesus' resurrection, his shameful death on a cross did not quickly yield up its meaning and purpose. Initially they could only say that the crucifixion happened according to the plan and foreknowledge of God (Acts 2: 23), which is as minimal an interpretation as a believer might offer. However quickly or slowly the divine message comes through, (a) negative episodes of suffering, sin, and other evil can convey the divine self-manifestation, no less than (b) happier 'moments of glad grace' (W. B. Yeats, 'When you are old') initiated by quietly mulling over the Scriptures. The environment of revelation in which the Holy Spirit is at work embraces both (a) crucifying situations and (b) the context of liturgy, bible study groups, sacred concerts, and natural scenes of exquisite beauty.

Let me offer a final example of (a). Sir Alister Hardy (1896–1985), the Linacre Professor of Zoology at the University of Oxford, founded in 1969 the Religious Experience and Research Centre, housed since 2000 at the University of Wales, Lampeter. He and his colleagues put together a huge database of over 6,000 personal accounts of spiritual experiences provided by 'ordinary' people. Public worship, the beauty of nature, sacred concerts, and prayerfully reading the Bible could prove the environment for events of revelation. Yet even more these reports, over and over again, witnessed to the way in which painful and even tragic episodes had triggered a vivid sense of God's loving presence. A comforting revelation of divine support and love came through, even and often especially, at times when many felt themselves afflicted and tortured by evil.[24] These accounts form a kind of

[24] See A. Hardy, *The Spiritual Nature of Man: A Study of Contemporary Religious Experience* (Oxford: Clarendon Press, 1983). On the work of Hardy, see D. Hay, *Something There: The Biology of the Human Spirit* (London: Darton, Longman & Todd, 2006).

modern prose counterpart to the ancient poetry of the psalms of lamentation and thanksgiving.

THE MEDIATORS OF REVELATION

Like the means for the divine self-communication, the mediators and messengers of that saving revelation have been and remain indefinitively various. In the whole history of God's self-communication, both inside and outside the Jewish-Christian story, certain individuals enjoy an uncommon capacity to discern, interpret, and express revelatory experiences. They can play a special role in communicating the divine revelation and salvation. Whether institutionalized (e.g. as kings and priests) or non-institutionalized (e.g. as prophets), these individuals prove themselves to be chosen channels through which people at large can experience God's self-communication. Hence part of the answer to the question '*How* did/does the divine self-communication occur?' must consist in pointing to the rich variety of mediators and messengers.

Such mediators people the pages of the Old and New Testament: Abraham and Sarah, Moses, the prophets, the authors of wisdom literature, Mary of Nazareth, the apostles, and the supreme case, Jesus himself. Jesus was not simply a great messenger from God; he was not simply a very important word about God; he was *the* Word of God incarnate, the uniquely full and final mediator of God's revelation to human beings (1 Tim. 2: 5). In all that story prophets may stand out as those who receive and mediate the divine revelation. But it is at our peril that we neglect the other mediators—not least Jesus himself, a prophet but much more than a prophet.

The history of Christianity (and of other religions) shows a constant line of men and women whose special gifts enabled them to convey God's saving words to others: saints,[25] founders of religious movements, prophetic figures, martyred bishops, outstanding church

[25] In the Dogmatic Constitution on the Church, the Second Vatican Council describes the revelatory function of saints: 'In the life of those who, sharing with us the human condition, are more perfectly transformed into the image of Christ (see 2 Cor. 3: 18), God vividly manifests (*manifestat*) to human beings his presence and face God addresses (*alloquitur*) us in them and offers us a sign (*signum*) of the Kingdom, to which we are powerfully attracted' (*Lumen Gentium*, 50).

leaders, and the rest. Nor should we pass over the innumerable 'lesser' mediators: from Christian parents in Korea to catechists in Africa, from parish priests in California to the Little Sisters of Jesus in Papua New Guinea.

As we have noted, William Abraham called 'revelation' a 'polymorphous' activity, which like teaching involves a variety of means. To this analogy we can add that teachers themselves are 'polymorphous', ranging from pre-school teachers of tiny children through to research professors leading teams of doctoral students at world-class universities. The mediators of revelation, no less than the means conveying the divine self-revelation, have varied and continue to vary enormously.

Mediators of divine revelation may also include unexpected and even hostile and murderous figures, such as the high priest Caiaphas, who presided over the Sanhedrin or highest leadership group in Jerusalem. John's Gospel reports him as prompting the decision to kill Jesus rather than tolerate a situation that might lead to the Romans 'destroying our holy place and our nation': 'it is better to have one person die for the people than to have the whole nation destroyed'. The evangelist reflects on the irony contained in the 'pragmatic', ruthless advice offered by Caiaphas: 'he did not say this on his own, but being high priest that year he prophesied that Jesus was about to die for the nation, and not for the nation only, but to gather into one the children of God who had been scattered' (John 11: 47–52). Caiaphas unwittingly disclosed the true meaning of the death Jesus was about to undergo. Among modern writers of fiction Flannery O'Connor (1925–64) stands out for proposing freakish characters, even a serial killer, as those who can be used by divine providence to convey something of the self-revelation of God.

A CODA: EXPERIENCE AS A MEDIUM, NOT A SOURCE

Before moving on from the various means and mediators which bring the divine self-revelation to human experience, we should recall what Paul Tillich wrote about experience not being a source but rather a medium: 'experience is the medium through which the sources "speak" to us, through which we can receive them'. Experiencing in faith the self-disclosure of God (the topic for our next chapter) creates the possibility for theology. Once again, as Tillich warned, experience does not thereby become 'a' or even 'the' source of theology: 'experience is not the source from which the contents of systematic theology are taken but the medium through which they are existentially received'.[26]

Tillich's observation has become even more important and critical in the twenty-first century when seemingly more writers slip into naming experience as a source for their theology. The language, for instance, adopted by Kevin Kelly about 'making faith-sense of experience and experience-sense of faith' left me with the question: how does Kelly understand 'experience'? Does he think of it as a *source* for theological reflection? Or does he think of experience as the context in which the life of faith is exercised and the medium through which the source(s) of faith can be received? Yet he writes of 'an experience-based moral theology'. Is such an approach meant to replace a biblically (and doctrinally) based moral theology?[27] Is his 'experience-based moral theology' another name for an experience-sourced moral theology? Kelly is only one among a number of contemporary writers who call for scrutiny in the light of Tillich's penetrating dictum.

[26] P. Tillich, *Systematic Theology*, i (Chicago: University of Chicago Press, 1951), 40, 42. Here Tillich differs markedly from F. D. E. Schleiermacher. As P. D. L. Avis (ed.) remarks in *Revelation* (London: Darton, Longman & Todd, 1997), 53, 'Schleiermacher went wrong, Tillich believes, in making experience the source of theological statements; it is, rather, the unavoidable medium of theological reflection'.

[27] K. Kelly, *50 Years Receiving Vatican II: A Personal Odyssey* (Dublin: Columba Press, 2012), 19, 21.

6

Believers Receive Revelation and Are Themselves Revealed

Divine revelation happens only when it is received by human faith, and so can, at least in some minimal sense, be understood and interpreted.[1] There is a reciprocity to revelation that makes it resemble love; revelation and love are not yet truly there before they are reciprocated.

In several works Caravaggio (d. 1610) brilliantly caught this reciprocity. In a chapel dedicated to St Matthew found in the church of St Louis in Rome, you find three paintings of the apostle by Caravaggio. The first painting depicts Matthew sitting at his tax booth engaged in his unsavoury work of collecting taxes and being called by Christ to leave that disreputable occupation and become a disciple. On the one side, Christ stretches out his arm in a way that recalls the Sistine Chapel and Michelangelo's depiction of the creation of Adam. Behind the extended arm of Christ there is an open window; its woodwork takes the form of a cross. On the other side, there is Matthew sitting at his desk with light shining on his face. He has seen and accepted the divine Light that at the incarnation has come into the world. Most commentators note how Caravaggio has brought together creation, the incarnation, and the crucifixion. What they normally miss is the

[1] On faith, see D. A. Campbell, 'Faith', in S. E. Balentine (ed.), *The Oxford Encyclopedia of the Bible and Theology* (New York: Oxford University Press, 2015), 327–36; A. Dulles, *The Assurance of Things Hoped for: A Theology of Christian Faith* (Oxford: Oxford University Press, 1994); H. Joas, *Faith as an Option: Possible Futures for Christianity*, trans. A. Skinner (Stanford, CA: Stanford University Press, 2014); F. A. Murphy, B. M. Mezei, and K. R. Oakes, *Illuminating Faith: An Invitation to Theology* (London: Bloomsbury, 2013); M. Westphal, *Kierkegaard's Concept of Faith* (Grand Rapids, Mich.: Eerdmans, 2014).

way Christ's self-revelation takes place, since it has achieved its purpose and been received in faith by Matthew. Let us begin this chapter by exploring the reciprocity between revelation and faith.

AN ACHIEVEMENT VERB AND NOUN

Along with others, Charles Davis drew on the analytic philosophy of Gilbert Ryle (1900–76) to call 'reveal' an 'achievement verb', or a verb which describes the culmination of an activity, as with 'finish a job' and 'reach a goal'. As such, 'it [reveal] expresses the accomplishment of a communication between God and the recipient of the revelation'. Hence 'for revelation to be achieved, it demands faith on the part of the recipient'.[2] One may likewise call 'revelation' an 'achievement noun'. Revelation achieves its goal when, first, it elicits living faith and when, secondarily what is revealed enters the life of the individuals and communities to which the self-revelation of God was originally directed.

Chapter 1 quoted Joshua Kira's words about God's self-revelation being 'an inherently relational idea'. It would be more accurate to use the word 'reciprocal'. Some relations can be, or can be largely, unilateral, but revelation is always reciprocal. Revelation does not exist without a recipient of revelation. For the event of the divine self-disclosure to occur, it must be received by men and women responding to God in faith. Accepted in faith, the self-revealing God is open to being, at least in some sense, understood and interpreted.

To God's speaking (*locutio Dei*) there corresponds the hearing of faith (*fides ex auditu*).[3] Speaking and hearing belong reciprocally together. Here one should add that human hearing, like human experience in general, implies always and everywhere some measure of interpretation. Non-interpreted hearing seems as implausible as non-interpreted experience.[4]

[2] C. Davis, 'Revelation and Critical Theory', in P. D. L. Avis (ed.), *Revelation* (London: Darton, Longman & Todd, 1997), 87–99, at 87, 88. See Joseph Ratzinger's firm statement to the same effect in Chapter 3, n. 10 above.

[3] The anonymous *Epistle to Diognetus*, to be dated to the late second century, notes this reciprocity: 'He [God] has revealed himself only to faith, by which alone are we permitted to know God' (8. 5).

[4] On experience being always interpreted experience, see G. O'Collins, *Rethinking Fundamental Theology* (Oxford: Oxford University Press, 2011), 49–50.

Some scholars, like Kira, want to distinguish between objective and subjective revelation. He maintains: 'there are ways in which revelation appears to be revelation regardless of whether it is [actually] recognized or [whether even] the possibility of recognition exists'. Specifically and 'objectively, Christ is the revelation of God simply by the fact that God sent him in an act of revelation'.[5] But, since as Kira himself points out, the heart of revelation is an 'uncovering', always and from the outset, there is an uncovering *for someone* or disclosure *to someone*. Revelation cannot, so to speak, hang in the air. It always involves answering the question: revelation to whom? Elsewhere in theology distinctions between the objective and subjective side of matters enjoy many uses, but not here. Non-recognized and non-received revelation would be an oxymoron. The very language of 'revelation' implies reception and the establishment of a reciprocal relationship. God reveals Christ to those who accept this revelation and respond in faith. Before that response takes place, the divine revelation does not, so to speak, go through; without reaching and triggering its goal in the human response of faith, the act of revelation simply does not happen.

This also holds true of the way in which the media uses the language of revelation. Every now and then headlines or media services announce 'Startling Revelations' or 'The Real Truth of the Railway Link Revealed'. An investigative journalist can claim to have uncovered for the public some deals that may embarrass the current government. Such non-theological use of 'revelation' illustrates how it always implies X (here the journalist) reveals Y (some financial irregularities which had hitherto been widely unknown) to Z, the readers of the paper, some of whom at least accept the truth of what has been revealed. Without some involvement of Z, any purported revelation has not been achieved.

Recently Niels Gregersen has offered a comprehensive and very helpful description of what revelation involves theologically. 'The logic of revelation is inherently relational, insofar as a revelation is a revelation *of* something or somebody (God the Father) *to* somebody (human apprehenders of the revelation) *in and through* a medium of revelation (the Incarnate One) *by* a relational power (the Holy Spirit)'.[6]

[5] J. Kira, 'A Response to [Stephen] Davis', in I. U. Dalferth and M. Ch. Rodgers (eds.), *Revelation* (Tübingen: Mohr Siebeck, 2014), 65–72, at 66.

[6] N. H. Gregersen, 'The Extended Body of Christ: Three Dimensions of Deep Incarnation', in N. H. Gregersen (ed.), *Incarnation: On the Scope and Depth of Christology* (Minneapolis: Fortress Press, 2015), 225–51, at 238.

This shows how a fully fledged, properly trinitarian theology of divine revelation also calls for reflection on the recipients. It requires the development of a theology of human faith, which would set out the internal and external factors involved in coming to the faith by which one accepts the self-revelation of God.

THE WORKING OF THE HOLY SPIRIT AND A GRACED PREDISPOSITION

The inner working of the Holy Spirit and their own graced predisposition enable human beings to receive in faith the self-revelation of God. Here the first requirement should be considered uncontroversial.

(1) When they present the message of the divine revelation in the crucified and resurrected Christ, the New Testament witnesses expect the message to be accompanied by an interior divine illumination. The Book of Acts tells of Paul's first convert in Philippi, a woman called Lydia: 'the Lord opened her heart' as she listened to the apostle's words (Acts 16: 14). The apostle himself writes of the Holy Spirit 'revealing' interiorly 'the things of God', enabling believers to interpret them (1 Cor. 2: 10–13) and giving people the chance of sharing the vision of faith (2 Cor. 3: 17–18). It is when God 'shines' in the hearts of human beings that they can know 'the glory of God on the face of Christ' (2 Cor. 4: 6). The 'inner' testimony of the Holy Spirit opens people to accept the 'outer' word of witness to revelation. Paul and other New Testament writers always suppose the impact of a divine initiative; when revelation comes, it lets human beings experience the presence of the living God (see Matt. 16: 17).

(2) The second requirement raises the question: has God, despite their sinfulness, gifted human beings with a predisposition that preconditions the way their cognitive capacities and freedom are exercised and opens them up to a divine self-communication? Controversially, Karl Rahner proposes a 'supernatural existential'—that is to say, a graced, fundamental openness which predisposes human beings to be hearers of the divine word and accept in faith the revealing and saving self-communication of God.[7] However we express it, some kind of predisposition seems

[7] K. Rahner, *Foundations of Christian Faith*, trans. W. V. Dych (New York: Seabury Press, 1978), 126–33. Karl Barth and others (e.g. in the Calvinist tradition) do not accept that God's saving revelation is something for which we are existentially predisposed: see

required if human beings are to be capable of receiving the divine revelation. We need to ask: what makes them potential hearers of the divine word? What opens them up to receive God's self-revelation?

When expounding what makes a human being 'a [potential] hearer of the message', Rahner highlights 'man as transcendent being'. He is that, 'insofar as all his knowledge and all his conscious activity are grounded in a pre-apprehension (*Vorgriff*) of "being" as such, in an unthematic but ever-present knowledge of the infinity of reality'.[8] The mystery of what it means to be human, both in the darkness of suffering and in this dynamic outreach to infinite reality, is unveiled when faith responds to the divine revelation. The transcendent mystery of human existence, by being revealed, opens us to accepting in faith the disclosure of the absolute mystery of God. Thus Rahner correlates the two mysteries.

A similar (but not identical) correlation showed up when Paul Tillich expounded revelation: 'revelation is the *answer* to the *questions* implied in the existential conflicts of reason'. He then spent pages unpacking this scheme of 'answer/questions'.[9]

Without using the term, the Second Vatican Council in *Gaudium et Spes* (the Pastoral Constitution on the Church in the Modern World of 7 December 1965) adopted a method of correlation: 'At least in a vague way, human beings will always desire to know what is the meaning of their life, their activity, and their death'. The divine revelation correlates with our most serious questions: 'God alone, who created human beings in his own image and redeemed them from sin, offers the fullest answer to these questions; and does that through the revelation in Christ his Son who became man' (*GS* 41). Revelation answers the deepest reality and need of human beings who are essentially questioners. It also throws light on those who receive the divine revelation.

THE RECEIVER REVEALED

There is no self-disclosure of God without a concomitant revelation of those receiving in faith that revelation. As William Abraham puts it

P. Helm, 'John Calvin, the *Sensus Divinitatis* and the Noetic Effects of Sin', *International Journal for Philosophy of Religion* 43 (1998), 87–107.

[8] Rahner, *Foundations of Christian Faith*, 24–43, at 33.

[9] P. Tillich, *Systematic Theology*, i (Chicago: University of Chicago Press, 1951), 147–55.

briefly, 'we come to know the truth about God *and ourselves*'.[10] Acknowledging and receiving in faith the divine revelation is a profoundly self-involving experience; it is also a profoundly self-revealing experience. By disclosing God to them, any event of revelation also reveals human beings to themselves. The disclosure of the mystery of God simultaneously reveals the human mystery. Knowing God in a new way necessarily implies knowing oneself in a new way.

A now classic passage of the Second Vatican Council's Pastoral Constitution of the Church stated: 'it is only in the mystery of the Word made flesh that the mystery of human beings truly becomes clear... Christ the final Adam, in the very revelation of the mystery of the Father and of his love, fully reveals human beings to themselves and discloses their most high calling' (*GS* 22). The revelation of God in and through Christ simultaneously reveals our true nature and final destiny as human beings.

This claim about their own self-revelation experienced by those who in faith accept God's disclosure in Christ can be backed up with plenty of evidence from the history of Christian saints and, in particular, mystics. A lifetime of experiencing and growing in an intimate knowledge of God through Christ and the Holy Spirit has brought innumerable saintly men and women to an ever richer self-knowledge. The lives of Augustine of Hippo, Symeon the New Theologian, Julian of Norwich, Teresa of Avila, John Wesley, Dietrich Bonhoeffer, Dorothy Day, and countless others yield constant insights into the ways faith in divine revelation enriched not only their knowledge of God but also their self-knowledge. Christian mystics, in particular, offer shining examples of the continuing growth in self-knowledge initiated and intensified by knowing God through the revelation of Jesus Christ.[11]

This is an area where theology has signally failed to support an important characteristic in the theology of revelation by drawing on the best in the history of Christian spirituality. Thirty years ago a Russian archbishop alerted me to the loss produced by such a divorce between theology and spirituality. Together with his 'secretary' (obviously a KGB man), he visited the Gregorian University (Rome) to check courses and consider possible, further collaboration. The

[10] W. J. Abraham, *Crossing the Threshold of Divine Revelation* (Grand Rapids, Mich.: Eerdmans, 2006), 58; italics mine.

[11] See B. McGinn (ed.), *The Essential Writings of Christian Mysticism* (New York: Random House, 2006).

president of a theological academy in Moscow, the archbishop was pleasantly surprised that the Gregorian had no officially prescribed philosophy. We offered courses and seminars in analytic, Aristotelian, existentialist, idealist, Marxist, Thomist, and other forms of philosophy. He was not so happy to find that we had an institute of spirituality, which was separate from our theology faculty: 'Shouldn't all theology be spiritual?', he asked. I had to agree that the relationship between theology and spirituality should be much closer.

In particular, studying the lives of saints—not least such masterpieces of autobiographical writing as Augustine's *Confessions*—throws much light on the self-knowledge brought by embracing the divine revelation in Jesus Christ. A direct connection with the spiritual classics would yield rich clues about the gift of divine self-revelation promoting a radical self-knowledge. Examining, not least, the threefold way of purification, illumination, and union through which mystics characteristically pass when they grow in self-knowledge, along with a knowledge of the self-revealing God, shows us how such self-knowledge in fact unfolds under the influence of divine revelation mediated by the Holy Spirit.[12]

[12] Ibid. 150–87.

7

Evidence for Revelation and Human Freedom

When human beings accept in faith the self-revelation of God, do or should evidential considerations play their role? Can we make a credible case for claims about the supreme divine revelation having occurred in Jesus Christ and so in some sense 'justify' faith in him? *Pace* Karl Barth and others, should we engage in the task of constructing such a case?[1] What role does human freedom play in accepting in faith the divine self-revelation?

VARIOUS SITUATIONS

As regards accepting revelation, we need to distinguish various situations. (a) There are those who personally experience the presence of Christ (when, for instance, they attend the celebration of a Good Friday liturgy or a full-choired Eucharist in a majestic cathedral) and afterwards ask themselves: 'In this experience was I genuinely meeting and coming to know God? What evidence points to this being an authentic encounter with the self-revealing God?'

We find a partial parallel for such a situation in the experience of the apostle Andrew, as depicted in John's Gospel (1: 35–42). At one level the initial question Jesus puts to Andrew and his anonymous

[1] Barth argued for the human incapacity for revelation, which included the human incapacity to establish a case for revelation having taken place. See G. Hunsinger, *How to Read Karl Barth: The Shape of His Theology* (New York: Oxford University Press, 1991), 92–5.

companion (the beloved disciple?) is straightforward: 'What are you looking for?' Jesus has turned around and seen two men trailing along behind him, and asks them what they are after. What is their purpose in following him? But the question plays on a possible, deeper meaning: 'what are you seeking in life? What are your hearts set on?' Without forcing himself on them, Jesus confronts and gently challenges their most fundamental aspirations and intentions. Andrew and his friend respond to Jesus' question by calling him 'Rabbi', and asking: 'Where are you staying?' This counter-question seems mundane, but hints at deeper dimensions. C. K. Barrett catches the profound sense of what is at stake: 'Nothing is more important than to know where Jesus abides and where he may be found'.[2] Then the two verbs that make up Jesus' seemingly matter-of-fact reply ('come and see') likewise convey a deeper meaning. 'Coming' in John's Gospel may express 'believing' in Jesus (e.g. 6: 35, 37, 44–5, 65); 'seeing' can be equivalent to personally knowing in faith (e.g. 9: 37–8; 12: 45; 14: 6–7, 9). To complete the picture, 'staying/abiding' (*menein*) communicates more than the merely superficial meaning of stopping or hanging around somewhere. Andrew and his companion want to know where Jesus is 'staying'; after 'coming' and 'seeing' where he is 'staying', they 'stay' with him for the rest of the day. The Gospel hints at the way in which the two men initiate a relationship of 'staying/abiding' with Jesus and 'in' Jesus, who will be disclosed to them as 'the true vine' in whom they will allow themselves to be incorporated (15: 1–11, a passage which uses the verb *menein* ten times).

After passing some hours with Jesus, Andrew is evidently satisfied that he has experienced God's Messiah or—to put it somewhat anachronistically—anointed Revealer and Saviour. He invites his brother Simon Peter to share that personal experience of God's self-disclosure in the person of Jesus. When discussing such an (a) situation, we are dealing with revelation in the *primary* sense of events in which individuals somehow find themselves in personal dialogue with the self-disclosing God. Whether or not they go on to question themselves about reasons for identifying this experience as an authentic self-manifestation of God, they remain convinced that this has been the case.

[2] C. K. Barrett, *The Gospel According to John*, 2nd edn. (London: SPCK, 1978), 181.

Another situation, situation (b), recurs innumerable times; it involves those who initially acknowledge the divine self-revelation in Christ and are invited to open themselves to further events involving such self-disclosure. This, for example, is the case not only with Andrew, but also with Simon Peter and Philip who follow Andrew in joining Jesus (John 1: 40–6). Later in John's Gospel these three disciples are named as witnessing the multiplication of loaves and fishes and hearing the subsequent discourse on 'the bread of life' (John 6: 5–9, 68). Like innumerable followers of Jesus, over and over again they will be drawn into situations in which Jesus will be revealed to them (here as 'the bread of life'), and they will be drawn into a further experience of the divine self-revelation. Then on the night before he dies, after washing the feet of the disciples, he challenges them with the question: 'Do you know what I have done to you?' (John 13: 12). In other words, have they opened themselves to this further revelation and its meaning—the disclosure of the startling humility of their divine 'Lord'? (John 13: 12–17).

There is also situation (c), the case of those who examine reports of purported revelation and ask, for instance: 'what reasons do I have for concluding that Andrew's encounter with Jesus reported a credible experience of the self-revealing God?' Here we put the focus on propositions (the *secondary* meaning of revelation) ultimately coming from those who claimed to have experienced, in the story of Jesus and the outpouring of the Holy Spirit, the climax of God's self-communication to human beings. This sense of revelation takes centre stage in Richard Swinburne's *apologia* for God's revelation in Christ. He is interested in 'the original propositional revelation'[3] communicated by Christ, rather than in any original self-disclosure of Christ.

EVIDENCE FOR REVELATION

Instead of examining events of revelation in the primary or personal sense (for instance, the encounters in John's Gospel between Jesus and various men and women who meet him), Swinburne sets himself

[3] R. Swinburne, *Revelation: From Metaphor to Analogy*, 2nd edn. (Oxford: Oxford University Press, 2007), 135, 136.

to establish the truth-value of propositions, or statements expressed in sentences, which derive from the biblical witnesses: 'revelation' in the *secondary* sense (see Chapter 1 above). He adduces significant evidence which supports and adds to the probability of these sentences being true.

Few modern authors have devoted more attention to the apologetical task than Richard Swinburne. His work *Revelation* explicitly dedicates two chapters to 'evidence of a revelation'.[4] The whole book has no other aim than justifying faith in the divine revelation communicated in its fullness by Jesus Christ. This work belongs with other publications by Swinburne on the divinity of Jesus, his miracles, his resurrection, the atonement, and so forth, which form a set of volumes making a multi-faceted case for accepting the central claims of Christian revelation.[5] Where some others have produced one or two books in support of such a case,[6] Swinburne has made the project a life-long, personal programme. He also stands apart from those who indulge a spurious credibility in a kind of triumph of alleged relevance over real, life-giving orthodoxy. He would never allow himself to eviscerate Christian claims and so make them 'compatible' with (scientific) reason. Swinburne is nothing if not sturdily orthodox in the beliefs he expounds and supports.

What is missing, however, with Swinburne and some other writers on the credibility of revelation, is a willingness to add an argument in 'another direction'. Let me explain. They normally argue, so to speak, 'from above' and tell their readers in general how this credibility can and should be established. They fail to reckon also with the evidential considerations 'from below', provided directly or indirectly by leading authors, who describe their personal journey from unbelief to belief and/or the experiences that kept them believing in the God revealed in Jesus Christ.[7]

[4] Ibid. 79–131.

[5] See e.g. Swinburne, *The Existence of God* (Oxford: Clarendon Press, 2004); *Is There a God*, rev. edn. (Oxford: Oxford University Press, 2010); *Was Jesus God?* (Oxford: Oxford University Press, 2008); *The Resurrection of God Incarnate* (Oxford: Clarendon Press, 2003).

[6] E.g. P. Copan and P. K. Moser (eds.), *The Rationality of Theism* (New York and London: Routledge, 2003); A. Plantinga, *Warranted Christian Belief* (New York: Oxford University Press, 2000).

[7] See e.g. G. M. Anderson, *With Christ in Prison* (New York: Fordham University Press, 2000); J. W. McLendon, *Biography as Theology: How Life Stories Can Remake Today's Theology* (Nashville: Abingdon, 1979).

The last century did not lack notable figures who came and/or continued to accept that God has been finally and fully revealed in the life, death, and resurrection of Jesus. Often they themselves or people close to them have documented their experiences and convictions and the reasons for them. I think here, for instance, of G. K. Chesterton (1874–1938), Paul Claudel (1868–1955), Dorothy Day (1897–1980), Avery Dulles (1918–2008), T. S. Eliot (1888–1965), Ronald Knox (1888–1957), C. S. Lewis (1896–1963), Rose Macaulay (1881–1958), Thomas Merton (1915–68), Malcolm Muggeridge (1903–90), Flannery O'Connor (1925–64), Dorothy L. Sayers (1893–1957), Evelyn Underhill (1875–1941), and Charles Williams (1886–1945). Their testimony about the evidential considerations that led them to believe in the divine self-revelation in Christ merits a hearing and counts in favour of the case for that revelation being true. I have in mind not merely their initial step to faith but also of the way that faith continued to prove its truth for them in practice.

Years ago I examined the prison writings of Dietrich Bonhoeffer (1906–45) which yielded clues about the conditions and nature of the continuing divine self-revelation which is experienced now and looks back to unique apostolic experience of foundational revelation which took place 'then'.[8] This saintly martyr experienced more fruitfully than many others the divine self-communication, as well as possessing a special talent for expressing the ways God spoke and acted in the last months of his life. Sadly, after this initial work, I did not press on to examine the autobiographical writings of similar Christians. That might have enriched the theology of revelation with further evidential considerations.[9] I did, however, encourage and supervise a number of doctoral students whose dissertations, in various ways, contributed to such a project: John Balluff on Charles Williams, Michael Heher on Flannery O'Connor, Michael Howlett on Patrick Kavanagh (1904–67), Anne Murphy on the prison writings of St Thomas More (1478–1535), Antonio Spadaro on Pier Vittorio Tondelli (1955–91), and Milton Walsh on Ronald Knox.

[8] G. O'Collins, *Fundamental Theology* (Ramsey, NJ: Paulist Press, 1981), 107–13. See F. Schlingensiefen, *Dietrich Bonhoeffer 1906–1945: Martyr, Thinker, Man of Resistance*, trans. I. Best (London: Continuum, 2010).

[9] Yet I did examine the revelatory power of Scripture in the story of St Antony of Egypt, St Augustine of Hippo, and Girolamo Savonarola: 'The Inspiring Power of Scripture: Three Case Studies', *Irish Theological Quarterly* 79 (2014), 265–73; reprinted as an appendix to this book.

When writing in support of the existence of God, Swinburne summarizes significant evidence under four main headings: the very existence of the physical universe, its conformity to intelligible laws, the moral awareness of human beings, and their experiences of the presence of God.[10] With the necessary adaptations, the fourth source of evidence deserves hearing when we scrutinize the credibility of divine revelation. The experiences and testimony of those who have accepted Jesus as the human face of God belong to the evidential considerations to be heard and evaluated.

ACCEPTING HISTORICAL REVELATION

Apropos of the credibility of the divine revelation communicated through Jesus Christ, we must attend to history. This revelation was conveyed through historical events that made up his story. Let me spell out *four theses* that illuminate this conviction.

(1) First, faith in God revealed through the story of Jesus cannot exist without some historical knowledge. The amount of such knowledge enjoyed by those who come to accept in faith God's self-revelation in Jesus obviously varies a great deal. They may be writers like Muggeridge who recorded his passage to such faith in several books on Jesus which examined what can be known historically about him. Other new believers, such as those adults who receive baptism in the liturgy on Holy Saturday evening, often pick up their historical knowledge of Jesus in less academic ways and not necessarily through reading works by professional New Testament scholars. But in all cases, accepting the divine revelation communicated through him means being able to say something about his history: from conception to death and resurrection.

(2) Secondly, faith in God who is revealed by Jesus does not depend simply on historical knowledge. While requiring some exercise of reason and not being simply 'a blind leap in the dark' that disdains any evidence provided by history or other sources, faith depends and draws on things that go beyond reason and, specifically, beyond

[10] These four themes provide the issues discussed in Swinburne, *The Existence of God*; he summarizes them in *Revelation*, 347–8.

historical reason (or reason exercised in historical matters). It is not mere historical evidence that justifies and supports one's faith. Without the grace of an interior divine illumination which accompanies the external presentation of the message about the divine self-disclosure in Christ, no amount of historical knowledge, even the most extensive and sophisticated knowledge and even the best biblical exegesis, will never merely *by itself* bring about that faith. Professional historians enjoy no such head start over others in the 'race' for faith. As with others, accepting God's self-manifestation in Christ does not depend simply and solely on how well that acceptance is supported by historical evidence.

In particular, such an acceptance in faith entails a loving commitment and a trusting hope that freely goes beyond the limited evidence and enters into a personal relationship with God revealed through Christ and his Holy Spirit. Knowledge, even the most critically acquired knowledge, so long as it remains bereft of graced illumination, love, and hope can never result in faith. Such faith in Christ and his revelation may be compared with a life-long commitment to family and friends. Mere historical research into their previous activities and achievements could never provide the grounds for our commitments to them. Most people would, I believe, consider it insulting even to think of founding such loving relationships on the basis of background checks.

To sum up this second thesis: faith in the divine Revealer neither bases itself simply on historical knowledge nor forms a simple prolongation of such knowledge, as though the critical examination of history (e.g. evidence from biblical historians) could by itself establish and maintain such faith. Christian faith in Christ the Revealer does not exist independently of historical knowledge, but it cannot be reduced to it. 'Mere' historical evidence is not commensurate with the questions being asked and the issues at stake for such faith.

It is intriguing that Wolfhart Pannenberg, who famously insisted on faith in divine revelation being grounded upon historical evidence,[11] introduced other considerations when he elaborated the way in which the first disciples rightly understood what the resurrection of Jesus revealed. Since they already hoped for a general resurrection at the end of history, they were in a position to grasp something new: that the

[11] See W. Pannenberg et al., *Revelation as History*, trans. D. Granskou and E. Quinn (London: Sheed & Ward, 1969).

general resurrection and the end of all history had already been anticipated by Jesus' personal resurrection. Thus the truth of God was now revealed. But, even though solid historical evidence supports Pannenberg in crediting Jesus' disciples with such prior hopes for a general resurrection, how can people two thousand years later accept their prior hopes and expect a future fulfilment for human beings in a general resurrection?[12] Pannenberg argued that such a hope for future resurrection proves its meaning and truth by being acted upon and standing 'the test today in the decisions of life'.[13] In other words, accepting now the expectations of the first disciples, which vitally shaped their full interpretation of Jesus' resurrection, comes through living with hope and (perhaps Pannenberg implied) love. Thus a key element in his total picture of accepting Christ's resurrection and the revelation that it brought goes beyond historical truth to include trusting hope and perhaps loving commitment.

(3) A third thesis argues for the mutual interaction between (a) knowing revelation and (b) loving and the imagination of hope. Love facilitates knowledge, just as knowing makes it possible to love someone or something already known. This holds true also of historical knowledge. Believers know the historical truth and find meaning in the history of Jesus and the climax of revelation it conveyed because they love him and find in him the object of their deepest hopes. Yet it is also true that they commit themselves to him in love and trust, after they have come to know something of him and the historical revelation he conveyed. Thus the historical knowledge of faith accepting revelation exemplifies two principles operating reciprocally in opposite directions, not only '*nihil volitum nisi precognitum* (nothing can be wanted/loved unless it is already known)' but also '*nihil cognitum nisi prevolitum* (nothing can be known unless it is already wanted/loved)'.

St Augustine of Hippo (354–430) famously stressed the latter principle, when he wrote about the interaction of love and knowledge: '*nemo nisi per amicitiam cognoscitur*' (*De diversis questionibus*, 83. 71. 3). This could be paraphrased as 'you need to be a

[12] W. Pannenberg, *Jesus–God and Man*, trans. L. L. Wilkins and D. A. Priebe (London: SCM Press, 1968), 67, 83–8.

[13] Ibid. 107.

friend of someone before you truly know him or her'. The eyes of love let us see reality and know the truth of Christ's revelation or anything else.

(4) Fourth, the certainty of faith's acceptance of the divine self-disclosure in Christ embraces but goes beyond historical knowledge. Let me explain at some length this thesis. For several centuries now, firm claims about such matters as Jesus' death and resurrection have faced routine censure. How can the certainty of faith tolerate pervasive uncertainties in historical knowledge or what Wilhelm Herrmann, Rudolf Bultmann's teacher at the University of Marburg, called 'the continually changing' results of historical study?[14] What his censure presupposes, among other things, is that any assurance about matters of past history can be detached from other characteristics of faith which accepts divine self-revelation. However, faith's firm answer to the question 'What can I know' belongs to the *one* act in which it also answers those other two questions, 'What ought I to do?' and 'What may I hope for?'[15] and gives its allegiance to the person of Christ. A firm confession of the historical truth about Jesus (summed up in the Nicene Creed) belongs together in a lived unity with a commitment to his ethical teaching and a trusting hope in his person.

Herrmann made an exaggerated claim (often repeated in later decades) when he declared that 'the results of historical study are continually changing'. The claim prompts the questions: All the results? Or only some of them? Are they changing substantially or only in secondary details and interpretations? Herrmann's version of the results of historical research calls out for some heavy qualifications.

One spots in Hermann's denigration of historical knowledge the long-term influence of Gotthold Ephraim Lessing (1719–81), whose minimalizing approach to such knowledge took a two-pronged from: 'If no historical truth can be demonstrated, then nothing can be

[14] W. Herrmann, *The Communion of the Christian with God*, trans. J. S. Stanyon (London: Williams and Norgate, 1895), 76.

[15] These three questions are taken from Immanuel Kant, *Critique of Pure Reason*, A805/B833, trans. P. Guyer and A. W. Wood (Cambridge: Cambridge University Press, 1997), 677. Kant's three questions help to place the three distinguishable but inseparable dimensions of faith, even it would be preferable to move them away from individualism, give them a Jesus-orientation, and make them read: 'What can we know of Jesus? What ought we to do about Jesus? What may we hope for through Jesus?'

demonstrated by means of historical truths. . . . . Accidental truths of history can never become the proof of necessary truths of reason.'[16] Against this one should argue that, although they cannot be demonstrated by mathematical calculations, philosophical logic, or repeated scientific experiments, many historical truths can be established beyond any reasonable doubt. Mathematical calculations cannot demonstrate the existence and career of Alexander the Great in the fourth century BC. But converging historical evidence makes it absurd to deny that he lived and changed the political and cultural face of the Middle East. We cannot run the film backwards to regain contact with the past by literally reconstructing the assassination of Julius Caesar in 44 BC or the crucifixion of Jesus almost one hundred years later. Such historical events cannot be re-enacted in the way in which we can endlessly repeat scientific experiments in the laboratory. But only the lunatic fringe would cast doubt on these two violent deaths. A priori logic cannot demonstrate the existence of Augustine of Hippo. But to deny his existence and massive influence on subsequent European thought and society would be to exclude yourself from normal academic discussion about the history of Western ideas. The available data let us know a great deal that went on in the ancient world, even if we cannot and should not try to 'demonstrate' our conclusions along the lines appropriate to mathematics, philosophy, and the natural sciences. There are very many historically certain truths from which we can argue and draw conclusions, including those which support events of divine self-revelation and so give rise to faith.

The main thrust of Lessing's case comes, however, in his second assertion: 'accidental truths of history can never become the proof of necessary truths of reason'. Even if we know with certainty many historical truths, they always remain contingent and accidental. These historical events, the truth of which we have established or—much more frequently—have simply learned from others, neither had to happen at all nor had to happen precisely the way they did. In principle things could have gone differently in the lives of Alexander the Great, Julius Caesar, Jesus, and Augustine. Jesus might have been lynched and killed by stoning; he could have been crucified along with a dozen others; he might have appeared after this death to a group of

[16] G. E. Lessing, *Historical Writings*, selected and trans. H. Chadwick (Stanford, Calif.: Stanford University Press, 1967), 53.

five thousand and not to a group of five hundred (1 Cor. 15: 6). As such, historical truths neither enjoy the status of necessary, universal truths of reason, nor can they work to prove such truths of reason. But is that so tragic? Is it, for instance, a fatal admission to grant that our knowledge of Jesus' death, burial, and post-resurrection appearances does not rise 'above' the level of contingent truths? Strictly speaking, things could have gone differently.

Only someone like Lessing who was bewitched by the pursuit of necessary, universal truths of reason would deplore this historical situation. In the strict sense of the word, 'necessary truths of reason' are tautologies, mathematical truths, and other a priori deductions which are in principle true always and everywhere and do not need the support of any empirical evidence. But how many people base their lives on such truths? Historical experience and contingent truths have a power to shape and change human existence in a way never enjoyed by Lessing's timeless, universal truths of reason. In particular, 'accidental' truths from the story of Jesus and his most heroic followers have played a crucial role in the lives of millions of Christians. They have heard the reports of Jesus' life, death, and resurrection and found themselves awed, moved and changed by what they believe to be the self-revelation of God. Both within Christianity and beyond, the concreteness of history repeatedly proves far more persuasive than any necessary truths of reason.

Furthermore, when historical claims are scrutinized, we face a range of possibilities about our conclusions: from the utterly certain, through the highly probable, the solidly probable, the probable, and various shades of possibilities, right down to the genuinely indeterminate. There is a range of historical conclusions which responsible scholars can firmly hold, even when they do not reach the status of utter certainty. They can construct solidly probable cases and reach firm conclusions, without pretending to enjoy the complete certainty that would discount even a remote possibility that further evidence might come to light and disprove or seriously qualify their conclusions.

Does this leave the assurance of faith in God's self-revelation in Christ—and its dependence on knowing events from the past—vulnerable, when historical knowledge may not be utterly certain about some important details (for instance, the emptiness of Jesus' tomb) and may be open to the possibility of revision? And is it particularly shocking that Christians are 'at the mercy' of history, in much the same way as we all live at the mercy of reality itself, above all the human reality of other people, and yet continue to put our trust in them? In a large variety of ways we relate deeply to others, rely on their testimony, and remain 'at their mercy'.

One of these ways concerns the history of revelation and, in particular, the life, death, and resurrection of Jesus. When I trust that new evidence from research scholars will not shatter the picture which I cherish of Jesus' history, I am no more indulging reckless confidence than when I trust that I have not been, for instance, horribly mistaken in family matters by accepting that 'this man' was my father. Life would be made intolerable, if we decided to live with the persistent fear of being confronted with the startling news that the reality around us is not what we have taken it to be and that we have been proved horribly wrong. We may admit that it could be logically possible that we have been deluded, but we are confident that it is not so. It is possible, for example, that my mother had a secret lover and that I have been mistaken for decades over my paternity. But I am confident that this is not so, and would never dream of digging up my father's remains to exclude any possible doubt by having a DNA test performed. Such 'definitive' evidence would betray and not enhance my parents' memory.

To spend my life morbidly preoccupied with the possibility that someone else fathered me would destroy my relationship with my parents. Similarly, nothing could be more destructive of my relationship with my spouse than constantly and anxiously entertaining the possibility of emotional rejection and unfaithfulness by asking myself, 'What will I do if she gets tired of me and has an affair with someone else?'

The case of faith in the self-revelation of God in Christ seems similar. To focus persistently on the possibility that new historical evidence could turn up and refute our acceptance of this revelation would exclude any workable and worthwhile faith. In other words, the 'risk' of faith is not unlike our basic human belief in the identity of our parents and in the fidelity of our spouse, friends, and relatives, inasmuch as such belief also involves historical claims that, strictly speaking, remain vulnerable in principle.

Here we might make the analogy more precise by distinguishing our relationship to (a) parents and siblings from (b) our relationship to spouse and friends. Both (a) and (b) are vulnerable in principle, but in different ways. In the case of (a), we grow up within a given situation rather than within a relationship we have personally chosen for ourselves; our commitment to parents and siblings comes from our being born into a particular family. This case resembles that of 'cradle Christians', who grow up with some commitment to God's self-revelation in Christ. In their adult years they can reflect on this faith relationship and allow it to deepen or else can let it slip and even reject it outright. But in their earlier years this relationship has been a 'given' of their existence. In the case of (b), we choose our spouses and friends. Along with spontaneous feelings and desires, such reasonable grounds as shared interests, common values, and similar expectations usually play their part in making such commitments. We come to these commitments, rather than being born and raised with them, just as non-believers can come to accept the divine revelation in Christ and commit themselves to him. They do so usually because they have *also* found the evidence (both historical and otherwise) and motives for such an acceptance to be reasonable and convincing. In short, the analogy proposed can be refined to cover those who start life as 'insiders' to faith and those who start life as 'outsiders' and may become 'insiders'.

What I am arguing for is the view that accepting in faith God's self-revelation in Christ involves an historical risk, inasmuch as we believe the testimony of others—in this case, testimony about the history of Christ.[17] But we need to add at once two riders. (a) Such faith does not depend simply upon historical knowledge. Faith is neither totally made nor, we should add, totally unmade by the answer to the question: what can we know historically about the past events of revelation history? (b) And the historical risk is part of the general risk involved in understanding and accepting reality.

HUMAN FREEDOM AND SIGNS

The self-revelation of God, above all its supreme highpoint with the resurrection of the crucified Jesus and the outpouring of the Holy Spirit, does not coerce the response of faith; it leaves room for the exercise of human freedom. There are signs, both miraculous and

[17] On accepting testimony in general, see C. A. J. Coady, *Testimony: A Philosophical Study* (Oxford: Clarendon Press, 1993).

otherwise, counting in favour of divine self-revelation and encouraging the assent of faith. These invite scrutiny.

On a priori grounds, Swinburne expects evidence in favour of the truth of revelation, but argues that 'too much evidence' would 'make the attainment of salvation so easy' that it would become 'available to those who had not formed a settled determination to pursue it as their supreme goal'. But, Swinburne objects, 'salvation is so important that there is reason not to give it to those who do not have a settled will to pursue it above all other goals . . . overwhelming evidence in the form of successive miracles would defeat the purpose of revelation'.[18] But prescribing that God would have no reason to give salvation to those who do not show 'a settled will' to pursue salvation as 'their supreme goal', above 'all other goals', seems a trifle presumptuous. In fact, how many people reveal a settled will to pursue salvation above all other goals? Swinburne seems to set the salvation bar far too high. Furthermore, such requirements hardly fit many of the people to whom Jesus conveyed divine mercy. Had they all shown a settled determination to pursue salvation as their supreme goal before he acted to bring them salvation?

But what kind of evidence would I point to? Let me deploy one theme from the Old Testament that Swinburne does not mention, and then one major piece of evidence from the New Testament that he does invoke.

(1) We begin with one remarkable result from the religious experience of the prophets, the psalmists, and others: their *image of God.*[19] Israelite religious experience bred an image of God that set Judaism quite apart from other peoples. At first the Israelites made room for the gods of other peoples. But with increasing clarity they came to acknowledge the exclusive nature and identity of their God. The gap between YHWH and other 'gods' opened up to the point that the Israelites denied the reality of other gods. Yet the difference between Judaism and other religions was more than just monotheism. Echn Aton's *Song of the Sun* clearly acknowledged only one God. And the

[18] Swinburne, *Revelation*, 125; see id., *Faith and Reason*, 2nd edn. (Oxford: Clarendon Press, 2005), 204–16.

[19] See J. J. Scullion, 'God in the Old Testament', *ABD* ii, 1041–8; M. S. Smith, *The Early History of* God, 2nd edn. (Grand Rapids, Mich.: Eerdmans, 2002); id., *The Memoirs of God: History, Memory, and the Experience of the Divine in Ancient Israel* (Minneapolis: Fortress Press, 2004).

Greek philosophers reached the notion of the Absolute or the Unmoved Mover. We spot some fundamental differences when we recall that Echn Aton's one god was the sun god. And over against the conclusions of Greek thought, YHWH, if utterly transcendent, was experienced not as a remote Unmoved Mover but as a tender, loving God who invited exclusive love and loyalty from human beings and, especially, from Israel.

The Old Testament image of God combined in an extraordinary way two elements: *majestic transcendence* and *loving closeness*. While initially and partly associated with sanctuaries and other such places, YHWH was experienced as transcending the normally accepted limits of space and time and went beyond the usual 'frontiers', bringing Israel on its exodus 'from the land of Egypt and the Philistines from Caphtor and the Syrians from Kir' (Amos 9: 7; see Chapter 5). Unlike gods of other Middle-Eastern nations, Israel's deity was not identified in *space* as the sun or another heavenly body. The sun, the moon, and the stars were among the things created by God (Gen. 1: 14–18). YHWH also passed beyond the limits of *time*. Other Middle-Eastern deities issued from chaos, and various myths proclaimed their genesis. Israel's God was known to be simply and always there, 'the first and the last' (Isa. 44: 6), the God who 'in the beginning created the heavens and the earth' (Gen. 1: 1). The Israelites admitted neither a birth nor an ageing process for their God.

Despite this transcendence of space and time, however, Israel did not shrink from mythical language when speaking of the divine deeds. God crushed 'the head of the Leviathan', 'cut Rahab into pieces' (Ps. 74: 13–14; 89: 10; Isa. 51: 9), and came riding on a storm in a spectacular scenario: 'Smoke went up from his nostrils, and devouring fire from his mouth; glowing coals flamed forth from him. He bowed the heavens, and came down; thick darkness was under his feet. He rode on a cherub, and flew; he came swiftly upon the wings of the wind' (Ps. 18: 7–10; see 29: 3–10; 77: 17–20). Aristotle would have admired the transcendence of Israel's God, but he could not have accepted the lively, mythical language of the psalmists. Israel's Middle-Eastern neighbours accepted such mythical language, but did not recognize a God who transcended space and time.

As regards sexuality, we likewise find a striking blend of elements in Israel's account of God. On the one hand, YHWH had no spouse and offspring, and remained beyond the sexual activities typical of other ancient deities. But, on the other hand, Hosea and other prophets talked of God as a husband who revealed a tender and wounded love when his people acted like a harlot: 'Behold, I will allure her, and bring her into the wilderness, and speak tenderly to her' (Hos. 3: 14). Second Isaiah pictured God as 'a woman crying out in travail' (Isa. 42: 14; see 46: 3–4; 49: 15). YHWH was known to transcend sexuality, and yet the prophets felt free to introduce masculine and feminine imagery by describing God as spouse, mother, and father.[20]

To sum up: the Israelites experienced YHWH as a loving and tenderly devoted God. At the same time, they treasured an elevated notion of their deity. Being so utterly transcendent, YHWH was not to be represented in any carved, moulded, or painted form. Such divine images were strictly forbidden (Exod. 20: 4–5; Lev. 19: 4; Deut. 4: 15–20). This highly elevated and yet intensely personal notion of God was the most extraordinary 'product' coming from the prophets and others in the Old Testament who experienced the divine self-communication. I would argue that this notion was an intellectual miracle. It could have arisen only from special, authentic experiences of God and was not to be explained through the 'merely' human powers of a tiny nation which enjoyed no formidable philosophical or other mental talents.

(2) *Miracles* attributed to Jesus and his *resurrection from the dead* obviously invite scrutiny from those concerned to adduce evidential considerations in favour of the divine self-revelation.[21] Swinburne attends to miracles in various publications,[22] and to the resurrection of Jesus, above all in his *The Resurrection of God Incarnate.*[23]

While sharing Swinburne's desire to make a case for Jesus' miracles and resurrection, I regret his regularly reducing the resurrection to

[20] See G. O'Collins, *The Tripersonal God*, 2nd edn. (Mahwah, NJ: Paulist Press, 2014), 12–23.

[21] On miracles of Jesus, see my *Jesus: A Portrait* (London: Darton, Longman & Todd, 2008), 51–80; on the case for his resurrection, see my *Believing in the Resurrection: The Meaning and Promise of the Risen Jesus* (Mahwah, NJ: Paulist Press, 2012), 127–39. On miracles see also P. R. Eddy and G. A. Boyd, *The Jesus Legend: A Case for the Historical Reliability of the Jesus Tradition* (Grand Rapids, Mich.: Baker Academic, 2007), 39–91; T. D. Sullivan and S. Menssen, 'Revelation and Miracles', in C. Taliaferro and C. Meister (eds.), *The Cambridge Companion to Christian Philosophical Theology* (New York: Cambridge University Press, 2010), 201–15.

[22] See e.g. his *Revelation*, 112–21.

[23] Oxford: Oxford University Press, 2003.

the category of a 'super-miracle',[24] as well as his following the language of David Hume in describing purported miracles as 'violations of natural laws'.[25] First, the purported resurrection of Jesus should not be called a miracle or even a 'super-miracle'. Miracles, like the healing miracles of Jesus, may be understood as signs anticipating what he would do for human beings in the final kingdom of God (in the perfect bodily 'healing' of the resurrection). Nevertheless, they happened and happen within our world of space and time, even if they point to what is to come. The resurrection simply goes beyond any such miracles. It was and is *the* event that initiates a series of final events that will fulfil and complete his personal rising from the death and the whole of human history (e.g. 1 Cor. 15: 20–28). Secondly, '*violate*' has four meanings, all of them negative and even ugly: (a) disregard or fail to comply with; (b) treat with disrespect; (c) disturb or break in upon; and (d) assault sexually. Presumably Swinburne uses 'violate' in sense (a). But when working miracles occasionally and for good reasons, God is surely better described as suspending or overriding the normal working of natural laws. Since it is God who created the precise shape and functions of the laws of nature, it seems odd to speak of God 'disregarding' or 'failing to comply with' them. Why should we continue to accept Hume's language? 'Suspending' or 'overriding' seems more appropriate language.

(3) As regards appealing to such evidential considerations, many people seemingly refuse to acquire knowledge about historical 'signs' that might suggest God's being revealed to human beings. It reminds me of reactions to the style of abstract painting that emerged at the end of the nineteenth century. Some people learn to appreciate it, by acquiring knowledge of the background from which such painting came and of what artists wanted to achieve in this format. Others, however, continue to dismiss it, without wanting to know what could be intended by creating compositions often free of figurative, recognizable, or visual references. Cognitive freedom persists in the matter of acquiring knowledge, whether in the world of art or in historical claims to have experienced God's self-revelation.

[24] Swinburne, *Revelation*, 121, 162, 165, 168.

[25] Swinburne, *The Resurrection*, 162, 186, 190; see id., *Revelation*, 112.

Add too that in many parts of the advanced industrial world a busy, even frenetic, life style leaves little space for serious reflection on 'signs' that suggest God's being manifested to us. Leisure time can be taken up with an intense preoccupation with sport. If Karl Marx were to return today, he might well suggest that sport, not religion, is 'the opium of the people'.

It can also be argued that the primary barrier to accepting divine self-disclosure in and through Christ is not precisely lack of knowledge but sinfulness. Accepting this revelation involves surrendering to his person and becoming his disciple—in a word, being converted. In the twentieth century few writers explored more expertly than Bernard Lonergan (1904–84) the intellectual, moral, and religious dimensions of conversion. His call to conversion was complex: be attentive, be intelligent, be reasonable, be responsible, and be loving.[26] Those ready to practise what Lonergan preached are, in effect, accepting the invitation of Jesus: 'repent and believe in the good news' (Mark 1: 15). Such a repentant conversion opens the way to accepting in faith the good news of what God was revealing in and through what Jesus was saying and doing.

This chapter opened by setting out various situations in which the divine revelation comes to human beings. In our next chapter we turn now to the different 'time zones' (past, present, and future) of revelation.

CODA: THE PARADOXES OF REVELATION

Swinburne remarks that revelation involves 'claims that we cannot possibly *confirm* by mere human reflection or ordinary historical investigation'.[27] Here one thinks above all of the claims about the Trinity (three divine persons sharing one divine nature) and the incarnation (one divine person enjoying two natures, one divine and the other human). F. D. E. Schleiermacher and his latter-day followers have declared such doctrines to be not merely unconfirmed by reason and research but simply logically incoherent or a contradiction in terms. Many contemporary Christian philosophers and theologians,

[26] B. J. F. Lonergan, *Method in Theology* (Minneapolis: Winston Press, 1979; orig. edn. 1972).

[27] *Revelation*, 111; italics mine.

far from attempting to confirm by human reason (including historical arguments) the truth of these doctrines, remain content to rebut the objections and argue that the incarnation, for instance, may be a paradox but is not a blatant logical contradiction.

In *Incarnation*, I set myself not only to expound the doctrine positively but also to point out weaknesses in objections to it.[28] A number of contributors to two joint works did just the same. They argued that the belief in the Trinity and the Incarnate Son of God which emerges from revelation remains deeply mysterious and paradoxical, but is not logically incoherent or absurd.[29]

[28] G. O'Collins, *Incarnation* (London: Continuum, 2002).

[29] S. T. Davis, D. Kendall, and G. O'Collins (eds.), *The Trinity* (Oxford: Oxford University Press, 1999); Davis, Kendall, and O'Collins (eds.), *The Incarnation* (Oxford: Oxford University Press, 2002).

8

Revelation Then, Now, and To Come

Chapter 1 of this book quoted James Dunn as asking: 'Can a prophetic religion survive unless it is open to the Spirit of prophecy, to inspire afresh *and reveal new things*?'[1] The question leaves us with an ambiguity. Does Dunn want Christian prophets of today, under divine inspiration, to disclose new (propositional) truths and so add fresh content ('new things') to the revelation confessed in the Nicene Creed (revelation in the secondary sense)? Or does he merely envisage such prophets through their fresh insights helping believers to experience again what they already know through revelation and to follow this experience up with new forms of practice?

Where Dunn may be making room for continuing and incremental revelation (in the propositional sense), others have confined revelation to the apostolic past. Through the twentieth century many Roman Catholics, prompted by a decree of the Holy Office *Lamentabili* of 3 July 1907, insisted: 'revelation ended with the death of the last apostle'.[2] They rejected any talk of revelation as a reality in the present, admitting only a growth in the collective understanding of the revelation completed and closed once and for all with Christ and his apostles. Yet this denial of present revelation seems incompatible with the language and practice of the liturgy[3] (which enacts a constant dialogue with the Father, through the Son, and in the Holy Spirit), and, more generally, with the activity of the Spirit actualizing God's living revelation in the Church and through her in the world.

[1] J. D. G. Dunn, 'Biblical Concepts of Revelation', in P. D. L. Avis (ed.), *Revelation* (London: Darton, Longman & Todd, 1997), 1–22, at 14; italics mine.

[2] See DzH, 3421.

[3] Matthew Levering calls the liturgy 'the primary context for the proclamation, interpretation, and *enactment* of God's revelation': *Engaging the Doctrine of Revelation* (Grand Rapids, Mich.: Baker Academic, 2014), 3; italics mine.

As much as anything, clarity in terminology promises to remedy this confusion about the 'when?' of revelation. Let us begin by looking at suggestions coming from Paul Tillich and some others.

TERMINOLOGICAL PROPOSALS

In the history of revelation, Tillich distinguished between 'original' and 'dependent' revelation. *Both* 'Peter and the other apostles' who first received Christ *and* 'all the following generations' have 'entered into a revelatory correlation' with him. There is a 'continuous revelation in the history of the church', which has been generated by the original revelation and is to be described as 'dependent revelation'. 'The history of church', while it has 'revelatory power', is not 'a locus of original revelations' but of 'continuous, dependent revelations, which are one side of the work of the divine Spirit in the Church'. The Spirit, 'illuminating believers individually and as a group, brings their cognitive reason into revelatory correlation with the event on which Christianity is based'.

'A dependent revelatory situation', Tillich explains, 'exists in every moment in which the divine Spirit grasps, shakes, and moves the human spirit. Every prayer and meditation, if it fulfills its meaning, namely, to reunite the creature with its creative ground, is revelatory in this sense'. Thus 'the marks of [dependent] revelation' are 'present in every true prayer'.[4]

Although he never mentions Tillich, Richard Swinburne adopts the terminology of 'original' revelation (for what was disclosed 'then'), without, however, also writing of subsequent, post-apostolic, *dependent* revelation. He dedicates an entire chapter to the 'original revelation',[5] and shows here and elsewhere how he is focused, above all, on the propositional content of (past) Christian revelation and its

[4] P. Tillich, *Systematic Theology*, i (Chicago: University of Chicago Press, 1951), 126–7. Karl Rahner also names the history of revelation as 'original', but he does not match Tillich by speaking of 'original' and 'dependent' revelation; see Rahner, *Foundations of Christian Faith*, trans. W. V. Dych (New York: Crossroad,1978), 173.

[5] R. Swinburne, *Revelation: From Metaphor to Analogy*, 2nd edn. (Oxford: Oxford University Press, 2007), 135–72.

truth (rather than on the Spirit initiating revelatory situations here and now).[6]

Thus Swinburne differs sharply from Tillich, who 'radically excludes a non-existential concept of revelation. Propositions about a past revelation give theoretical information; they have no revelatory power.' 'Revelation', Tillich adds, 'whether it is original or dependent, has revelatory power only for those who *participate* in it, who enter into the revelatory correlation'.[7]

Aylward Shorter has proposed the terminology of 'foundational' revelation that occurred then and 'participant' revelation that occurs now.[8] 'Participant' echoes Tillich's language about 'those who participate' in revelation. Levering has written of 'our ability to hear and participate in divine revelation'.[9] But he does not follow Shorter or myself in contrasting 'participant' with 'foundational' revelation. Recently Philip Caldwell first queries but then seems to accept the language of 'foundational' and then 'dependent' revelation.[10]

Whatever precise form it takes, we need a terminology that adds an essential third point and distinguishes between (1) revelation inasmuch as it reached an unsurpassable, once and for all fullness with Christ, his apostles, and the outpouring of the Holy Spirit, (2) inasmuch as it continues today and calls people to faith in a living encounter with God, and (3) inasmuch as it will be gloriously and definitively consummated in the life to come. In one sense revelation is past (as 'foundational'), in another sense it is present (as 'dependent'), and in a further sense it is a reality to come (as 'future', 'final', or 'eschatological'). The Book of Revelation witnesses to God revealed as 'the One who is, who was, and who is come' (Rev. 1: 4, 8; 4: 8). As foundational, revelation 'was'; as 'dependent', it 'is'; and as final, it 'is to come'.

[6] Avis, who is knows Tillich's work well, adopts his term 'original' as in 'original revelation' (Avis, *Revelation*, vii), but does not take up the matching term 'dependent revelation'.

[7] Tillich, *Systematic Theology*, i, 127; italics mine. Tillich clearly exaggerates when he asserts that 'propositions about a past revelation' have 'no revelatory power'. The Nicene Creed is nothing if not a set of propositions about past revelation; set to music and sung, it has repeatedly shown its revelatory power, and so been transformed from what I call revelation in the secondary sense (propositions coming from events of revelation) to revelation in the primary sense (events of living revelation received in faith; see Chapter 1 above).

[8] A. Shorter, *Revelation* (London: Geoffrey Chapman, 1983), 139–43.

[9] Levering, *Engaging the Doctrine of Revelation*, 3.

[10] P. Caldwell, *Liturgy as Revelation* (Minneapolis: Fortress, 2014), 299, 401.

THE NEW TESTAMENT WITNESS

Before expounding the second-order language of this triple terminology, we should recall how the witness of the New Testament in its first-order language speaks in a triple time-key of the divine self-revelation in Christ.

(1) First, the prologue of the Letter to the Hebrews announces a past revelation that was in some sense perfect and complete, rather than provisional and fragmentary: 'Long ago God spoke to our ancestors in many and various ways to the prophets, but in these last days he has spoken to us by the Son' (1: 1). Hebrews attributes the fullness of the divine revelation communicated through Jesus to his identity as *the Son of God*.

John's Gospel also understands the historical revelation through Christ as full and unsurpassable: 'the Word became flesh and pitched his tent among us, and we have seen his glory, the glory of the Father's only son, full of grace and truth' (1: 14). In the logic of John's prologue, the divine revelation in and through Christ is full and complete, because he is *the Word of God*. To be sure, the language of sonship turns up in the same verse (1: 14). This Gospel will go on to highlight Christ as the Son who reveals the Father (John 14: 9), right through to the end when it announces its central purpose: 'these things have been written so that you may come [or continue] to believe that Jesus is the Messiah, *the Son of God*, and that through believing you may have life in his name' (John 20: 31). Yet, at least in the prologue, it is because he is the Word who 'was in the beginning', who 'was with God', and who 'was God' (John 1: 1) that he could communicate the fullness of 'grace and truth'.

Paul approaches the incarnational language of John when he writes in hymnic terms of the self-emptying and self-humbling involved in Christ 'being born in human likeness', 'being found in human form', and 'taking the form of a slave' before dying on the cross. This self-abasement led to the universal revelation that made it possible for 'every tongue to confess that Jesus Christ is Lord, to the glory of God the Father' (Phil. 2: 6–11). With their different accents, Hebrews, John, and Paul converge in professing a past, divine self-revelation that was somehow full, complete, and unsurpassable.

John of the Cross (1542–91), biblical scholar and mystic, brought out the implications of what the evangelist John had written. In his one and only Word, God has once and for all said everything to us, and now has nothing more to say. Jesus has proved not merely *a* revelation of God but *the* full revelation of God: 'In giving us his Son, his one Word (for he [God] possesses no other), he spoke everything to us at once and in this sole Word—and he has nothing more to say'.[11] This famous comment on the divine self-revelation should not, however, lead us to deny or ignore revelation as continuing to happen, which Hebrews, the Johannine corpus, and Paul all attest.

(2) Second, in a classic passage on faith Hebrews states: 'now faith is the assurance of things hoped for, the proof of things not seen. By this [faith] the elders [our ancestors] received approval. By faith we understand that the universe was fashioned by the word of God, so that from what cannot be seen that which is seen has come into being' (11: 1–3). Hebrews does not explicitly invoke the self-revealing activity of God that continues to give rise to faith. But it implies such revelation, notably by calling faith 'the proof of things not seen'. As C. R. Koester comments, 'the unseen realities of God give proof [present tense] of their existence by their power to evoke faith'.[12] It is the divine reality that creates faith, the invisible power of God that evokes hope ('the assurance of things hoped for'). In other words, ongoing faith is called into existence by the ongoing, revealing, 'proof-giving' activity of God or, in Tillich's terms, by the Holy Spirit that 'moves the human spirit'.

The Johannine corpus also represents revelation as happening here and now. The Book of Revelation, on the one hand, looks back to what Christ achieved and revealed (e.g. 1: 5–6, 17–18; 5: 9–10) and to those associated with him in that saving and revealing work, 'the apostles of the Lamb' (21: 14). On the other hand, Revelation represents the divine self-disclosure as happening here and now: for instance, in the messages that the risen and exalted Christ addresses through the Holy Spirit to seven churches in Asia. The faithful should hear in faith 'what the Spirit is saying' to them right now (2: 1–3: 22). Here the divine revelation comes across as being a living event and continuing reality. Likewise, the First Letter of John recalls how in the past 'the eternal life that was with the Father was revealed to us' (1: 2).

[11] John of the Cross, *Ascent of Mount Carmel*, 2. 22. 3; *The Collected Works of Saint John of the Cross*, trans. K. Kavanaugh and G. Rodriguez, rev edn. (Washington, DC: ICS Publications, 1991), 230.

[12] C. R. Koester, *Hebrews* (New York: Doubleday, 2001), 480.

To convey this divine self-revelation to its readers and hearers, the Johannine community now 'testifies to' and 'declares' in the present what has been revealed (1: 1–3).

Paul expounds faith as the 'obedience of faith' given to God as he continues to communicate himself through the apostolic preaching (Rom. 16: 26). God's 'righteousness is revealed' to elicit the faith of human beings and bring them into a right relationship with God (Rom. 10: 16–17). In a lyrical passage the apostle portrays faith as responding to what is heard, 'the word of Christ' (Rom. 10: 14–17). The good news that Paul preaches is nothing less than 'the [revealing] word of God' working to bring about faith and keep it alive (1 Thess. 2: 13). The heart of the apostolic preaching remains the message of the crucified Christ's resurrection, the already achieved climax of divine revelation to which believers look back and to which, in faith, they here and now continue to respond (1 Cor. 15: 3–11).

(3) Yet, thirdly, when Paul and other New Testament witnesses use the language of revelation, they heavily slant it towards *the future divine manifestation* that will be the second coming of Christ, the fulfilment of the human race, and the end of all history.[13] Thus Hebrews announces that Christ 'will appear a second time' to 'save those who are eagerly waiting for him' (9: 28). First John comforts its readers with the promise, 'when he [God] is revealed, we will be like him, for we shall see him as he is' (3: 2). Paul proclaims that 'the revealing of the Lord' will be on 'the day of his final coming' (1 Cor. 1: 7–8), and reckons 'the sufferings of the present time' not 'worth comparing with the glory that will be revealed to us' (Rom. 8: 18).

Further New Testament witnesses disclose the same tendency to link the language of revelation with the future. First Peter, while recognizing a past divine self-disclosure when Christ 'was revealed at the end of the ages' (1: 20), repeatedly refers to the 'salvation ready to be revealed in the last time' (1: 3) and 'the grace that Jesus Christ will bring you when he is revealed' (1: 13; see 1: 7). We find a similar tension between revelation as past and as future in the Letter to Titus. On the one hand, it rejoices that 'the grace of God has appeared, bringing salvation to all' (2: 11). On the other hand, two verses later it looks towards the future revelation: 'we wait for the blessed hope and

[13] See A. Dulles, *Models of Revelation* (New York: Doubleday, 1983), 228–9.

the manifestation of the glory of our great God and Saviour Jesus Christ' (2: 13).

To sum up: the New Testament presents the divine self-revelation as something that has happened (past), that is happening (present), and that will happen (future). What terminology will allow us to relate these three sets of teaching which at first sight might seem mutually exclusive? If, for instance, revelation has been completed in the past, how can it happen today and reach its final fullness in the future? If revelation is a present event, how can we speak of it as having reached its perfect culmination two thousand years ago?

FOUNDATIONAL REVELATION

Before summarizing the role of the apostolic church for later generations of Christians, I need (a) to dwell on the appropriate terminology to use before (b) considering those who personally witnessed the foundational revelation later in this section. I propose naming past revelation completed with Christ and his Holy Spirit as 'foundational' rather than as 'original' revelation (so in their different ways, Avis, Rahner, Swinburne, and Tillich).

'Original' may seem to express the purely factual standing of this revelation, as existing at/from the beginning. Yet, in general usage, what is 'original' can also serve as a pattern for what comes later, even as a normative pattern. This might support the case for following Tillich's terminology and speaking of 'original' revelation.

Nevertheless, in the context of Christian theology, 'original' could easily evoke the opening words of Genesis ('in the beginning, when God created the heavens and the earth', echoed by the opening words of John's Gospel: 'in the beginning was the Word'). It was only *after* these 'beginnings' (which signalled, the 'pre-existence' of God and that of the Word, respectively) that the revelation recorded, interpreted, and applied by the Old Testament Scriptures—not to mention the decisive revelation mediated by Christ and his Holy Spirit—began. The use of 'original' in the terminology of 'original revelation' can too readily bring up Genesis, the book of 'origins' or 'the book of beginnings', which the prologue of the Fourth Gospel deliberately recalls. These origins did not yet constitute the full history of saving revelation; they preceded it.

'Foundational', as in 'foundational revelation', has the advantage of echoing a New Testament summarizing vision of what the history of revelation and salvation brought with the foundation of the Church, a vision which includes the mediation of that history through the apostles and early Christian prophets, with 'prophets' inevitably suggesting also the Old Testament prophets. The Letter to the Ephesians speaks of 'the household of God', which has been 'built upon the *foundation* of the apostles and the prophets, Christ himself being the cornerstone' (Eph. 2: 19–20), The image of the New Jerusalem in the Book of Revelation proposes a city rather than a house to describe the foundational role of the Twelve: 'the wall of the city has twelve *foundations*, and on them the names of the twelve apostles of the Lamb' (21: 14).

Such foundational imagery includes not only a house and a city but also 'a spiritual house' or temple that, when the history of revelation and salvation reached their highpoint, God built through Jesus Christ. 'A living stone chosen and precious in God's sight', Christ is the 'cornerstone' of this temple (1 Pet. 2: 4–8).[14] The image of the 'cornerstone', used here and, as we have just seen, in Ephesians (and in the Synoptic Gospels and Acts, see n. 14) has the advantage of drawing attention to the centrality of Christ in whom the whole history of the divine self-revelation reaches its highpoint. He is the reliable basis on which all that makes up the saving revelation of God has been built. He will continue to support all that happens in the history of saving revelation. 'Foundational' seems an appropriate epithet for the historical revelation in, with, and through Christ.

In the years that followed the publication on 18 November 1965 of the Second Vatican Council's Constitution on Divine Revelation, *Dei Verbum*, some Roman Catholics represented it as teaching the revelation that came through Christ to be 'definitive'. I did so myself, mistakenly commenting that *Dei Verbum* describes 'revelation as something which reached its full *and definitive* climax' through the self-manifestation of Christ.[15] In fact the text spoke rather of the 'fullness' (*DV* 2) of the revelation which he 'completes and perfects'

[14] Here 1 Pet. cites Ps. 118: 22–3, as does Mark 12: 10–11 (with parallels in Matt. 21: 42 and Luke 20: 17–18, and Acts 4: 11).

[15] G. O'Collins, *Retrieving Fundamental Theology* (Mahwah, NJ: Paulist Press, 1993), 90; other pages wrongly apply 'definitive' or 'definitively' to the historical, divine revelation in Jesus Christ: 87, 89 (twice), and 94.

(*DV* 4). But neither here nor elsewhere did Vatican II ever allege that the divine self-disclosure in Christ is 'definitive' (and 'final'). To be full, complete, and perfect is one thing, but to be definitive goes further. It would mean that this revelation has proved unconditionally full, totally complete, and simply conclusive, so that all of God's self-manifestation is simply over and done with. There is no further revelation to wait for. Such a position is incompatible with the New Testament teaching on the final revelation to come, which we summarized in the previous section.

Apropos of inappropriate use of 'definitive', I felt cheered when I discovered that I shared this 'mistake' with Rowan Williams. Writing on 'Trinity and Revelation', he declared: 'the claim that Jesus of Nazareth "reveals" God . . . is a statement affirming that what is thought to be characteristic of God alone . . . has been experienced in connection with the life and death of a human being: that *direct and immediate knowledge of God* is to be had *definitively* in the leading of a life governed by the memory and presence of Jesus'.[16]

Dei Verbum referred rather to the 'new and *definitive covenant*' (but not the 'new and definitive revelation') inaugurated by Christ. Then it went on at once to speak of expecting 'the glorious manifestation of our Lord Jesus Christ', citing the Letter to Titus 2: 13 and 1 Timothy 6: 14 (*DV* 4).

The Congregation for the Doctrine of the Faith (CDF), in its declaration of 2000, *Dominus Iesus*, diverged from the teaching of *Dei Verbum* when it slipped into speaking of 'the *definitive* and complete character of the revelation of Jesus Christ' (art. 4; italics mine). This statement, Jacques Dupuis commented, ignores 'the gap that remains between the historical divine revelation which took place in Jesus Christ and God's final revelation at the *eschaton*. However complete the historical revelation in Jesus Christ may be, it belongs to the "already," not to the "not yet." While it is decisive as God's full historical manifestation, it is not definitive . . . as will be God's final manifestation at the end of time'.[17] Notice how Dupuis applied both

[16] R. Williams, *On Christian Theology* (Oxford: Blackwell, 2000), 138; italics mine. I would think 'direct and immediate knowledge of God' fits better the final vision of God beyond death. It is that vision which will definitively bring full knowledge of God.

[17] J. Dupuis, 'The Declaration *Dominus Iesus* and My Perspectives on It', in William Burrows (ed.), *Jacques Dupuis Faces the Inquisition; Two Essays by Jacques Dupuis on* Dominus Iesus *and the Roman Investigation of His Work* (Eugene, OR: Pickwick Publications, 2012), 32.

'definitive' and 'final' only to the eschatological revelation to come at the end.

In its most recent document the Pontifical Biblical Commission, like the CDF, writes of Jesus' relationship with God being 'definitively revealed and confirmed through his death and resurrection'. By 'raising Jesus from the dead', God the Father 'shows his complete and definitive approval of the person of Jesus in all his activities and claims'.[18] The document continues to qualify the historical revelation in and through Christ as 'definitive'.[19]

Paul Avis, like the CDF and the Biblical Commission, applies 'definitive' to the historical self-disclosure of God in Christ: revelation 'is embodied supremely and *definitively* in the person and ministry of Jesus Christ'. The same adverbs are turned into adjectives when Avis attributes to Tillich the language of 'definitive': 'The supreme and *definitive* revelation is (as Tillich puts it) the appearance in history of the New Being in Jesus as the Christ as our ultimate concern'.[20] While naming Christ as 'the miracle of the final revelation', Tillich, however, does not claim a 'definitive' revelation.[21] A revelation can be 'final' (in the way Tillich and others understand this adjective) without being 'definitive'. William Abraham, however, clearly makes the two adjectives synonymous when he writes: 'He [Jesus Christ] operates as the final, definitive access to the truth about God'.[22]

Before leaving the historical revelation in Jesus Christ, let me note that calling it 'absolute', as I did in *Retrieving Fundamental Theology*, is also misleading. There I wrote of the apostles witnessing to 'the *absolute* climax of God's self-revelation which they had experienced in the crucified and risen Christ'.[23] In an earlier book, I had also written of Christ as 'the absolute climax of the divine self-communication'.[24] Although I did not press on and explicitly call Christ 'the absolute Revealer', I implied that. I was led astray by Karl Rahner, with his

[18] *The Inspiration and Truth of Sacred Scripture*, trans. E. Esposito and S. Gregg (Collegeville, Minn.: Liturgical Press, 2014), 24, 28.

[19] Ibid. 43, 44, 58, 158.

[20] Avis, *Revelation*, vii, 56; italics mine.

[21] Tillich, *Systematic Theology*, i, 136; in a section on 'The Final Revelation in Jesus as the Christ', 135–7.

[22] W. J. Abraham, 'Revelation and Reason', in I. U. Dalferth and M. Ch. Rodgers (eds.), *Revelation* (Tübingen: Mohr Siebeck, 2014), 29–46, at 31.

[23] O'Collins, *Retrieving Fundamental Theology*, 94.

[24] G. O'Collins, *Fundamental Theology* (Ramsey, NJ: Paulist Press, 1981), 98.

language of Christ as 'the absolute Saviour', and his statement that with the incarnation 'the history of revelation has its absolute climax'.[25] He did not speak of Christ, in what happened from the incarnation until the outpouring of the Holy Spirit, proving himself 'absolute Revealer', but that was implied. Revelation and salvation, let us remember, while distinguishable in the history of God's self-communication, remain inseparable. To name Christ as 'the absolute Saviour' implies that he was also 'the absolute Revealer', and vice versa.

Appealing to the usage of Thomas Aquinas, Dupuis expressed serious difficulties with Rahner's talk of 'the absoluteness of Christianity' and Christ as 'absolute Saviour'. His reason was 'that absoluteness is an attribute of the Ultimate Reality of Infinite Being, which must not be predicated of any finite reality, even the human existence of the Son of God made man. That Jesus Christ is "universal" Saviour does not make him the "Absolute Saviour", who is God himself.'[26] Dupuis did not also direct his criticism towards any claim about the historical Christ being 'absolute Revealer', but it applied there as well. Such language about the past, historical revelation is better avoided, inasmuch as 'absolute', in the strict theological sense, means what is simply 'unlimited' and 'unconditional'. Only God as such is just that in the work of revelation and redemption.

(b) I have defended the choice of 'foundational' (over 'original', 'definitive', and 'absolute') as the most suitable term for the divine self-revelation in the past. What of those who personally witnessed to that foundational revelation which, for all future generations, took place through a specific set of events and the experiences of a specific set of people? God's saving self-disclosure came in the history of Israel, through the prophets ('the Holy Spirit has spoken through the prophets'), and then—in a full, perfect, and unsurpassable fashion—through Jesus of Nazareth and the experiences in which he and his first, apostolic followers were immediately involved. The foundational role of the apostles (and the apostolic generation) in transmitting revelation included *four, overlapping functions*.

(1) The summary formulas of preaching, recorded in Paul's letters (e.g. 1 Cor. 15: 3–5), the Acts of the Apostles (e.g. 2: 22–4,

[25] See Rahner, *Foundations of Christian Faith*, 174, 193–5.

[26] J. Dupuis, *Toward a Christian Theology of Religious Pluralism* (Maryknoll, NY: Orbis, 1997), 282.

32–3, 36; 3: 13–15; 4: 10–12; 5: 30–2)[27] and elsewhere in the New Testament (e.g. Luke 24: 34), reflect a primary function of Peter, Paul, and other apostolic witnesses. Their basic message ('the crucified Jesus has been raised from the dead and of that we are witnesses') gathered the first Christians. Through their Easter preaching, the apostles testified to the self-manifestation of God they had experienced in the life, crucifixion, and resurrection of Jesus, along with the outpouring of the Holy Spirit. Those who had not seen Jesus and yet believed in him (John 20: 29) depended upon the testimony of these witnesses for their coming, through the power of the Holy Spirit, to experience revelation and express faith in the risen Jesus.

(2) Believers entered the community through being baptized 'into' Christ's death and resurrection (Rom 6: 3–11). Together they celebrated eucharistically the death of the risen Lord in expectation of his final coming (1 Cor. 11: 26). Thus the post-Easter and post-Pentecost proclamation initiated the liturgical life of the Church and the liturgical experiences of revelation it triggered.

(3) The apostolic leaders made the normative decision not to impose on Gentile converts specifically Jewish obligations of the Mosaic law (Acts 15: 1–30; see Gal. 2: 1–21). The resurrection of the crucified Christ brought the new covenant which both confirmed God's promises to the chosen people (Rom. 9: 4; 11: 29; 2 Cor. 1: 20) and liberated Gentile believers from the obligation of circumcision and other burdens of the Jewish law (Gal. 5: 1).

(4) Finally, the apostles and other Christians of the apostolic age wrote the Gospels and further New Testament texts. These inspired writings perpetually witness to the climax of divine self-revelation in Christ and to the origins of the Church.

In short, the apostles and their associates shaped once and for all (1) the essential faith, (2) sacramental life, and (3) moral practice for Gentile members of the Church. Through (4) the books of the New Testament, they left for all subsequent ages of believers a divinely

[27] On these verses, see J. A. Fitzmyer, *The Acts of the Apostles* (New York: Doubleday, 1998), 254–6, 258–61, 284–6, 300–2, 336–8.

inspired record and interpretation of the unsurpassable revelation in Christ and its reception in the opening decades of Christian life. We can sum up these once-and-for-all, apostolic functions by speaking of their witnessing to the 'foundational revelation' and acting in the light of it. The 'faith that comes to us from the apostles' (Roman Canon) is, equivalently, the (foundational) revelation that comes to us from them.

DEPENDENT REVELATION

We have seen how Shorter recommended naming present revelation as 'participant' revelation. Yet we should recall how the members of the apostolic generation themselves received a 'participant revelation', by participating in the events that climactically embodied God's self-revelation: Christ's life, death, and resurrection, along with the coming of the Holy Spirit at the first Pentecost. Hence one could talk of a participatory revelation involving the apostles. In these terms later believers would participate in a participation. Or should we rather say that, as regards God's self-communication in Christ, the apostolic generation participated in a foundational way, while later believers participate in a dependent way—that is to say, in dependence upon the apostolic witnesses? It seems simpler and clearer if we distinguish between the *foundational revelation* communicated to the apostolic community and the *dependent revelation* experienced by later believers.[28]

At the start of this chapter we referred to those who claim that any 'present revelation' is not revelation in the proper sense, but only a growth in the collective understanding of that revelation completed and 'closed' once and for all with Christ and his apostles. They sometimes appeal to Jude 3–4. The writer urges his readers to 'contend for the faith' against certain 'ungodly intruders who have perverted the [apostolic] faith that was once and for all entrusted to the saints'. Does this once-and-for-all 'entrusting' of revelation that

[28] Specifically with reference to the apostolic experience of the risen Christ and believers' experience of the same risen Lord, Rahner writes of 'dependence' on the apostolic witness, and adds: 'our faith remains tied to the apostolic witness' (*Foundations of Christian Faith*, 274–6).

triggered the apostolic faith imply that no further communication of revelation takes place, and that later generations of Christians merely have the task of remembering, interpreting, and applying the historical revelation?

Undoubtedly such a growth in understanding takes place. How could I say otherwise at a time when an interest in Blessed John Henry Newman (1801–90) and his writings flourishes as much as ever? His *Essay on the Development of Christian Doctrine* of 1845 espouses the growth in collective interpretation and understanding that tradition has brought. Nevertheless, we would not do justice to tradition if, while accepting the development it has effected towards understanding past revelation, we denied that it continues to produce everywhere an actual revelation of God. In the next chapter we will reflect on the role of the Holy Spirit as the 'soul' of the living, Christian tradition. The witness of the Spirit brings it about that the divine self-revelation recorded in the Scriptures is not only more fully understood but is also actualized as God's living revelation to the Church and though her to the world.

To deny revelation in the present is to doubt the active power here and now of the Holy Spirit in guiding tradition and mediating the living presence of the risen Christ. This also means reducing faith to receiving some revealed truths, inherited from the past, rather than acknowledging faith in its integral sense as being full obedience given to God revealed here and now through the living voice of the good news. In short, to deny such present revelation of God involves selling short its human correlative, faith.

To be sure, if one persists in holding that revelation entails *primarily* the communication of revealed truths about God (rather than the personal self-disclosure of God), it becomes easier to relegate revelation to the past. As soon as the whole set of revealed doctrines was complete, revelation ended or was 'closed'. For this way of thinking, later believers cannot immediately and directly experience revelation. All they can do is remember, interpret, and apply truths disclosed long ago to the apostolic church.

Those who think this way should learn to recognize how present revelation (effected through the reading and proclaiming of the Scriptures,[29] the Church's sacramental worship ('announcing the death of

[29] See how the Scriptures serve to 'instruct for salvation through [arousing] faith in Christ Jesus' (2 Tim. 3: 15).

the Lord until he comes'—1 Cor 11: 26), preaching, the witness of Christian living, and very many other means) actualizes the living event of the divine self-manifestation, and continues to do so in innumerable contexts and for innumerable people who respond in faith. The past events and experiences which affected the chosen people, the prophets, Jesus, his apostles, and other founding fathers and mothers of Christianity are recalled and re-enacted. God is not silent but continues to speak and call forth faith. Just as, in the liturgy, 'the work of our redemption is [continually] exercised (*opus nostrae redemptionis exercetur*)', so 'the work of revelation to us is [continually] exercised (*opus nostrae revelationis exercetur*)'. The classic statement about the liturgical mediation of salvation *in the present* may be applied equally well to the (liturgical and extra-liturgical) mediation of revelation *in the present*: the work of revelation, the inseparable counterpart of salvation, is constantly 'exercised' or performed.

This present mediation of revelation (and salvation) depends essentially upon accepting the foundational and authoritative testimony about the past self-disclosure of God in Christ. Revelation, as believers experience it and accept it now, remains 'dependent' revelation. The adjective 'dependent' expresses a permanent relationship to the witness of the apostolic generation, whose faith in and proclamation of the gospel sprang from their special, immediate experience of Jesus during his lifetime and after Easter. This apostolic witness to foundational revelation continues to be determinative and normative for the post-apostolic history of Christians and their experience of God in Christ.

This ongoing revelation *does not add* to the essential 'content' of what was fully disclosed through Christ's life, death, resurrection, and the sending of the Holy Spirit. As a living encounter with Christ through his Spirit, this divine self-communication never stops. Yet this encounter adds nothing essentially new to what the apostolic generation came to know through their experience of Christ and his Spirit.

THE START OF DEPENDENT REVELATION

To complete this account of the essential link between ongoing (dependent) revelation and past (foundational) revelation, we need to ask: when did foundational revelation end and the period of dependent revelation start?[30] Or was there a partial overlap between the two periods?

Here the traditional answer refers to the end of the apostolic age. Rightly understood, this response recognizes that the *full reception of revelation* by the first Christians *also* included the phase of discerning and expressing their experiences. Peter, Paul, Mary Magdalene, and other founding fathers and mothers of the Church spent a lifetime reflecting on and articulating their experience of the crucified and risen Christ and his Holy Spirit. Collectively and personally, they gave themselves to interpreting the meaning, truth, and value of their total experience of Jesus and the Spirit. That experience had lodged itself profoundly in their memory to live on powerfully and productively until the end of their lives.

Understood this way, the period of foundational revelation covered not merely the climactic events (the life, death, and resurrection of Jesus, together with the outpouring of the Spirit) but also the decades when the apostles and their associates assimilated these events, fully founded the Church for all peoples, and wrote the inspired books of the New Testament. During those years the apostles were not receiving new truths from Christ, as if, through his ministry, death, and post-resurrection appearances, he had failed to reveal to them all that he wanted to reveal. Rather they were led by the Holy Spirit to interpret normatively and apply what they had experienced of the fullness of revelation in Christ (John 15: 26; 16: 13).[31] The activity of the Spirit during the apostolic age also entered into foundational revelation and its phase of immediate assimilation. That age belonged to the revealing and redemptive Christ-event, and did so in a way that would not be true of any later stage of Christian history.[32]

[30] See J. Schumacher, *Der apostolische Abschluss der Offenbarung Gottes* (Freiburg im Breisgau: Herder, 1979).

[31] On these verses, see A. T. Lincoln, *Gospel According to St John* (London: Continuum, 2005), 411–12, 421.

[32] In 'The Death of Jesus and the Closure of Revelation', *Theological Investigations*, xviii, trans. Edward Quinn (London: Darton, Longman & Todd, 1983), 132–42, at 140–1, Karl Rahner argued that 'it would be better and more exact to say that revelation closed with the achievement of the death of Jesus, crucified and risen'. This view does not do justice to (a) the special activity of the Holy Spirit guiding the Church through the apostolic age, and (b) the apostolic witnesses' discernment and interpretation of their experience (of Jesus' death and resurrection) which lasted through their lives.

When the apostolic age closed—roughly speaking at the end of the first century—there would be no more founding of the Church and writing of inspired Scriptures. The last period of foundational revelation, during which the original, Christian witnesses brought into being the visible Church and completed the written word of God, was ended. Through the apostolic Church and its Scriptures, later generations could share dependently in the saving self-communication of God mediated by unrepeatable events involving Jesus and his first followers. All later believers would be invited to accept the witness of those who announced what they had personally experienced of the full, divine revelation in Christ: 'we proclaim to you the eternal life which was with the Father and was made manifest to us' (1 John 1:2). As this verse shows, the period of dependent revelation was already inaugurated with the experience of those who accepted in faith the proclamation of the original witnesses in the Johannine community—not to mention those who responded (dependently) in faith to the (foundational) preaching of Paul. Not surprisingly, there was a partial overlap between the periods of foundational and the dependent revelation.

FUTURE AND FINAL REVELATION

Chapter 2 above reflected on the mysteriousness of God, which is enhanced rather than removed by past and present revelation. A future and final revelation[33] in which, through the risen Christ and the Holy Spirit, the divine self-communication will reach its definitive climax seems even more mysterious and incomprehensible.

To be sure, the Gospels and other New Testament books promise a final, saving revelation that will affect not only individuals and the human community: not only 'all the nations' gathered for what the Son of Man will disclose in judgement (Matt. 25: 32) but also the cosmos itself ('the new heaven and the new earth' to be revealed at the end (Rev. 21: 1)). Jesus speaks of a final heavenly banquet (Matt. 8: 11; Mark 14: 25) and a marriage feast (Matt. 25: 1–13),[34] when the

[33] As is obvious, I refer 'final' revelation to the future and not to the past, as Tillich did when expounding the appearance of Christ in history; see n. 21.

[34] See Rev. 19: 7–9; 21: 2, 9; Rev. 22: 17 on the final marriage feast.

coming kingdom of God will be manifested (Matt. 8: 11; Mark 14: 25) and his disciples will finally be at home with him in the house of the Father (John 14: 1–3; see Rev. 21: 3–9). Some New Testament authors follow up Jesus' language about the coming Son of Man (e.g. Mark 13: 24–7) by promising the final manifestation of the now glorified Christ at the end of history (Tit. 2: 13; Heb. 9: 28). Paul expects that, when we come to God at the end, 'we will see face to face' and 'will know fully even as we have been fully known' (1 Cor. 13: 12). First John consoles its readers with the hope that they will enjoy the intimate divine presence when they will 'see' God revealed 'as he is' (3: 2). Seeing the 'face' of God (Rev. 22: 4), the community of all who have reached a blessed fulfilment will live forever in the heavenly Jerusalem (Rev. 21–2). Note that Paul, John, and Revelation converge in picturing the 'beatific vision' primarily as a collective transformation rather than an individual, self-sufficient completion of salvation to come. The heavenly Jerusalem is utterly unimaginable apart from our relationship with (a) the Father, Son, and Holy Spirit, and (b) one another. Images of angels, thrones, trumpets, heavenly music, and similar language from Revelation provide a scenario for this final manifestation of God at the resurrection of the dead. But what will '*revelation* after death' as distinct (but not separable) from resurrected '*life* after death' be like?[35]

None of this New Testament testimony to the final revelation of God constitutes reports coming in, as it were, from the future, 'eyewitness accounts of a future which is still outstanding'.[36] Here this testimony differs sharply from that arising from past figures who mediated revelation (e.g. Isaiah, Peter, and Mary Magdalene) or from later, 'dependent' Christians (e.g. Teresa of Avila and Dietrich Bonhoeffer). They encountered the living God and witnessed to what was communicated by those revealing and redemptive episodes. We pray 'thy kingdom come', but do not have testimony that might tell us clearly what that final kingdom will reveal itself to be.

Daniel, Ezekiel, the psalms, and other Old Testament sources provide Mark 13 and the Book of Revelation with rich symbolic

[35] See S. T. Davis, *After We Die: Theology, Philosophy, and the Question of Life after Death* (Waco, TX: Baylor University Press, 2015); F. J. Matera, *Resurrection: The Origin and Goal of Christian Life* (Collegeville, Minn.: Liturgical Press, 2015); A. C. Thiselton, *Life After Death: A New Approach to the Last Things* (Grand Rapids, Mich.: Eerdmans, 2012).

[36] Rahner, *Foundations of Christian Faith*, 431.

imagery. This apocalyptic language, found previously in canonical and non-canonical texts, aims to evoke religious feelings (about the present and the future) rather than to provide descriptions of what will be revealed at the end. Paul and John point us to the central Christian claim about, and hope for, the future and final self-revelation of God: risen from the dead, human beings will see God 'as he is' or 'face to face'.[37]

Without specifying what shape 'scientific predictions' take, William Abraham has written of 'the potential conflict between scientific predictions about the future and Christian eschatological claims'. He adds: 'amazingly, this has received next to no attention'.[38] Such potential conflict does not bear on hopes for a beatific vision in the final divine self-manifestation of God, but rather on the tension between scientific views and Christian hopes for the resurrection of human beings and a transformed cosmos. This latter tension has, *pace* Abraham, been addressed in a number of works: for instance, a theological and scientific study of bodily resurrection produced by an international team in 2002.[39] The Easter promise of the new creation to come may seem threatened, for example, by two major scientific scenarios for the future: the universe will either freeze itself out of existence or it will collapse back into a dense fireball. But, it was argued, we may not presume that the laws of nature that have governed the past and continue to govern the present will also necessarily govern the future. In the final history of the cosmos, God is free to act in new ways and transform the laws which he has created. Yet while resurrection is the necessary condition, seeing God 'face to face' remains the core claim for those who hope for a future and final revelation.

The beatific vision of God to come remains mysteriously hidden, an experience that, through faith, hope, and love, we can glimpse only 'dimly' (1 Cor. 13: 12). Yet glimpses and anticipations are already available—proleptically, as those who adopt Wolfhart Pannenberg's terminology would say—through the life of grace, the Holy Spirit, the

[37] For details and bibliography on apocalyptic literature, see J. T. Hibbard, 'Apocalypticism', in S. E. Balentine (ed.), *The Oxford Encyclopedia of the Bible and Theology*, i (New York: Oxford University Press, 2015), 42–7; see also C. J. Roetzel, 'Eschatology', ibid. 262–73.

[38] Abraham, 'Revelation and Reason', 29–46, at 32–3.

[39] T. Peters, R. J. Russell, and M. Welker (eds.), *Resurrection: Theological and Scientific Assessments* (Grand Rapids, Mich.: Eerdmans, 2002).

resurrection of Jesus, and the Eucharist. Through faith and love, 'eternal life' has already begun for believers (e.g. 1 John 2: 25; 3: 15; 5: 13). The gift of the Holy Spirit is a 'pledge' of the glorious vision and existence promised for the final future (2 Cor. 1: 22; 5: 5; Eph. 1: 14). The risen Christ constitutes the 'first fruits' or first instalment of coming resurrection for those who die (1 Cor. 15: 20). The Eucharist 'announces' the death of the risen Lord 'until he comes' (1 Cor. 11: 26).

To this list, Augustine of Hippo would add the experience of beauty. In our present life we experience and love beauty in many, partial forms. Earthly beauty reflects and participates in the utterly perfect, fully harmonious, and radiantly splendid divine beauty. The life to come will bring the final revelation of God, who is supremely and infinitely beautiful, 'the Beauty of all things beautiful' (*Confessions*, 3. 6; see 9. 4). Experiencing beauty here and now communicates to us something of the risen Christ's beauty and draws us towards and into that final revelation of beauty.

For eight chapters now we have kept the focus steadily on the divine self-revelation and its characteristics. We turn now to the closely related realities of tradition, biblical inspiration, and scriptural truth.

9

Handing on Revelation

The Role of Tradition

Responding with faith to events of revelation and shaped by their experiences of the divine self-communication, believers from the start of biblical history followed up their encounters with God by handing on to the next generation some account of what they had experienced. Thus Abraham, Sarah, and other half-glimpsed figures in the earliest period, prompted by their experiences of the divine self-communication, set going the narrative of the believing community, with its ethical and worshipping practices and forms of leadership.

The prophets typically heard the word of God (revelation in the primary sense) and passed on the messages they received (revelation in the secondary sense). Sometimes consoling and supportive but sometimes dramatically unsettling, the prophetic messages shaped and reshaped the biblical tradition. In less dramatic ways, the authors of wisdom literature educated the people in what they had learned from God and about God.

The story of Moses, with its movement from revelation in the primary sense to revelation in its second sense, suggests paradigmatically the constant reframing of tradition. In Midian the God of his ancestors appears to Moses at the burning bush and commissions him to accept a leadership role in delivering the people (Exod. 2: 23–4: 17). Moses is to take a message to 'the elders of Israel' and say to them: 'The Lord, the God of your ancestors, the God of Abraham, of Isaac, and of Jacob, has appeared to me, saying . . . "I will bring you up out of the misery of Egypt"' (Exod. 3: 16–17). He takes the message to the people and assumes his leadership role. The divine appearance or theophany at Horeb prefigures a second theophany (at Sinai), when God establishes a covenant with Israel (Exod. 19–31)—a life-changing set of experiences that reframes forever the people's tradition.

The climax of biblical history and foundational revelation came with Jesus and his Holy Spirit, the apostles, and other first-century disciples. What they received through their experience of God re-interpreted and re-framed what they handed on. We saw at the close of Chapter 1 above how the divine self-revelation radically modified, for instance, the monotheistic tradition and made it a trinitarian monotheism. The apostolic generation's experience of Christ and the Holy Spirit led them, not to abandon monotheistic faith, but to recast it as faith in Father, Son, and Holy Spirit. In this and in other ways, by building into the tradition their experiences of God's new messages to them and actions on their behalf, Jesus and the apostolic generation formed and fashioned the normative tradition of Christianity which they launched.[1]

Some members, of the apostolic age, inspired by the Holy Spirit, set down in writing the story of the making of the foundational tradition

[1] On tradition, see D. Braithwaite, 'Vatican II on Tradition', *Heythrop Journal* 53 (2012), 915–28; Y. Congar, *Tradition and the Life of the Church*, trans. A. N. Woodrow (London: Burns & Oates, 1964); id., *Tradition and Traditions: An Historical and Theological Essay*, trans. M. Naseby and T. Rainborough (London: Burns & Oates, 1966); G. Ebeling, *The Word of God and Tradition*, trans. S. H. Hooke (London: Collins, 1968); J. F. Kelly (ed.), *Perspectives on Tradition and Scripture* (Notre Dame, Ind.: Fides, 1976); G. O'Collins and D. Braithwaite, 'Tradition as Collective Memory: A Theological Task to be Tackled', *Theological Studies* 76 (2015), 29–42; H. J. Pottmeyer, 'Normen, Kriterien, und Strukturen der Überlieferung', *HFTh* iv, 124–52; K. Rahner and J. Ratzinger, *Revelation and Tradition*, trans. W. J. O'Hara (London: Burns & Oates, 1966); M. Rösel et al., 'Tradition', *TRE* xxxiii, 689–732; O. Rush, *The Eyes of Faith: The Sense of the Faithful and the Church's Reception of Revelation* (Washington, DC: Catholic University of America Press, 2009); D. Sarisky, 'Tradition', in S. E. Balentine (ed.), *The Oxford Encyclopedia of the Bible and Theology*, ii (New York: Oxford University Press, 2015), 384–7; J. E. Thiel, *Senses of Tradition: Continuity and Development in Catholic Faith* (New York: Oxford University Press, 2000); P. Valliere, 'Tradition', in M. Eliade (ed.), *Encyclopedia of Religion*, xvi (New York: Macmillan, 1987), 1–18; K. J. Vanhoozer, 'Scripture and Tradition', in K. J. Vanhoozer (ed.), *The Cambridge Companion to Postmodern Theology* (Cambridge: Cambridge University Press, 2003), 149–69; D. Wiederkehr, 'Das Prinzip der Überlieferung', *HFTh* iv, 100–23; id., *Wie geschieht Tradition? Überlieferung im Lebensprozess der Kirche* (Freiburg im Breisgau: Herder, 1991); A. N. Williams, 'Tradition', in J. Webster, K. Tanner, and I. Torrance (eds.), *Oxford Handbook of Systematic Theology* (Oxford: Oxford University Press, 2007), 362–77; D. H. Williams, *Retrieving Tradition and Renewing Evangelicalism: A Primer for Suspicious Protestants* (Grand Rapids, Mich.: Eerdmans, 1999).

and how they had understood, expressed, and acted upon (or sinfully failed to act upon) their encounter with God through Jesus and his Spirit. These inspired Scriptures (like the Old Testament Scriptures) emerged *from* tradition, and were interpreted and actualized *within* the living tradition of the community. Much more will be said about the relationship between tradition and the Sacred Scriptures, as well as about biblical inspiration (both related to and different from revelation). Here I wish only to point out how the inspired Scriptures originated from (and within) the tradition that had been triggered by experiences (in faith) of the divine self-revelation. Thus tradition both preceded the composition of the Sacred Scriptures, included those Scriptures, and extended beyond them. Tradition transmits, interprets, and applies the inspired texts, but it also transmits much more besides—in the ways of worshipping, living, and believing of the whole community.

Richard Swinburne rightly acknowledges how revelation preceded the writing of the inspired Scriptures, but omits the process of tradition when he writes: Scripture 'is a true record of revelation which existed before it'.[2] But the sequence is revelation, tradition, and then the writing of inspired Scripture. Swinburne has little or nothing to say about the key, mediating role of tradition. His limited view of tradition concerns itself only with 'unwritten traditions'.[3] Moreover, Scripture includes much more than 'a true record of revelation'; we will come to this in the next chapter. Biblical inspiration (which Swinburne does not discuss), as we shall see, is a special God-given impulse to set down in writing various things, which include much more than simply events and words of revelation.

THREE PRELIMINARIES

Before examining directly the relationship between revelation and tradition, we need to clarify terminology, indicate the full scope of tradition, and introduce the principle of 'the tradition always in need of reform (*traditio semper reformanda*)'.

[2] R. Swinburne, *Revelation: From Analogy to Metaphor*, 2nd edn. (Oxford: Oxford University Press, 2007), 137.

[3] Ibid. 188–9, 212, 310, 313, 315.

(1) Right from the outset it is important to alert readers to the way 'tradition' may designate either a process (the act of handing on, *actus tradendi*) or what is handed on (the content, the *traditum*). It would waste time to remark constantly whether it is the process or the content that is meant. The context will make it clear which meaning is intended: either the act of transmission or the content of what is transmitted.

(2) Understood either as process or content, tradition, when spoken of in the singular, involves innumerable 'actors'. The protagonists who transmit post-New Testament tradition include, as well as the invisible Holy Spirit (to whom we return below), official leaders, charismatic figures, and millions of believers of every kind. It is the whole community of the baptized that hands on tradition.[4]

Such a total view of tradition allowed Pope Francis to recognize as a gift to Catholics things 'sown' by the Holy Spirit and transmitted by the living tradition of other Christians: 'we can learn so much from each other. It is not just about being better informed about others, but rather about reaping what the Spirit has sown in them, which is also meant to be a gift to us.' The Pope offered an example in the area of leadership: 'in the dialogue with our Orthodox brothers and sisters, we Catholics have the opportunity to learn more about the meaning of episcopal collegiality and their experience of synodality'.[5] It is the whole Christian Church that hands on the living tradition. As principal agent of tradition, the Holy Spirit is active everywhere in Christian churches.

Here, at least by implication, Pope Francis evoked the vision enunciated by Vatican II (in the Constitution on Divine Revelation) of *the whole Church* transmitting tradition: 'what was handed on by the Apostles includes everything that contributes to making the People of God live their lives in holiness and grow in faith. In this way the Church, in her doctrine, life, and worship, perpetuates and transmits to every generation all that she herself is, all that she believes' (*DV* 8). What 'contributes to making the People of God

[4] This is the basis of what John Henry Newman argued in his remarkable essay of 1859, 'On Consulting the Faithful in Matters of Doctrine', ed. J. Coulson (London: Sheed and Ward, 1961).

[5] Pope Francis, *Evangelii Gaudium* (The Joy of the Gospel) (Vatican City: Libreria Editrice Vaticana, 2013), art. 246; available on the Vatican website and in numerous print editions.

live their lives in holiness and grow in faith' will also be found in other Christian churches. A total view of the living tradition involves learning from other Christians.[6]

(3) The content of tradition or *traditum* itself includes all manner of beliefs, forms of worship, and ranges of practice. This raises the question, within the Catholic Church and beyond: how do we know whether and to what extent this complex *traditum* remains faithful to and authentically expresses the foundational, apostolic experience of the divine self-revelation? The question will be taken up in this chapter.

A principle endorsed by Vatican II's Decree on Ecumenism (*Unitatis Redintegratio*, art. 6) should direct our response: the whole Christian Church requires constant 'reformation' and 'renewal' (*ecclesia semper reformanda*). The council acknowledged that 'every renewal of the Church essentially consists in an increased fidelity to her vocation'. In fact, 'the Church is called by Christ' to 'a constant reformation, which she invariably needs inasmuch as she is a human and earthly institution' (art. 6). That teaching necessarily invites us to accept the principle of *traditio semper reformanda*; the whole Christian tradition requires constant reformation and renewal.

To recognize the Holy Spirit as the primary agent of tradition brings up the question: Is the Spirit somehow then responsible for the wounds in tradition that call for purification and healing? The holiness of the primary agent of tradition is not jeopardized by the wounds left by the secondary agents of the traditionary process. After all, Paul writes about the Holy Spirit 'dwelling in you [plural]' (1 Cor. 3: 16) and making the Christian community the temple of the Spirit,

[6] After *Dei Verbum*, it is the Decree on the Eastern Catholic Churches that deals most with tradition, significantly using the noun *traditio* twelve times and its near equivalent *patrimonium* (heritage) five times. Like the Constitution on Divine Revelation, it understands tradition broadly as comprising 'institutions, liturgical rites, ecclesiastical traditions', and, significantly the whole discipline of 'Christian life' (*OE*, 1). While explicitly concerned with 'Eastern Catholic Churches', the decree expresses 'esteem' for the way in which 'the heritage of the whole Church of Christ' shines forth in those churches (art. 5). Since (a) other 'Eastern' churches, which are not in communion with the Catholic Church but share with (b) those that are in communion with Rome, very many of the same 'institutions, liturgical rites, ecclesiastical traditions', and way of 'Christian life', the Vatican II decree implies esteem for and willingness to learn from group (a). However, it was left for Pope Francis to say just this explicitly.

while using the same letter to call on that community to turn away from various sins that have wounded them and needed healing.

Let us turn now to examine the human reality of tradition, some relevant features of the history of Christian tradition, an ecumenical convergence over the link between tradition and Scripture, and the task of discerning 'the (authentic) Tradition' (upper case and in the singular) within particular traditions (lower case and in the plural).

TRADITION AS A HUMAN REALITY

Inasmuch as the experience of the divine self-communication is also a human phenomenon, it necessarily involves tradition. The social, historical, and religious existence of all human beings is situated firmly within tradition. Human life is simply unthinkable outside the matrix of tradition.[7] Over and above being a religious phenomenon that marks Christianity and other world religions, tradition—and this is a reality often ignored by those who write about it in a theological context—shapes the entire cultural existence of men and women. Tradition is almost synonymous with a society's whole way of life or, in a word, with its culture. Let me recall how tradition functions as a human reality which secures a society's *continuity*, *identity*, and *unity*.[8]

Tradition fashions the bond between *successive generations* of a society. From the past we receive our language, laws, customs, beliefs, practices, and further symbolic realities that are generally accepted without question and provide Italy, Japan, Madagascar, or any other society with its characteristic cultural values. Even if members of a given society rarely stop to reflect on what they have taken over, they remain radically indebted to the past for their inherited values and

[7] Experts in the broad disciplines of sociology and cultural anthropology (e.g. Robert Bellah, Peter Berger, Clifford Geertz, Anthony Giddens, Thomas Luckmann, David Martin, Talcott Parsons, Rodney Stark, and their successors) frequently study tradition, even when they do not explicitly introduce the term as such.

[8] Yves Congar wrote: 'tradition is like the consciousness of a group or *the principle of identity* which links one generation to another: it enables them to remain . . . the same people as they go forward through history'. In short, tradition is 'a principle that ensures . . . *continuity and identity*' (*Tradition and the Life of the Church*, 8; italics mine).

expectations which give life its meaning and provide ideals to be practised. Thus one generation passes on to another norms, attitudes, and behaviour patterns by which society has hitherto functioned. From the past we receive the stories we live by and live for. Of course, newcomers can challenge, reject, or modify traditions they have received, but they can never do so totally. They cannot start from scratch. Any such *complete* break with the past is never a genuine option. At least initially, these newcomers to an existing society are taught to live by the existing ways. Otherwise they would be incapable of altering or rebelling against what the previous generation has handed on to them.

In 1968, North Atlantic countries experienced a massive rejection of tradition, especially among their student populations. But then the 1970s saw many young people becoming disillusioned with change and revolution. Around the same time, large segments of the Muslim world began returning to traditional values and practices, which they felt to be threatened by secularizing trends. The pendulum swings backwards and forwards. But neither total revolution nor frozen tradition will ever finally dislodge the other. Permanence and a hunger for permanence seem as essential a feature of human experience as change and a yearning for change. Tradition and change, so far from being mutually exclusive, stand in function of each other.

Besides effecting continuity within the flow of history, inherited tradition *identifies* us here and now at our deepest levels. The power of culture in our lives is the power of tradition in our lives. Traditional values and conventions help establish our cultural identity as Italians, Japanese, Scots, Vietnamese, or whatever, and then effectively *unite* our societies. In short, tradition works as the principle of continuity, identity, and unity in any human community—between generations and within generations.

Sometimes, to be sure, tradition may be demonically misused by unscrupulous politicians who aim to secure the identity and unity of a nation or particular group, so as to promote some unworthy and even criminal project. They may do so by retrieving a past 'victory' and calling for continuity with this 'glorious' tradition. It is at our peril that we ignore the ways in which traditions may be exploited in an evil cause.

Paul Ricoeur reminds us that collective memory and the traditions which it preserves can prove pathological, even dangerously pathological. Ricoeur calls such memory 'haunted', 'a past that does not pass', 'collective traumatisms', or 'wounds in the collective memory'.[9] At times such pathological memories derive from 'acts of violence' that founded the history and traditions of some ethnic or national group.[10] Pathological memories may characterize certain traditions.

It is clear from positive and negative examples that tradition transcends not only individuals but also the present history of a group. It shapes the collective experiences of a group and its interpretation of such experiences, as well as all those expressions of experience which one generation transmits to another. In receiving, changing, and handing on its tradition, a society acts as a collective subject, interpreter, and administrator of the tradition. This collective subject experiences and hands on something that goes beyond the mere sum total of individual experiences: namely, some collective experience.[11]

When we move to discuss Christian tradition, we should not imagine that it simply conforms to the typical trajectory of tradition in 'ordinary' human affairs. Christians look back through their history and tradition to an enduringly normative point of reference, an unsurpassable climax in the first century of our era. Admittedly other groups and societies cherish the memory of some foundational events, like a war of independence, the landing of their first settlers, or a glorious revolution, which they recognize or at least believe to have shaped the subsequent, 'successful' course of their history. In ways that offer an analogy to the Christian model, people can cling to the spirit of their national patrimony and seek to renew themselves through traditions derived from their origins and/or from some radical transformation of their country's history.

Yet no nation has security of tenure. Any nation could go out of existence or be recreated through events that will provide a radically new point of departure. Christians, however, believe the coming of Jesus Christ to be the lasting, normative climax of the divine self-communication, trust that the Church which he founded will not disappear in the course of human history, and acknowledge the Holy Spirit as the invisible and effective 'bearer' of their essential tradition.

[9] P. Ricoeur, *Memory, History, Forgetting*, trans. K. Blamey and D. Pellauer (Chicago: University of Chicago Press, 2004), 54, 78.

[10] Ibid. 79.

[11] See O'Collins and Braithwaite, 'Tradition as Collective Memory', *passim*.

CHRISTIAN TRADITION

How then has Christian tradition functioned (or failed to function) when the period of *foundational* revelation ended with the apostolic age and gave way to the era of *dependent* revelation in which all subsequent believers have lived? The Church had been founded and the writing of inspired Scriptures (which recorded the foundational experience and a normative interpretation of the divine self-revelation through Christ and his Spirit) had come to a close. Through many particular traditions, the foundational witnesses handed on to subsequent generations their experience of God and the ways in which they lived out of that experience. They did this, above all, through the New Testament Scriptures (which drew on and incorporated the Old Testament Scriptures); the celebration of baptism and the Eucharist; the practice of regular prayer and help to those in need; the creation of community leaders by the imposition of hands and the invocation of the Holy Spirit; and other traditions. Constantly re-actualizing the past tradition, as 'the law of praying, believing, and living (*lex orandi, credendi, et vivendi*)' that triggered moments of divine self-disclosure (revelation in the primary sense),[12] maintained and clarified the group identity and continuity of early Christians. Tradition, above all the memory of the living Jesus, continued to define Christians and tell them who they were.

Commemorative ceremonies as ritual performances, above all baptism and the Eucharist, embodied and maintained an essential continuity in the Christian tradition.[13] By ritually re-enacting such events as the baptism of Jesus and his Last Supper and by aiming to nourish a life-style required by those basic sacraments, Christian memory provided access to revelation and served the continuity of tradition. The examples of baptism and the Eucharist, along with other examples about to be listed, vindicate what Levering writes: 'our ability to hear and participate in the divine revelation is inseparable

[12] M. Levering rightly recognizes the primacy of liturgy or 'lex orandi': 'the liturgy is the primary context for the proclamation, interpretation, and *enactment of God's revelation*' (*Engaging the Doctrine of Revelation* (Grand Rapids, Mich.: Baker Academic, 2014), 3); italics mine. See also Philip Caldwell, *Liturgy as Revelation* (Minneapolis: Fortress Press, 2014).

[13] See P. Connerton, *How Societies Remember* (Cambridge: Cambridge University Press, 1989), 41–71.

from the tradition process',[14] which, we might add, is eminently a process of memory.[15]

From the second and third centuries and later, further traditions emerged and spread in the Christian Church: for instance, the biblical canon, settled by recognizing *these* Scriptures as inspired, apostolic, and authoritative (rather than, e.g., the Gnostic texts castigated in the second century by Irenaeus of Lyons); the threefold, ordained ministry of bishop, presbyter, and deacon; the holding of synods and councils that produced at times such enduring creeds as the Nicene-Constantinopolitan Creed of 381 (a set of true propositions that have remained normative for all later Christians);[16] pilgrimages to the Holy Land and to the tombs of martyrs; the composition of various liturgical texts (notably the Eucharistic prayers of Western and even more of Eastern Christianity); the emergence of such key sacramental practices as infant baptism; obligations about celibacy, fasting, and abstinence; the founding and spread of monastic life for both men and women; prayers for the dead; the unfolding story of Christian art (e.g. Eastern icons); architecture (e.g. Romanesque and then Gothic cathedrals and churches); liturgical music in East and West; developments in devotion to the Virgin Mary and other saints; particular structures for ecclesiastical governance (e.g. the dioceses in the West and eparchies in the East); and worship of Christ that took form in devotion to his presence in the Blessed Sacrament, to his five wounds, and to his love expressed through the symbol of the Sacred Heart.[17]

Along with such particular traditions, one should also note some traditions that were less than worthy of Christians and sometimes downright scandalous: the formation of ecclesiastical tribunals for tracking down, examining, and punishing heretics; ways in which

[14] Levering, *Engaging the Doctrine of Revelation*, 3.

[15] See O'Collins and Braithwaite, 'Tradition as Collective Memory', *passim.*

[16] This and other early creeds, notably the Apostles' Creed (revelation in the secondary sense), summarized and clarified the divine revelation expressed through the Sacred Scriptures and did so in consistently biblical language. Usually '*homoousios* (of one being)' is cited as the solitary non-biblical term in the Nicene Creed. Some scholars, however, relate it to God's self-disclosure as 'I am who I am' of Exod. 3: 14. Such monuments of tradition, so far from being a 'dead letter', can, in their turn, actualize further events of divine self-disclosure (revelation in the primary sense).

[17] On these and similar development in traditions, see G. O'Collins and M. Farrugia, *Catholicism: The Story of Catholic Christianity*, 2nd edn. (Oxford: Oxford University Press, 2015), 1–101.

indulgences (or remittance in purgatory of temporal punishment due to sins, for which sorrow had been expressed and forgiveness received) were blatantly misused; multiple benefices or properties attached to church offices that led, for instance, to bishops enriching themselves and depriving whole dioceses of spiritual leadership; forms of papal leadership that indulged power and greed and failed to exercise an authentic pastoral ministry derived from St Peter. Some of these particular traditions seriously wounded the Church, helped spark the sixteenth-century Reformation, and raised the issue of tradition and Scripture for the Council of Trent (1545–63).[18]

SCRIPTURE AND TRADITION(S)

In its decree of 8 April 1546 (Bettenson, 275–6; DzH 1501–9; ND 210–15), the Council of Trent acknowledged 'the Gospel' (which approximates to foundational revelation) to be 'the source [singular] of all saving truth and [all] regulation of conduct'. It then pointed to the written books of Scripture and unwritten (apostolic) traditions (plural) as 'containing' this saving truth and regulation of conduct. Against attempts to make the Bible the only guide to revelation and faith, Trent maintained that the tradition of the Church also preserved and disclosed 'the Gospel'. We can expect to find revelation expressed, recorded, and actualized through various traditions, as well as through the inspired Scriptures.

The Reformers, when they rediscovered central themes of the New Testament (forgiveness, grace, and freedom), turned against such human enactments as the laws of fasting, the rule of annual confession, the practice of indulgences, and the obligation of celibacy for religious and Latin-rite priests. Understanding the Bible and not human traditions to

[18] On the Reformation and Trent, see R. Bireley, *The Refashioning of Catholicism 1450–1700* (Basingstoke: Macmillan, 1999); H. J. Hillerbrand (ed.), *The Oxford Encyclopedia of the Reformation*, 4 vols. (Oxford: Oxford University Press, 1996); R. Po-Chia Hsia (ed.), *A Companion to the Reformation World* (Oxford: Blackwell, 2004); id. (ed.), *Reform and Expansion 1500–1660* (Cambridge: Cambridge University Press, 2007); J. W. O'Malley, *Trent and All That: Renaming Catholicism and the Early Modern Age* (Cambridge, Mass.: Harvard University Press, 2000); id., *Trent: What Happened at the Council* (Cambridge, Mass.: Belknap Press of Harvard University Press, 2013).

be the only authoritative rule for faith, Luther made *sola Scriptura* a battle cry in the campaign to reform the Catholic Church.

The main thrust of the principle could be put as follows. Within the limits of the biblical text, the Holy Spirit actively expresses the truth of revelation and brings into play the saving reality of Jesus Christ. The Bible alone takes on the role of being the exclusive rule of faith. A 1963 conference of Faith and Order (a theological think-tank for the World Council of Churches) was to sum up the scope of *sola Scriptura* this way: 'The Protestant principle has been an appeal to Holy Scripture alone, as the infallible and sufficient authority in all matters pertaining to salvation, to which all human tradition should be subjected'.[19] By the time of this conference, which took place during the Second Vatican Council, a sea change had occurred over the question of tradition and Scripture and brought a movement towards an ecumenical convergence. Before discussing that change, let us recall some pertinent issues that came up during the sixteenth century and subsequently.

DIFFERENT ECCLESIOLOGIES

The controversy over tradition and Scripture involved divergent views of the Church. To make a risky generalization, Protestants differed from Catholics by distinguishing or even separating the Holy Spirit from the visible, historical community with its inherited traditions and authoritative magisterium, or office needed to teach the good news of Christ in changing contexts and new cultures.[20] In

[19] P. C. Rodger and L. Vischer (eds.), *The Fourth World Conference on Faith and Order, Montreal 1963* (London: SCM Press, 1964), 51.

[20] Apropos of this need, Richard Swinburne writes: 'if revelation is to answer new questions raised by a new culture, it needs a church to interpret it, [at least] in one of the ways compatible with *the original meaning* rather than in other ways, so as to give true answers to the questions of the new culture' (*Revelation*, 106; italics mine). We may well wonder, however, about 'the' original meaning of revelation. Could anyone have ever clearly pinned down what the revelation of God to Moses originally meant or what the resurrection of the crucified Jesus originally meant? Surely those great events of fundamental revelation yielded and yield, not one original meaning, but a multiplicity of meanings? When Jesus united the commands to love God and love neighbour (Mark 12: 28–34) and at the Last Supper said 'this is my body' (Mark 14: 22), did he intend his words to bear only one, original meaning, by which all of his followers were to be subsequently constrained?

the short or the long run, the rejection of the magisterium meant *either* giving exclusive autonomy to the Scriptures (interpreted privately through the light of the Holy Spirit, or in dependence upon the 'latest' results of biblical research), *or* allowing reason to take full charge, as typically happened in the Enlightenment. Against such trends, Catholics believed that the Holy Spirit supported the wider community with its traditions and empowered the bishops, including the Bishop of Rome, to teach authoritatively, as well as to guide and sanctify believers. In other words, they acknowledged the Spirit's active presence to extend beyond individual believers reading the Scriptures, preachers expounding the Scriptures, and ministers using the Scriptures in celebrating the sacraments.

While footnote 20 puts me into debate with Swinburne, he rightly argues that God can be expected to provide some kind of permanent and authoritative means for interpreting revelation. It does not seem plausible to represent God as revealing himself in Christ and the outpouring of the Holy Spirit, and then 'stepping back' by failing to provide ongoing and reliable assistance towards remembering, interpreting, and applying to action the foundational revelation and the closely related inspired Scriptures. To be enduringly effective, foundational revelation calls for some kind of 'magisterium' that will preserve and formulate it in creeds and further forms of official teaching.

EXCLUSIVE NORM OF FAITH?

Apart from a basic divergence over ecclesiology, Catholics and other Christians (e.g. Orthodox and many Anglicans) questioned further the *sola Scriptura* view that the Bible by itself should determine Christian faith and practice.[21] To begin with, the Bible itself nowhere claims to function, independently of tradition, as the exclusive norm of faith. Emerging from the Jewish and apostolic traditions, the Bible would never have come into existence without them. If the

[21] See A. Dulles, 'Reflections on "Sola Scriptura"', in *Revelation and the Quest for Unity* (Washington, DC: Corpus Books, 1968), 65–81; W. Pannenberg, 'The Crisis of the Scripture Principle', in *Basic Questions in Theology*, trans. G. H. Kehm, i (London: SCM Press, 1974), 1–14.

community's tradition, along with the inspiration of the Holy Spirit, led to the formation of the Scriptures, one would expect tradition to remain active in interpreting and applying the Scriptures, in bringing about experiences of (dependent) revelation, and in guiding the response of faith.

Some Catholic and other apologists insisted, moreover, that it took (post-apostolic) tradition to acknowledge *these* Scriptures as inspired and trustworthy witnesses to (foundational) revelation and to exclude other books from the biblical list or canon. In other words, it took tradition to identify just where the authoritative Scriptures were to be found. Yet one should not ignore Karl Rahner's view that recognizing the extent of the canon was in some ways a special affair which did not exemplify the general relationship between tradition and Scripture.[22] The general relationship is seen rather in two different settings: (a) where the Bible was first formed through Jewish and apostolic tradition, and (b) where it was later interpreted and applied through post-apostolic tradition, as well as challenging and purifying particular later traditions.

Critics came to point out how the overwhelming majority of Protestant Reformers never in fact drew their belief and practice solely from their experience of the Scriptures. As was argued above in the section 'Tradition as a Human Reality', even in the rejection of tradition some traditional 'substratum' is always preserved, no matter how many factors are new. Thus nearly all the Reformers maintained, for example, the traditional belief in the Trinity, even though a properly articulated doctrine of the Trinity was worked out only at two fourth-century councils (held in 325 and 381, respectively). Moreover, most Protestants did not appeal to the *sola Scriptura* principle and abandon infant baptism, a practice which does not enjoy a clear and compelling warrant in the New Testament alone.

The difficulty of basing belief and practice merely on the Scripture became more acute when modern biblical scholarship began in the seventeenth century. Once historical exegetes started confining the sense of Scriptures to their strictly literal meaning and offered historical reconstructions of how these texts arose, it became more problematic to support Christian faith simply and solely on the basis of the Scriptures. What learned professor should one follow in

[22] For those interested in his reasons, see 'Scripture and Tradition', in K. Rahner et al. (eds.), *Sacramentum Mundi*, vi (London: Burns & Oates, 1970), 54–7.

acknowledging the 'literal' meaning or accepting the reconstruction of the genesis of various biblical texts? Add too the rise of modern hermeneutics or theories about the 'right' methods for interpreting scriptural and other text, launched by F. D. E. Schleiermacher (1768–1834) and Wilhelm Dilthey (1833–1911).[23] Do we understand texts by recovering the intentions and creative processes of the authors themselves? Or can texts carry more meaning than the original authors consciously intended? Which theory of hermeneutics should one adopt?

Some Protestants and others have pointed out that the Bible can bring as much multiplicity and even division as unity. If the literal meaning of the biblical texts were to emerge with the simple clarity of basic mathematics, the Scriptures might have effected general agreement in interpreting the foundational Jewish and Christian experience of the divine self-communication. But we *create*, as well as discover, meaning when we read biblical and similar texts. Not only changing public contexts but also what individuals bring to the reading of the Scriptures—their deep questions, previous experiences, inherited assumptions, actual commitments, and whole personal history—affect the meaning they proceed to champion. Right from the early centuries of Christianity, protagonists of division and of such heresies as Arianism have supported their interpretation of (foundational) revelation by appealing to the Scriptures. The verdict of history is clear. The principle of *sola Scriptura*, if taken strictly, can hardly promise to bring agreement about right ways to interpret the experience of the divine self-communication in Christ.

Moreover, it seems too much to expect the Scriptures by themselves to provide answers, especially full and convincing ones, to new questions and fresh challenges. How could the Bible by itself respond to issues that arose only after the close of the apostolic age? Greek philosophy, for instance, raised questions about the 'person' and 'nature(s)' of Christ that the New Testament could not be expected to answer clearly. The authors of the New Testament and the

[23] See E. Charry, 'Hermeneutics, Biblical', in S. E. Balentine (ed.), *The Oxford Encyclopedia of the Bible and Theology*, i (New York: Oxford University Press, 2015), 457–70; B. C. Lategan, 'Hermeneutics', *ABD* iii, 149–55. See also R. E. Palmer, *Hermeneutics: Interpretation Theory in Schleiermacher, Dilthey, Heidegger, and Gadamer* (Evanston, Ill.: Northwestern University Press, 1969); D. Sarisky (ed.), *Theology, History, and Biblical Interpretation: Modern Readings* (London: Bloomsbury, 2015).

traditions they drew on did not face such questions and hence could hardly be expected by themselves to provide the appropriate answers.

INAPPROPRIATE LANGUAGE

As we saw above, the Council of Trent spoke of 'all saving truth and [all] regulation of conduct' being 'contained' in the inspired Scriptures and 'unwritten [apostolic] traditions'. So long as Catholic theologians understood revelation as God manifesting certain (otherwise undisclosed) truths, they remained comfortable with such language (see Chapter 1 above). They were concerned to establish where various revealed truths were to be found, and could raise the question: even if the Bible is not 'formally sufficient' (inasmuch as it needs to be interpreted by tradition), is it 'materially sufficient' in communicating the truths of revelation? That is to say, does it 'contain' all the revealed truths? Or are some of them (e.g. the doctrines of the immaculate conception and assumption of the Blessed Virgin Mary) 'contained' only in tradition?

Interpreting tradition and Scripture in this 'material' way degraded both tradition and revelation. Tradition became a mere vehicle for carrying revealed contents, and precisely as such turned into something extrinsic to revelation. Revelation itself became primarily something to be transported from one generation to the next. After the apostolic generation (which had received all the truths of revelation but did not record all of them in the inspired Scriptures) had died out, subsequent Christians had the duty of handing on through tradition the full list of revealed truths. Faithful tradition, along with the survival of the Bible, was understood to preserve all the truths revealed at the foundation of Christianity.

Post-Tridentine Catholic theology read Trent's decree as if it were teaching two 'materially' separate and equally valid 'sources' of revelation, one being tradition and the other Scripture. J. R. Geiselmann (1890–1970), even if some details of his case had to be corrected, firmly established that the 'two-source' theory of revelation could not claim support from Trent.[24] That council reserved the term

[24] J. R. Geiselmann, *The Meaning of Tradition*, trans. W. J. O'Hara (Freiburg im Breisgau: Herder, 1966).

'source' exclusively for 'the Gospel', or the one message of salvation communicated by Christ.

A propositional view of revelation lay behind the typical Catholic version of the tradition/Scripture issue. Once the shift came to an interpersonal model of revelation (Chapter 1), the whole discussion was reshaped. Whether in the foundational or in the dependent stage, revelation primarily means a gracious call to enter by faith into a relationship with the tripersonal God. Revelation is something which happens and is not, properly speaking, 'contained' in a book (the Bible) or in traditions that Christians inherit from previous generations of believers. Since revelation is the living reality of a personal encounter with God, it cannot be happily described as 'contained' in anything, whether it be Scripture or tradition.

THE MOVE TO MONTREAL

The 1963 Faith and Order meeting in Montreal signalled a shift in Protestant views on tradition and Scripture. Take, for instance, the case of Gerhard Ebeling (1912–2001). When maintaining how reflection on proclamation is the proper task of theology, he stated that theology should also be concerned with 'the proclamation that has already taken place' and wrote: 'the task which theology is given to do is identical with the gift it receives from tradition'. Hence 'the task of handing on this tradition . . . is clearly constitutive of theology'.[25] Ebeling approached theology in the spirit of 'tradition seeking understanding (*traditio quaerens intellectum*)'. In a long essay '"Sola Scriptura" and Tradition', he stated clearly: 'the Scripture principle necessarily involves a doctrine of tradition'.[26] The change that we see here was partly due to the hermeneutics of Hans-Georg Gadamer (1900–2002). This Protestant philosopher rehabilitated tradition by incorporating it in interpretation, and explained it not as an obstacle but as a necessary context for the recovery of meaning. Tradition is

[25] G. Ebeling, *Theology and Proclamation*, trans. J. Riches (London: Collins, 1966), 22–3; see also 15–16, 25–31. Paul Tillich understood tradition to be an indispensable feature of human and Christian life; see his *Systematic Theology*, iii (Chicago: Chicago University Press, 1963), 183–5. On the place of tradition in modern Protestant theology, see Congar, *Tradition and Traditions*, 459–82.

[26] Ebeling, *The Word of God and Tradition*, 102–47, at 144.

'the way we relate to the past' and the way 'the past is present'. Hence 'we are always situated within traditions'; tradition 'is always part of us'.[27] Wolfhart Pannenberg, in a long study 'Hermeneutic: A Method for Understanding Meaning', also reflects the influence of Gadamer when adopting a positive attitude to the principle of tradition.[28]

The 1963 Faith and Order conference disclosed several lines of convergence with Catholic reflection on tradition, which were to be incorporated in Vatican II's 1965 document, *Dei Verbum*. Some of what was endorsed in Montreal and Rome echoed Yves Congar's magisterial *Tradition and Traditions*, which originally appeared in French in two volumes (1960 and 1963). In view of the Montreal conference (July 1963), the Bossey Ecumenical Institute (funded and run by the World Council of Churches) hosted a consultation between Faith and Order and the Catholic Conference for Ecumenical Affairs (18–23 March 1963) to discuss reports prepared for Montreal. Congar attended and commented on a report, significantly entitled 'Tradition and traditions'.[29] He did not go on to attend the Montreal conference, but he had already made his input through the Bossey consultation and previously in other ways. At Vatican II he was the leading Catholic theological expert (*peritus*), and had a hand in drafting eight out of the sixteen documents, including *Dei Verbum*—specifically, its Chapter 2 (on tradition). Let me signal five lines of convergence.

(a) The *model of revelation* as the divine self-communication was decisive for the Montreal report, Congar, and *Dei Verbum*. Since it was agreed that revelation is *primarily* a personal encounter with God (who is Truth) rather than the communication of a body of truths, the heat went out of any 'quantitative' debate about some revealed truths being 'contained' in Scripture and others being possibly 'contained' only in tradition.

(b) Both the Montreal document and *Dei Verbum* embodied 'total' views of tradition as the *whole living heritage* which is passed on. From this point on, let me talk of 'the Tradition' or *Tradition* (with a capital T) when I use the word in this sense. Thus *Dei Verbum*

[27] H.-G. Gadamer, *Truth and Method*, trans. J. Weinsheimer and D. G. Marshall, 2nd edn. (New York: Crossroad, 1989), 282.

[28] W. Pannenberg, *Theology and the Philosophy of Science*, trans. F. McDonagh (London: Darton, Longman & Todd, 1976), 156–224, esp. 197–8.

[29] See Y. Congar, *My Journal of the Council*, trans. M. J. Ronayne and M. C. Boulding (Collegeville, Minn.: Liturgical Press, 2012), 283–5.

declared: 'What was handed on by the Apostles includes *everything* that contributes to making the People of God live their lives in holiness and grow in faith. In this way the Church, in her doctrine, life, and worship perpetuates and transmits to every generation *all* that she herself is, *all* that she believes' (art. 8; italics mine). The Montreal report likewise described Tradition in global terms as 'the Gospel itself, transmitted from generation to generation in and by the Church'.[30]

The Montreal report leaned towards interpreting the essential *Traditum* (or what is handed on) as 'Christ himself present in the life of the Church'.[31] It preferred to move beyond the *visible* human realities which make up the Christian life of faith and emphasize the (invisible) truth and reality of the risen Christ present among believers. That presence constitutes the heart of the *Traditum*: 'what is transmitted in the process of tradition is the Christian faith, not only as a sum of tenets [equivalent to "all that she [the Church] believes" of *DV* 8], but [also] as a living reality transmitted through the operation of the Holy Spirit. We can speak of the Christian Tradition (with a capital T), whose content is God's revelation and self-giving in Christ, present in the life of the Church.'[32] Then the report echoed what Ernst Käsemann had said in a lecture at the conference: 'the Tradition of the Church is not an object which we *possess* but a reality by which we are *possessed*'.[33] More than merely the visible sum of beliefs and practices which Christians hand on, Tradition is the saving presence of Christ, engaged in a process of self-transmission through the Holy Spirit in the ongoing life of the Church. To echo the language of *Dei Verbum*, through the Holy Spirit, Christ provides 'everything that contributes to making the People of God live their lives in holiness and grow in faith' (art. 8).

(c) This brings us to a third item in the converging lines of agreement: *the invisible role of the Holy Spirit*. If the people of God form the visible bearers of *Tradition*, the transmission takes place through the power of the Holy Spirit.[34] Ultimately, as Congar insisted, it is Christ's Spirit who maintains the integrity of the Tradition and thus guarantees the Church's essential fidelity to the foundational experience of the divine self-communication in Christ.[35] *Dei Verbum* introduced what amounted to the same point: 'the Holy

[30] *Montreal 1963*, 50. [31] Ibid. [32] Ibid. 52.
[33] Ibid. 54; italics mine. [34] Ibid. 52.
[35] Congar, *Tradition and Traditions*, 338–46.

Spirit, through whom the living voice rings out in the Church and through her in the world, leads the believers into all truth, and makes the word of Christ dwell abundantly in them' (art. 8).

I have noted the total view of the Tradition or *Traditum* which both *Dei Verbum* and the Montreal report endorsed. The one *Traditum*, however, is expressed through *many tradita* or *traditions.* The Montreal report illustrated how this expression in different traditions takes place in the spheres of liturgy, doctrine, and life: 'Tradition taken in this sense is actualized in the preaching of the Word, in the administration of the sacraments and worship, in Christian teaching and theology, and in mission and witness to Christ by the lives of members of the Church'.[36]

In this terminology the specific traditions become 'expressions and manifestations in diverse historical forms of the one truth and reality which is Christ'.[37] Vatican II's decree on ecumenism, *Unitatis Redintegratio*, suggested similarly how the one *Traditum* gets expressed in the many *tradita*: 'this whole heritage (*patrimonium*) of spirituality and liturgy, of discipline and theology, in its various traditions belongs to the full catholicity and apostolicity of the Church' (art. 17).

(d) This actualizing of the one Tradition in the many traditions entails not only a rich diversity but also a recurrent challenge. Granted that we never find the Tradition 'neat' but always embodied in various traditions, do all of those particular traditions actualize authentically the essential *Traditum*? The Montreal report put the issue this way: 'Do all traditions that claim to be Christian contain the Tradition? How can we distinguish between traditions embodying the true Tradition and merely human traditions? Where do we find the genuine Tradition, and where impoverished tradition or even distortion of tradition?'[38]

At least explicitly, *Dei Verbum* did not address this question of discerning 'the Tradition within the traditions'. It was left to other documents from Vatican II to spell out principles that should guide such a discernment: for instance, the Constitution on the Sacred Liturgy (*Sacrosanctum Concilium*), the Decree on the Renewal of Religious Life (*Perfectae Caritatis*), and the Declaration on Religious Freedom (*Dignitatis Humanae*). The Decree on Ecumenism (*Unitatis Redintegratio*) clearly implied the need to discern and purify various

[36] *Montreal 1963*, 52. [37] Ibid. [38] Ibid.

traditions. It spoke of 'the Church called by Christ' to 'a constant reformation which she invariably needs' (art. 6).[39]

(e) *Dei Verbum* alerted its readers to the difficulty of using the inspired Scriptures as the only source of certainty in assenting to given truths—or to transpose matters into the precise point of our question—as the sole means for establishing where the authentic Tradition is to be found among the diverse traditions. *Dei Verbum* declared: 'The Church does not draw her certainty about all revealed matters through the holy Scripture alone' (art. 9). The Montreal report stated the same difficulty this way: 'Loyalty to our confessional understanding of Holy Scripture produces both convergence and divergence in the interpretation of Scripture.... How can we overcome the situation in which we all read the Scripture in the light of our own traditions?'[40] Inherited traditions and other presuppositions cause Christians to *create* meaning, as well as discover it, when they read and interpret the Bible. Hence it is neither feasible nor even possible to use the Scriptures as the *sole* criterion for sorting out defective and authentic traditions, so as to find the Tradition within the traditions. What other criteria might support the Scriptures in the task of discernment and interpretation?

DISCERNING THE TRADITION WITHIN THE TRADITIONS

What particular traditions truly express the foundational revelation and so help the good news of Christ to remain living and effective in the life of the Church? *Four questions* can pull their weight in the work of discernment. First, does some particular tradition contribute to the faithful being led more clearly by the Holy Spirit and Christ? Secondly, does it help them when they worship together? Thirdly, is any decision about this or that tradition illuminated and supported by prayerful reflection on the Scriptures? Fourthly, does the decision inspire believers to serve the needy more generously?

[39] See G. O'Collins, *The Second Vatican Council: Message and Meaning* (Collegeville, Minn.: Liturgical Press, 2014), 25–56.

[40] *Montreal 1963*, 53–4.

(1) The first question relates the work of discernment to the experience of growing, through the Holy Spirit and as adopted brothers and sisters of Christ, more deeply into the life of God. Do some inherited traditions (e.g. inherited liturgical customs and texts) allow believers to experience more vividly what Christ has brought them: the forgiveness of sins, the new life of grace, and the hope of glory? Do these traditions facilitate the sanctifying work of the Spirit?

(2) The second question centres squarely on common worship. Do particular liturgical practices and texts help the worshipping community to give glory to the Father, Son, and Holy Spirit? Do such traditions enhance or frustrate the experience of those being baptized and confirmed and, in particular, those sharing actively in the celebration of the Eucharist?

(3) Thirdly, the Bible provides the normative, written witness to the foundational revelation which created the Christian community. In the period of dependent revelation, the Scriptures must continue to guide, nourish, and challenge the Church and every aspect of Christian life. The Scriptures are essential for evaluating current traditions. What conclusion should we reach when we put under the Word of God various traditions?

(4) We come, lastly, to the fourth question, which has a special terminological link with the second. In the New Testament and works of early Christian writers, *leitourgia* referred both to the community worship and to the obligation to meet material needs of others. This double usage suggests the essential bond between worship and the service of the suffering. Those Jesus expected his followers to help included the hungry, the thirsty, strangers, the naked, the sick, and prisoners (Matt. 25: 31–46). His parable of the Good Samaritan powerfully illustrated what he wanted from all: the willingness to help any human being in distress (Luke 10: 30–7).The words of Jesus from Matthew 25 and Luke 10, along with the parable of the rich man and the poor Lazarus (Luke 16: 19–31), should influence the conscience of Christians discerning traditions they have inherited from the past. Do these traditions support and embody Christ's call to minister to the destitute? Do they encourage us to recognize the crucified Jesus in those who suffer terrible need?

These then are four daunting questions Christians should put to themselves when evaluating the array of traditions the previous generation has handed on to them. I am not alleging that the four questions can be answered easily and at once. But if we do not even ask these questions, it seems difficult, if not impossible, to discern faithfully the traditions that embody the true Tradition and what Christ is calling us to change, reform, or strengthen in all that we have received from the past.

REVELATION, TRADITION, AND SCRIPTURE

Before moving to examine biblical inspiration, let me pull matters together and outline in seven ways the complex relationship between revelation, tradition, and the Scriptures.

(1) First, the apostles and those closely associated experienced the fullness of foundational revelation and salvation (through Christ and the Holy Spirit) and faithfully responded by expressing, interpreting, and applying this once-and-for-all experience through their preaching. In and through this preaching, the conferral of baptism, and the celebration of the Eucharist, they fully founded the Church. The apostolic age brought not only the founding of the Church but also the composition of the twenty-seven inspired books of the New Testament. Under the guidance of the Holy Spirit these books (which drew on experiences and memories as well as on oral and written traditions) fixed for all time the apostolic preaching as the normative response to the complete revelation of God in Christ and through the Holy Spirit.[41]

(2) Secondly, the books of the New Testament, together with the inspired writings of the Old Testament, do not as such coincide with revelation. The difference between revelation and Scripture is the difference between a lived reality and a written (and inspired) record. We cannot simply identify revelation with the Bible. In a normative way the Scriptures report the human experience of foundational revelation, as well as the ways in which men and women responded to, interpreted, and remembered that experience. The scriptural witness remains distinct from the experience of revelation itself, just as a written record differs from a lived reality.

[41] The sacred authors were not necessarily aware of doing all that. The results of their activities cannot be simply measured by their conscious intentions. They never lived to witness what they had achieved.

Where foundational revelation came *before* the Scriptures, dependent revelation continued *after* the writing of these Scriptures ended. Hearing, reading, and praying over the Scriptures can bring about now the experience of (dependent) divine revelation. The biblical texts help initiate what believers experience today of God's self-communication. Yet in this period of dependent revelation, the Scriptures differ from revelation in the way that an 'inspired and inspiring', written record differs from the living reality of encounter with God.

(3) Thirdly and similarly, *tradition* never literally coincides with revelation.Tradition can hand on revealed truths (or propositional revelation), but cannot precisely 'hand on' the experience of revelation. It may prove revealing in the sense of recalling moments of revelation, interpreting those moments, and offering means to experience revelation. Yet revelation remains different from tradition as a lived experience is to be distinguished from the community's expression of that experience which is transmitted through history. To sum up: we cannot identify *tout court* either tradition or Scripture as such with the experience of God's revealing and saving presence.

(4) Fourthly, how should the post-apostolic tradition of the Church be understood and how does it relate to Scripture? All active members of the Church are, in fact, engaged in the *process* of transmitting tradition and bringing about for others the experience of the divine self-communication. They do so by pondering the Scriptures, celebrating the Eucharist, administering and receiving the sacraments, preaching and evangelizing, composing sacred music, writing catechisms, teaching prayers, involvement in religious education, and through all the other beliefs and practices that make up the total reality of the Church and give Christians their continuity, identity, and unity. Seen as such an active process (*actus tradendi*), the tradition of the post-apostolic Church includes but obviously goes well beyond the Scriptures. Handing on, interpreting, and applying the Scriptures is only one, albeit major, part of tradition's activity.

(5) Fifthly, in this active process there exists a *mutual priority* between tradition and the Scriptures. On the one hand, authentic tradition seeks to remain faithful to the normative account of Christian origins and identity that it finds in the inspired Scriptures. On the other hand, fresh challenges and a changing content require tradition to do what the Scriptures cannot do for themselves. It must interpret and apply them, so that they can become the revealing word of God to

new readers and hearers today. In this way tradition (and the Christian life to which it gives shape and force) not only forms an extended commentary on the Scriptures but also allows them to come into their own and let Christ speak to people.

(6) Sixthly, in this whole process the members of the *magisterium* have a special but not exclusive role as 'carriers' of tradition and (subordinate) mediators effecting the living event of divine self-revelation. Tradition as an action is thus exercised in a particular way by the bishops, inasmuch as they transmit matters of faith and Christian practice. By formulating statements of faith and taking practical decisions which affect the life of the Church, they introduce some fresh elements into the tradition and its narrative that will be transmitted to the next generation of believers.

The exercise of the magisterium at the Second Vatican Council, for example, influenced and modified what has been handed on. As an engine for far-reaching change in the Catholic Church and beyond, Pope Francis is currently influencing the traditions of church governance and life that will be transmitted to the next generation. A living tradition necessarily means a tradition that changes, with the changes maintaining the apostolic identity of the Church and coming not only from bishops but also, and often even more, from others who are charismatically endowed.

(7) Seventhly, the whole people of God will not transmit all that they received exactly as they received it. Language shifts occur, the flux of experience calls forth fresh interpretations and activities, emerging signs of the times offer their special message to believers, and technological advances offer new challenges and possibilities (e.g. for preaching the gospel). Certainly an essential continuity is maintained. The dependent revelation which is experienced now remains essentially continuous with the original, foundational revelation which the apostolic generation received in faith. At the same time, the whole Church, no less than the members of the magisterium, modify to some degree the aggregate of beliefs, customs, and practices (tradition as 'object') which one generation of believers transmits to the next.

To draw all this together, understood *either* as the active process (*actus tradendi*) *or* as the object handed on (the *traditum*), tradition includes Scripture rather than simply standing alongside it. In both senses, tradition is much more extensive than Scripture.

10

Revelation and Inspiration

The last chapter engaged itself with the complex relationship between the Scriptures and tradition. The Second Vatican Council's document on revelation, *Dei Verbum*, summed up three essential moments in this relationship: tradition and Scripture 'flow from the same divine well-spring' (foundational revelation), 'in some fashion form together one thing' (dependent revelation), and 'move toward the same goal' (the final fullness of revelation and salvation) (art. 9). Revelation as foundational made tradition and Scripture possible. If there had been no well-spring of revelation, the Jewish-Christian tradition and Scripture would not have come into being. During the phase of dependent revelation, while tradition interprets and actualizes Scripture, in its turn Scripture challenges and purifies tradition. At the end, the face-to-face revelation of God will bring Scripture and tradition to their goal and replace them.

Kevin Vanhoozer fills out the laconic language about Scripture and tradition now 'forming together one thing'. He writes: 'Scripture and tradition are paired . . . norms for doing theology, for seeking knowledge of God and knowledge of self'.[1] Elsewhere he asks: 'What is tradition if not a form of life to know and glorify God? And what is Scripture if not a certain use of language to name God?'[2] Let me now turn to the relationship between revelation and biblical inspiration, and lay the ground for setting forth some characteristics of biblical inspiration and, its major consequence, biblical truth.[3] First,

[1] K. J. Vanhoozer, 'Scripture and Tradition', in K. J Vanhoozer (ed.), *The Cambridge Companion to Postmodern Theology* (Cambridge: Cambridge University Press, 2003), 149–69, at 166.

[2] Ibid. 149.

[3] As is the case with revelation and tradition, recent decades have not seen much writing on the topic of biblical inspiration. In a work of over 900 pages, J. W. Rogerson

how should we describe the relationship between the inspired Scriptures and foundational revelation?

THE FORMATION OF THE BIBLE

Let us begin by considering the *genesis* of the Bible, which illustrates some differences between the divine self-disclosure and the inspired Scriptures. We will then be in a position to reflect on the *content* of the Bible in relation to revelation.[4]

(1) The Bible should not be simply identified with the divine self-revelation.[5] As a living, interpersonal event, revelation takes place or happens. God initiates, at particular times and in particular places

and J. M. Lieu (eds.), *The Oxford Handbook of Biblical Studies* (Oxford: Oxford University Press, 2006) do not even have an entry 'inspiration' in the index. In a recent, 500-page selection of twenty modern readings on biblical texts, Darren Sarisky likewise does not include 'inspiration' in the index: *Theology, History, and Biblical Interpretation* (London: Bloomsbury, 2015). After discovering that 'they' were saying little or nothing about the topic, Philip J. Moller wrote an article, 'What Should They Be Saying about Biblical Inspiration?', *Theological Studies* 74 (2013), 605–31.

[4] W. J. Abraham, *The Divine Inspiration of the Holy Scriptures* (Oxford: Oxford University Press, 1981); P. Achtemeier, *The Inspiration of Scripture* (Philadelphia: Westminster Press, 1980); L. Alonso Schökel, *The Inspired Word*, trans. F. Martin (New York: Herder & Herder, 1965); R. E. Collins, 'Inspiration', in R. E. Brown, J. A. Fitzmyer, and R. E. Murphy (eds.), *The New Jerome Biblical Commentary* (London: Geoffrey Chapman, 1989), 1023–33; T. M. Crisp, 'On Believing that the Scriptures are Divinely Inspired', in O. D. Crisp and M. C. Rea (eds.), *Analytic Theology: New Essays in the Philosophy of Theology* (Oxford: Oxford University Press, 2009), 187–213; S. T. Davis, 'Revelation and Inspiration', in T. P. Flint and M. C. Rea (eds.), *The Oxford Handbook of Philosophical Theology* (Oxford: Oxford University Press, 2009), 30–53; C. Focant, 'Holy Scripture', in J.-Y. Lacoste (ed.), *Encyclopedia of Christian Theology*, ii (New York: Routledge, 2004), 718–25; H. Gabel, *Inspiriert und Inspirierend: Die Bibel* (Würzburg: Echter, 2011); T. M. McCall, 'Scripture as the Word of God', in Crisp and Rea (eds.), *Analytic Theology*, 171–86; S. M. Schneiders, 'Inspiration and Revelation', in K. D. Sakenfeld (ed.), *The New Interpreter's Dictionary of the Bible*, iii (Nashville: Abingdon Press, 2008), 57–63; B. Vawter, *Biblical Inspiration* (London: Hutchinson, 1972).

[5] Whenever the divine revelation is simply identified with the Jewish-Christian Bible, this makes it difficult, if not impossible, to recognize how the revelation of God is, in various ways, also offered to those who follow 'other' religious faiths and who do not accept or may not even know about the existence of the Bible. Such a simple identification would involve holding '*extra Scripturam nulla revelatio* (outside Scripture no revelation)'. A final chapter will discuss the presence of revelation for those who follow 'other' faiths or none at all.

and for particular persons, some form of self-disclosure. This divine initiative achieves its goal and revelation happens when human beings respond in faith to God's self-disclosure.

As such, the Scriptures are not a living, interpersonal event in the way just described. They are written records, which by a special inspiration of the Holy Spirit came into existence through the collaboration of some believers at certain stages in the foundational history of God's people. The Scriptures differ then from revelation in the way that written texts differ from something that actually happens between persons—in this case, between human persons and the divine Persons. Hence, while it makes perfectly good sense to say 'I left my Bible' on the bus, it does not make sense to say 'I left revelation on the bus'. One could say, of course, 'when travelling on the bus, God's revealing word reached me'. That was an event in my life, but it was not an object, namely, a book, which I could leave behind.

In the long history of the Bible's composition, the gift of revelation and the special impulse to write inspired Scriptures were not only distinguishable but also separable. Either directly or through such mediators as the prophets and, above all, Jesus himself, the foundational revelation was offered to *all* people; God's self-communication was there for everyone. The special impulse to write some of the Scriptures was, however, a particular charism given only to those who, under the guidance of the Holy Spirit, composed or helped to compose the sacred texts of what came to be known as the books of the Old and New Testament. To be sure, the Scriptures were written for everyone. But the charism of inspiration was given only to a limited number of persons.

Even in the case of the sacred authors themselves, the self-revelation of God and the charism of inspiration do not coincide. Receiving in faith the divine self-manifestation was one thing, being led by the Holy Spirit to set down certain things in writing was another. God's revelation impinged on their entire lives. In cases that we know, the charism of inspiration functioned only for limited periods of their history. The divine revelation was operative in Paul's life before and after his call/conversion (around AD 36). Around AD 50 he wrote his first (inspired) letter that has been preserved for us (1 Thessalonians), and went on to compose other letters during the 50s and into the early 60s. The divine self-communication affected Paul's entire history, the charism of biblical inspiration only the last decade or so of his apostolic activity.

(2) Reflection on the *content* of the Bible yields another angle on the difference I wish to express. The Bible witnesses to and interprets various persons, words, and events that mediated the divine self-revelation. The Letter to the Hebrews acknowledges the Son of God as the climax in a series of mediators of revelation (Heb. 1: 1–2). A wide variety of events manifested God and the divine will: from an exodus, an exile, births of various children, through to a crucifixion, resurrection, and descent of the Holy Spirit. Prophetic utterances, parables, creeds (e.g. Deut. 26: 5–9; Rom. 1: 3–4), hymns (e.g. Phil. 2: 6–11; Col. 1: 15–20), summaries of proclamation (e.g. 1 Cor. 15: 3–5), and—supremely—the words of Jesus himself disclosed the truth of God (and of human beings).

At the same time, the Bible *also* records matters that do not seem to be connected, or at least closely connected, with divine revelation. The language of courtship and human love fashions the Song of Songs, an inspired book that, paradoxically, has no explicitly religious content. Alongside lofty prescriptions to guide the worship and life of Israel as a holy people, Leviticus includes many regulations about wine and food, about the sick and the diseased (in particular, about lepers), about sexual relations, and about other matters that hardly seem to be derived from divine revelation. This book (that probably took its final shape in the sixth or fifth century) contains pages of rituals and laws, which usually look as if they came from old human customs rather than from some divine disclosure. The Book of Proverbs puts together the moral and religious instruction that professional teachers offered the Jewish youth in the period after the Babylonian exile. This wisdom of the ages is based on lessons drawn from common human experience, and is in part (Prov. 22: 17–24: 34) modelled upon the *Instruction of Amen-em-ope*, an Egyptian book of wisdom. Where religious faith supports Proverbs' view of an upright human life, Ecclesiastes seems to use reason alone to explore the meaning of existence and the (limited) value of life which ends in the oblivion of death.

Admittedly, one might argue that in human love, ancient religious traditions, the experience of the ages, and the use of reason, God is also at work to disclose the truth about our nature and destiny, and about the Creator from whom we come and to whom we go. Any theology that proposes dramatic, special events as the *only* appropriate means of mediating the divine would be a diminished version of revelation. God can certainly use 'ordinary' channels to communicate with human beings and shed light on the human and divine mystery (see Chapter 5 above).

Nevertheless, whole sections of the Bible (e.g. much of wisdom literature) speak more of our human condition and less vividly of divine revelation. That the inspiration of the Holy Spirit operated in the formation of these books is no immediate gauge of the 'amount' of divine self-revelation to which they witness. They may proclaim matters of revelation less intensely and closely than any other parts of the Bible. Simply from the activity of divine inspiration in the composition of a book, one cannot draw any necessary conclusions about the degree to which God's self-revelation shows through that book.

Add too the way many chapters of the Bible focus on the human story of individuals and groups: for instance, certain passages in the historical books of the Old Testament. Some of this material can seem a long way from God's saving self-communication. Take, for example, the story of the concubine's murder and the subsequent revenge on the Benjaminites (Judg. 19: 1–20: 48), Saul's visit to the witch of Endor (1 Sam. 28: 1–25), and, for that matter, the death of Ananias and Sapphira (Acts 5: 1–11). One might argue that such stories illustrate how people failed to respond to the overtures of divine revelation. Human failures, sins, and even atrocities were also things recorded under the impulse of divine inspiration. But that fact does not as such guarantee anything about their positive value for revelation. In short, an inspired record is one thing, revelatory 'content' is another.

The latest document from the Pontifical Biblical Commission, *The Inspiration and Truth of the Sacred Scripture*, describes the Scriptures as God addressing us in human words or, as its subtitle puts it: '*The Word that Comes from God and Speaks of God for the Salvation of the World*'. Serving the faithful transmission of revelation, the Bible is 'the authoritative source for knowledge about God'.[6] Recognizing different ways in which the inspired Scriptures originated from God, the document highlights the divine revelation becoming 'a written text' and focuses on the books of the Bible functioning as 'a privileged vehicle of God's revelation'.[7] It has to work hard to press into this scheme human matters that are less closely connected with the divine self-revelation,

[6] Biblical Commission, *The Inspiration and Truth of Sacred Scripture*, trans. T. Esposito and S. Gregg (Collegeville, Minn.: Liturgical Press, 2014), xxi, 4.

[7] Ibid. 47, 60.

such as the human love between a young woman and a shepherd vividly and even erotically celebrated in the Song of Songs. The document speaks of this biblical book being open to a more 'theological dimension' and 'additional meanings', which, in fact, the history and practice of Christian mysticism added later.[8] In its origins, however, the Song of Songs was an imaginative drama of human love, rather than some self-disclosure of God that became 'a written text'.

But, when they reach some classical challenges for biblical interpretation, the commission introduces the question of which passages should be 'considered perennially valid' and which 'relative', or 'linked to a culture, a civilization, or even the mentality of a specific period of time'. They add: 'the status of women in the Pauline epistles raises this type of question'.[9] The document then dedicates pages to what these epistles say about the submission of women to their husbands, the silence of women in ecclesial gatherings, and the role of women in the assembly.[10] Rather than being 'a word that comes from God' or a revelation that became 'a written text', such examples should be understood, yes, as items recorded under the impulse of divine inspiration, but with the content coming more from human beings and the culture of their world.

An acceptance of other (human) sources for the inspired texts of the Bible appears also in the general conclusions of *The Inspiration and Truth of the Sacred Scripture*. There the commission 'fully' recognizes that 'the literature of the Old Testament is greatly indebted to Mesopotamian and Egyptian writings, just as the New Testament books draw extensively on the cultural heritage of the Hellenistic world'.[11] Once again, while saying that the entire Scriptures were written under the divine inspiration, we should, nevertheless, acknowledge how not infrequently the Scriptures record what comes from human beings in their cultural diversity.

USING THE BIBLICAL TESTS

With a view to distinguishing between revelation and biblical inspiration, this chapter has so far directed attention to the past formation

[8] Ibid. 86–8. [9] Ibid. 150. [10] Ibid. 153–4. [11] Ibid. 166.

of the Bible. What does the relationship between revelation and inspiration look like if we turn to the role of the Scriptures in the life of the Church today?

(1) We will move in this section to interpret directly the nature of biblical inspiration, or the impact of the charism of inspiration on the scriptural authors themselves. But we should not neglect the inspiring impact of the Scriptures on those who read or hear them, and mull over them in prayer. Christian experience witnesses every day to the ways in which biblical texts can convey the divine revelation and even inspire dramatic changes in the lives of people. Passages from the prophets or the psalms, the words of Jesus from the gospels, and teaching from Paul let the truth about the divine and human mystery shine forth. Such scriptural texts repeatedly bring an inner light to those who ponder them prayerfully. They hear God speaking to them through these inspired words. What was long ago written down under the guidance of the Spirit can become inspiring and illuminating. As Ambrose of Milan said, 'when we read the divine oracles, we listen to him [God]'.[12]

Christian experience also shows how less 'promising' sections of the Bible can enjoy such a revealing impact. At first glance, some scriptural texts come across as 'primitive' (e.g. Saul's visit to the witch of Endor), 'boring' (e.g. the genealogies in 1 Chron. 1–9 or in the infancy narratives of Matthew and Luke), or so filled with hatred as to seem quite alien to the revelation of divine love (e.g. Ps. 137: 7–9). Such passages can, however, act as negative 'foils' which bring out the heart of divine revelation and our appropriate response to it. Saul's nocturnal visit to the witch is at least a cautionary tale: we should not try in that way to enter into contact with 'the other world'. In Psalm 137, we hear some exiled Israelites crying out for savage vengeance on their Babylonian and Edomite enemies. Their prayer for revenge works to illuminate God's loving concern for all (Jonah 4: 11) and Jesus' prayer that his executioners be forgiven (Luke 23: 34). As regards the biblical genealogies, they may not say much to many people in the North Atlantic world. But for some other cultures to lack knowledge of one's ancestors is to suffer diminishment in one's

[12] Ambrose, *De officiis ministrorum*, 1. 20. 88; PL 16. 50. In the words of Vanhoozer, 'the inspiration of the Scripture in the past and the illumination of the Scripture in the present are but twin moments in one continuous work of the Holy Spirit' ('Scripture and Tradition', 165).

personal identity. In any case, given the chequered career of some who feature in the biblical genealogies, including those of Jesus himself (Matt. 1: 1–17; Luke 3: 23–38), we are enabled to grasp more deeply the truth that 'God writes straight with crooked lines'.

In short, experience shows how any biblical text can lead people to know the truth about God and the human condition. Normally the 'great' sections of the Scriptures have this revelatory impact. But thoroughly unpromising scriptural texts can also trigger or renew people's living knowledge of God. This point has more relevance nowadays, since the lectionaries for the Sunday and weekday Eucharist contain a much broader selection from the Bible.

The history of Christianity also testifies to the revealing and inspiring impact of Scriptures. I think here of such figures as St Antony of Egypt (d. 356), St Augustine of Hippo (d. 430), and Girolamo Savonarola (d. 1498). In all three cases we know how specific biblical texts played a decisive role towards bringing them the revealing word of God and 'inspiring' dramatic changes in their lives. It was St Athanasius of Alexandria (d. 373) who recorded the occasion when Matthew 19: 21 turned around the existence of Antony and led him to become the founder of the eremitic monasticism of solitary hermits.[13] Augustine and Savonarola left in writing their own accounts of how Romans 13: 13–14 and Genesis 12: 1, respectively, profoundly illuminated and influenced the course of their lives. Without being the founder of collective or cenobitic monasticism—for which St Pachomius (d. 346) takes the credit—Augustine and a century later St Benedict of Nursia (d. around 550) helped to promote it widely in Western Christianity. Savonarola's heroic attempt to reform the Catholic Church in the heartland of Italy was brutally terminated by his execution. An appendix to this book takes up what we can glean about the ways in which scriptural texts shaped the story of these three figures.[14]

[13] Athanasius of Alexandria, *The Life of Antony: The Coptic Life and the Greek Life*, trans. T. Vivian and Apostolos N. Athanassakis (Kalamazoo, Mich.: Cistercian Publications, 2003). Despite some recent objections, the traditional attribution to Athanasius of this life of Antony should continue to be accepted; see D. M. Gwynn, *Athanasius of Alexandria: Bishop, Theologian, Ascetic Father* (Oxford: Oxford University Press, 2012), 15.

[14] For basic data about their lives and bibliographical information, see F. L. Cross and E. A. Livingstone (eds.), *The Oxford Dictionary of the Christian Church*, 3rd edn. (Oxford: Oxford University Press, 2005), 81 (Antony), 129–32 (Augustine), and 1468–9 (Savonarola).

(2) Having acknowledged the revealing power of the Bible, let me now call attention to some limits and qualifications. It is not and was not the only means for receiving divine revelation. Before the Hebrew Scriptures came to be written, God had already initiated the revealing and saving history of the chosen people. Christians recognized in Jesus the climax of that revelatory and redemptive history two decades before the first book of what came to be called the first book of the New Testament was composed (1 Thessalonians). Reading St Paul's Letter to the Romans triggered Augustine's conversion. But it was a night of reading St Teresa of Avila's autobiography that moved St Edith Stein (d. 1942) towards Christian faith and, eventually, martyrdom. An immense range of experiences can bring Christians the divine self-communication, even to the point of radically changing their lives. These experiences, at least initially, need not have anything directly to do with the Scriptures. The data gathered by Sir Alister Hardy's Religious Experience and Research Centre amply supports that conclusion (see Chapter 5).

God's revelation, as we shall see in the last chapter, reaches those of other faiths without their reading or hearing the Bible. To some extent at least, their religious environment and personal experience can mediate to them the truth of God and of our human condition. Only those out of touch with the followers of other living faiths and unaware of the testimony of the Bible itself[15] will deny the evidence for the divine saving and revealing activity on their behalf. God speaks to them and triggers their faith through means other than the Bible.

A final limit to be noted in the Bible's revelatory impact is a sad one. It is more than possible to read the Scriptures without being open to the Holy Spirit. A merely 'scientific' knowledge of the Bible might yield little by way of knowing the God to whom the Scriptures testify. Regrettably, someone's extensive 'technical' knowledge of the Bible does not automatically guarantee for him or her that the Bible will become a vehicle of revelation. One may know 'the letter' but not 'the spirit' of the Scriptures. In the words of the Biblical Commission, 'the inspired Word is of no avail if the one who receives it does not live by the Spirit who appreciates and savours the divine origin of the Bible'.[16]

[15] See G. O'Collins, *Salvation for All: God's Other Peoples* (Oxford: Oxford University Press, 2008).

[16] *The Inspiration and Truth of Sacred Scripture*, 162.

(3) To conclude: as an inspired text, the Bible illuminates constantly the divine and human mystery. It is indispensable for Christian existence, both individually and collectively. Nevertheless, revelation or the living word of God proves a larger and wider reality than the Bible and is not limited to the written text of the Bible. It is an error to identify *tout court* revelation with the Scriptures. God's living and authoritative word is not subordinated to a written text, not even an inspired one.

Nevertheless, three reasons justify calling the Scriptures 'the word of God' or 'the word of the Lord'—as is said to conclude the reading of biblical passages in the liturgy. (a) First, unlike any other religious texts available for Christian (and, in the case of the Hebrew Scriptures, Jewish) use, they were written under the special guidance of the Holy Spirit. In a unique way, God was involved in preparing and composing these texts. (b) Secondly, all the Scriptures have some kind of relationship to the *foundational* revelation—to the persons, events, and words that mediated God's self-communication to its fullness with Christ and his apostles. Even in the case of those books and passages which focus less immediately and vividly on the divine revelation, some link can be found. Thus the love poems that make up the Song of Songs relate themselves to the history of revelation and salvation by invoking key personages and places in that history (Solomon, David, and Jerusalem). The bridegroom of these poems suggests Israel's God, who like a loving husband wishes to woo again a faithless wife (Hos. 2: 14–23). (c) Thirdly, in the post-apostolic period of *dependent* revelation any section of the Scriptures could become for human beings a living word of God. John's Gospel formulates its revelatory and salvific scope in terms that can be applied to the whole Bible: 'These things have been written so that you may believe that Jesus is the Christ, the Son of God, and that believing you may have life in his name' (20: 31; see 2 Tim. 3: 15–17). Our 'believing' allows divine revelation to happen, and 'life' is the salvific consequence of accepting revelation.

BIBLICAL INSPIRATION

If it is an error to identify revelation *tout court* with the Bible, what are we to make of the divine activity of inspiration that produced the

Scriptures, the unique record of the foundational Jewish-Christian experiences of God and the human responses they evoked? By witnessing to collective and individual experiences and the new self-identity those experiences initiated, the Bible offers subsequent generations the possibility of sharing (to a degree) in those experiences[17] and accepting that new identity. Thus the Scriptures are both an effect and a cause of the divine self-revelation. The record of what was experienced *then* helps to instigate and interpret the experience of God's self-communication *now*.

We need to disentangle different uses of the word 'inspiration'. We might describe the essence of *biblical* inspiration as a special impulse from the Holy Spirit, given during the long history of the chosen people and the much shorter apostolic age, to set down in writing both experiences of the divine self-revelation and other things which are not closely tied to revelation. This distinguishes biblical inspiration from *prophetic* inspiration, a God-given impulse to speak (and act symbolically) in certain ways. Such prophetic inspiration to *speak* may be connected with the biblical inspiration to *write*. But characteristically the Old Testament prophets were speakers (and actors) rather than writers. It was generally left to others to collect, expand, arrange, and publish their prophetic utterances. These (frequently anonymous writers), as the immediate authors of the prophetic books of the Bible, received the charism of biblical inspiration. Nevertheless, their charism obviously presupposed that Isaiah, Jeremiah, Ezechiel, and others had received the prophetic charism to speak.

It was natural for the Second Letter of Peter to describe the written texts of the prophetical books as if they were the *spoken words* of the prophets: 'no prophecy of Scripture is a matter of one's own inspiration, because no prophecy ever came from the impulse of a human being, but human beings moved by the Holy Spirit spoke from God' (2 Pet. 1: 20–1). Both the spoken word and the written word enjoyed a divine origin and authority.[18] Distinctions between them were not firmly drawn. The author of the Book of Revelation likewise blurred distinctions between the spoken (prophetic) word and the written

[17] Believers today experience the risen Christ (in the liturgy and beyond) but not exactly in the same way as those who witnessed his appearances after his death and burial; see D. Kendall and G. O'Collins, 'The Uniqueness of the Easter Appearances', *Catholic Biblical Quarterly* 54 (1992), 287–307.

[18] See R. Bauckham, *Jude, 2 Peter* (Waco, Tex.: Word Books, 1983), 228–35; G. L. Green, *Jude & 2 Peter* (Grand Rapids, Mich.: Baker Academic, 2008), 229–34.

word when he called his book 'words of prophecy' to be listened to (Rev. 22: 18).[19] This blurring of distinctions between the spoken and the written was encouraged by the fact that many believers, rather than reading the texts, heard them proclaimed in their liturgical assemblies.

Hence, almost inevitably, the early Church understood the sacred writers to have the role of prophets, and later theologians like Thomas Aquinas interpreted biblical inspiration as prophetic.[20] However, precisely as such biblical inspiration was a God-given impulse to write rather than (merely) to say something. Therefore, from this point on, unless otherwise noted, 'inspiration' will be taken in the sense of biblical inspiration.

Since the books of the Bible were written under a special impulse and guidance of the Holy Spirit, we may call God the 'author' of these books and the Bible itself 'the word of God'. Thus the effect of inspiration was to invest human words with the authority of being also 'the word of God' and allow us to call the Scriptures 'sacred'. But what form did this 'special impulse' take? Any answer affects what is meant by calling God 'the author'. Eight points enter our account of inspiration.

(1) Various fathers of the Church and later theologians adopted the model of *verbal dictation* when describing how inspiration functioned. In this view, the inspired writers heard a heavenly voice dictating the words which they were to set down. They obediently reproduced the texts that were revealed to them. Christian art sometimes reflects this reduction of the inspired authors to the status of mere stenographers. In the Pazzi chapel of the Basilica of Santa Croce in Florence, Luca della Robbia represents the evangelists in terracotta. An eagle has arrived from heaven to hold the text for John to copy down. A lion performs the same service for Mark.

Such a view interprets inspiration in a mechanical way that dramatically reduces the human role in composing the Scriptures. The sacred writers cease to be real authors, and become at best mere secretaries who faithfully take down the divine dictation. A set of tape-recorders could serve God's purposes just as well. In the verbal

[19] See R. Bauckham, *The Climax of Prophecy: Studies on the Book of Revelation* (Edinburgh: T. & T. Clark, 2003); H. B. Huffmon et al., 'Prophecy', *ABD* v, 477–502, at 494–5, 500.

[20] See his treatise on prophecy in *ST* IIaIIae. 171–4.

dictation view, the divine causality counts for everything, the human causality for nothing or next to nothing.

Those who endorsed verbal dictation theories mistakenly believed that affirming the Sacred Scriptures to be the inspired word of God entailed denying that they are also a genuinely human word. They wrongly imagined that God and human writers compete rather than collaborate. Apart from this basic theological flaw, the verbal dictation approach could not satisfactorily explain the many differences of form and style exhibited by the inspired authors. Did the Holy Spirit's style change from the years when Paul's letters were written to the later period when the Gospels were composed? If the human writers played no real part in the literary process, such differences could come only from a mysterious, and even arbitrary, divine decision to vary the style and alter the form.

The naïve model of verbal dictation may linger on in the fantasy of fundamentalists. But it is an error to be dispelled. Most Christian circles have made their peace with the genuinely human activity involved in the literary process that produced the inspired Scriptures.

(2) Secondly, the inspired authors wrote in various genres but not in all possible forms of literature. They wrote psalms, proverbs, letters, gospels, apocalypses, and so forth. But the Bible contains, for example, no epic poetry (like Homer), no works for the theatre (like ancient Greek dramas), no novels (in the modern sense), and no 'scientific' history (in the modern sense).

The last point may be the most important. Christians have been prone to read biblical history through modern spectacles. Undoubtedly, the historical books of the Old and New Testaments convey much trustworthy information. The Gospels, for instance, provide a reliable guide to the last years of Jesus' life.[21] But this well-founded conclusion should not be pushed to the point of treating the Gospels as if they were *modern* biographies, or of glossing over the fact that the historical books of the Old Testament should be classed as

[21] See J. D. G. Dunn, *Christianity in the Making*, i: *Jesus Remembered* (Grand Rapids, Mich.: Eerdmans, 2003); P. R. Eddy and G. A. Boyd, *The Jesus Legend: A Case for the Historical Reliability of the Synoptic Jesus Tradition* (Grand Rapids, Mich.: Baker Academic, 2007); M. Hengel and A. M. Schwemmer, *Geschichte der frühen Christentum*, i: *Jesus und das Judentum* (Tübingen: Mohr Siebeck, 2007); C. S. Keener, *The Historical Jesus of the Gospels* (Grand Rapids, Mich.: Eerdmans, 2009); J. P. Meier, *A Marginal Jew: Rethinking the Historical Jesus*, i–iii (New York: Doubleday, 1991–2001), iv (New Haven, Conn.: Yale University Press, 2009).

popular history. In short, just as the Bible did not exemplify all the forms of literature extant in ancient times, it did not miraculously anticipate future genres, like modern, 'scientific' history.

(3) Some biblical authors deployed unusual resources as writers and produced works of literary power and beauty. The Bible has proved a rich source of imagery, language, and 'inspiration'—used not least in the world of music: for instance, in Gregorian chant, polyphony, the hymns of Martin Luther, the 'passions' according to Matthew and John by Johann Sebastian Bach, the *Messiah* of George Frederick Handel, biblical operas, and other musical works.[22] The Scriptures, through various translations (e.g. the Vulgate, the Luther Bible, the Douay Bible, and the Authorized Version) and through their use by such writers as Dante, Shakespeare, Milton, and Bunyan, have profoundly affected English, German, Italian, and other modern languages and literature.[23]

Nevertheless, the gift of inspiration did not mean that the *literary* level shown by the sacred writers was necessarily higher than that of other writers. This special divine impulse to write did not miraculously raise (but rather respected) the writing talents of those who received it. The first nine chapters of 1 Chronicles belong to the canon of inspired Scriptures, but these dreary genealogies will not excite too many readers in the modern world. Divine inspiration could be at work in a dull form of human writing. As such, this gift does not automatically guarantee anything about the literary standard of the product.

(4) We should likewise be cautious about claiming that inspiration necessarily entails a uniformly *high religious power and impact*, which lifts the Scriptures above non-inspired writings. Of course, the Gospels, the psalms, the letters of St Paul, and many other books of the Bible continue to fire readers with their special spiritual quality. But

[22] See J. A. Greene, 'Music and the Bible', in B. M. Metzger and M. D. Coogan (eds.), *The Oxford Companion to the Bible* (New York: Oxford University Press, 2003), 535–8. Here one should not ignore the extraordinary impact of the Bible and, in particular, of the Gospels on the visual arts; innumerable works held in great galleries around the world exemplify this impact.

[23] Besides various works by Robert Alter, see R. Atwan and L. Wieder (eds.), *Chapters into Verse: Poetry in English Inspired by the Bible*, 2 vols. (New York: Oxford University Press, 1993); D. Norton, *A History of the Bible as Literature* (New York: Cambridge University Press, 2000); L. Ryken et al. (eds.), *Dictionary of Biblical Imagery* (Downers Grove, Ill.: InterVarsity Press, 1998).

experience shows how Augustine's *Confessions*, *The Imitation of Christ*, and the works of Teresa of Avila consistently enjoy a greater religious influence than the Letter of Jude, 2 Maccabees, and purity regulations from Leviticus. A striking spiritual impact is not necessarily the result of some text having been written under the influence of biblical inspiration, nor is its limited spiritual impact an index that a text has not been inspired by the Holy Spirit.

The limits that we detect in the literary and even in the religious power of inspired writings stem from the themes being treated (e.g. genealogies and purity regulations) and from these books being generated by genuine human activity, albeit activity exercised under a special divine impulse. Inasmuch as they were human products, they inevitably reflected the limitations of a community's culture and of the writers' own individual capacities.

(5) Fifthly, like the charism of prophecy and apostleship, the gift of inspirations was *not strictly uniform*. Just as there were major and minor prophets and just as Peter and Paul clearly acted as more significant apostles than some of those listed among the Twelve, so it seems reasonable to hold that the evangelists, for example, enjoyed a 'higher' degree of inspiration than was the case for texts like 2 Maccabees.

All the inspired authors received a special divine impulse to express something in writing. Yet there could be different degrees of the Holy Spirit's presence and activity on their behalf. Secondly, one would expect the nature of the theme—for example, the life, death, and resurrection of Jesus in the case of the Gospels—to have affected the degree of inspiration. In general, as the revealing and saving self-communication of the tripersonal God reached its highpoint with the coming of Christ, a higher degree of inspiration would, we might expect, be associated with the written witness to that climax. Third, since divine gifts seem to be normally proportionate to the human qualities of the recipients, a 'higher' charism of inspiration would match a cultured and dramatic person like Paul of Tarsus.

When discussing 'some characteristic qualities of inspiration', the Biblical Commission agrees that the charism of inspiration was not uniform for 'all the authors of the biblical books'. It was only 'analogously the same'.[24] The remark remains quite isolated in the

[24] *The Inspiration and Truth of Sacred Scripture*, 53–5, at 55.

commission's text, which nowhere treats in any detail the 'the analogy of inspiration'. Yet this lonely remark reminds me that I could present my fifth point in terms of the analogy of inspiration. Instead of inspiration having been always monolithically the same, it was a reality that betrayed similarities and differences.

(6) A further, analogous *variation* concerns the *consciousness* of the inspired writers. Some, like Paul (e.g. Gal. 1: 1–24) and the author of the Book of Revelation (1: 3; 22: 7, 9–10, 18–19), knew themselves to be specially guided by the Holy Spirit or at least to be writing with particular divine authority. But other biblical authors, like Luke (1: 1–4) and the author of 2 Maccabees (15: 38), while claiming to have done their best with the sources available to them, showed no clear awareness that they were writing under a special divine guidance. Both then and now, the Holy Spirit can be at work in various ways, without the beneficiaries necessarily being conscious of such divine guidance (and authority) coming to them.

The Biblical Commission, in sketching a phenomenology of inspiration, helpfully gathered from the Scriptures 'the testimony of biblical writings to their origin from God'.[25] They state, for example: 'Luke explicitly indicates that the source of his gospel was "those who from the beginning were eyewitnesses and ministers of the word" (Luke 1: 2), suggesting, in this way, that his gospel comes from Jesus, the ultimate and supreme revealer of God the Father'. Even if Luke 'does not present the source of the Book of Acts and its divine provenance in the same explicit way', the divine provenance of the book is also 'the immediate, personal relationship' of 'the eyewitnesses and ministers of the word with Jesus'.[26]

The commission may well be right in examining the Scriptures for signs of the inspired authors showing, in one way or another, a sense of the divine origin of what they were composing. Some kind of *divine provenance* for their books can be widely established. Asking about the authors' precise consciousness of divine guidance opens up a more difficult quest.

(7) Seventhly, often it would be more accurate to speak of 'special impulses [plural]' to write, since *many books of the Bible emerged from a long process*. They did not necessarily come from a solo author. Frequently the case of those sharing in the charism of inspiration

[25] Ibid. 1–68. [26] Ibid. 33.

could be complex and varied. Inasmuch as they helped to shape the writing of some part of the Scriptures, a special impulse of the Holy Spirit moved all those who brought about the text.

The charism of inspiration guided, for instance, all those who contributed to the making of the historical books of the Old Testament and was not restricted to the final editor(s). Likewise the same charism touched all those Christians who handed on, as eyewitnesses or otherwise, the stories and sayings that came to be woven into the four Gospels. In the same way we should recognize the inspiration of the author(s) who created hymns subsequently incorporated into New Testament letters (e.g. Phil. 2: 6–11; 1 Tim 3: 16).

(8) Eighthly and finally, *we should not compare the authorship of biblical books too closely with the work of modern authors.* First, unlike many contemporary authors, the biblical authors often drew on oral and written material that had already taken some shape, and they did not fashion their books in a great blaze of creativity. Secondly, their aim was consistently religious: to communicate a message of faith, and not to win success for their literary prowess, as is the case with many, but not all, modern authors. Some of them showed a remarkable grasp of language and an intensity of human feeling. But they did not wish to be judged either by their artful expression or by their capacity to articulate deep personal experience.

The essential difference could be put this way. Modern poets, dramatists, and novelists normally write for themselves, often reflect their own individual background, and remain very much persons in their own right. The biblical authors, however, often wrote anonymously, drew on the general traditions and experiences of believers, and produced works to serve the community. Even if they were more, at times even much more, than mere mouthpieces of their communities (e.g. Paul), we would ignore at our peril the social setting, responsibility, and function of their writings.

THE FUNCTION OF INSPIRATION

Our eight points about biblical inspiration have clarified, hopefully, a little how the special impulse of the Holy Spirit worked through the sacred authors. Provided we acknowledge the real human role of these writers (point 1), we will be in a position to recognize various limitations in their activity (points 2 to 8). Admittedly what has been said so far about inspiration has largely attended to what the special guidance of the Holy Spirit did *not* involve. The biblical authors did not write in all possible styles; their works do not always enjoy a religious effect superior to that of all non-inspired texts; they were not necessarily conscious of being inspired; and so forth. It seems unreasonable to expect a fuller description of all the dynamics of inspiration, let alone a totally clear explanation of it. Such an account should not be looked for, once we acknowledge how this charism (which makes the biblical text both the word of God and the word of human beings) belongs to the total mystery of Christ, who was and is truly divine and fully human. If we cannot 'explain' the relationship between humanity and divinity in the incarnation, we should not hope to explain the similar (but not identical) relationship between divine and human found in the operation of inspiration.[27]

Nevertheless, Karl Rahner's interpretation of inspiration points towards a positive, if limited, account.[28] Without recalling and adopting in every detail his explanation, I want to present five considerations drawn from Rahner that indicate what made God the 'author' of the Scriptures and why we can call the Bible 'the word of God'.

First of all, the gift of inspiration belonged to the divine activity in the history of revelation and salvation which led to the founding of the Church, with all the elements (including the Scriptures) that constitute her total reality. Where the books of the Old Testament recorded various events, persons, and experiences that prepared the way for Christ and his Church, those of the New Testament witnessed to persons (above all, Jesus himself and his apostles), events, and experiences (above all the crucifixion, resurrection, and outpouring of the Holy Spirit) that immediately fed into the founding of the Church.

Hence, secondly, God could be called the 'author' of Scriptures, inasmuch as special divine activity formed and fashioned the Church. Creating the Church also involved 'authoring' the Bible.

[27] See G. O'Collins, 'The Incarnation: The Critical Issues', in S. T. Davis, D. Kendall, and G. O'Collins (eds.), *The Incarnation: An Interdisciplinary Symposium on the Incarnation of the Son of God* (Oxford: Oxford University Press, 2002), 1–27, at 6–12.

[28] See K. Rahner, *Foundations of Christian Faith*, trans. W. V. Dych (New York: Seabury Press, 1978), 369–78; id., *Inspiration in the Bible*, trans. C. H. Henkey (New York: Herder & Herder, 1961).

Third, the charism of inspiration was communicated primarily to the community, and to individuals inasmuch as they belonged to the community. The social dimension of biblical inspiration has been noted under points 7 and 8 above.

Since, fourthly, God communicated the charism of inspiration precisely as part of the divine activity in bringing the Church into existence, we can appreciate why that charism did not continue beyond the apostolic age. It belonged to the unique, non-transferable role of the apostles and the apostolic community in (a) witnessing to Christ's resurrection from the dead and the coming of the Holy Spirit and (b) founding the Church. In the course of Chapter 8 above, we saw how the first Christians and their leaders, acting as resurrection witnesses and church founders, shared in the once-and-for-all quality of the Christ-event itself. The biblical authors and, specifically, the New Testament writers likewise had a once-and-for-all function, whether they were apostles like Paul or simply members of the apostolic community. Since the charism of inspiration entered the divine activity of establishing the Church, it ceased to be given once the Church was fully founded. Inspired writing ended when the period of foundational revelation clearly gave way to the period of dependent revelation. The biblical texts continued to prove richly inspiring, but the production of new biblical texts was closed.

To sum up the change: later generations of Christians bear the responsibility of proclaiming Christ's resurrection, keeping the Church in existence, and living by the Bible. But they neither 'directly' witness to the risen Christ (as did those who met him gloriously alive after his death), nor do they found the Church, nor do they continue to compose inspired Scriptures.

Fifthly and finally, through the inspired record of their foundational experiences, preaching, and activity, the members of the apostolic Church remain uniquely authoritative for all subsequent generations of Christians. Thus the priority of the apostolic Church was and remains much more than a merely chronological one.

Besides offering some account of biblical inspiration—a task which much recent theology appears to ignore—this chapter has set itself to distinguish between inspiration and the broader (and prior) reality of revelation. As we have remarked more than once, identifying inspiration and revelation is an endemic mistake. While one should say that the Bible is the word of God, it cannot be simply identified with revelation. It generates confusion to say, as many do, that 'the Bible is the revealed word of God'. A similar and frequent mistake occurs when inspiration is identified with one of its major results, inerrancy (better called biblical truth). We move next to the truth of the Bible, along with the 'canonization' of its scope and authority.

11

The Canon and Truth of Scriptures

Christians expect to find in the inspired Scriptures the revealed truth by which they can live, worship, and be saved. Rather than focus on the historical discontinuities and theological diversities between the books of the Old and New Testaments in a way that would exclude a real unity, they read and hear these books together, and accept them as the canonical or authoritative guide for their existence. They express this belief by publishing them together as the one-volume Bible. In a metaphor that makes room for the unity of, along with the differences between, the Sacred Scriptures, Kevin Vanhoozer pictures the Christian respect for them: 'Scripture is the *polyphonic testimony* to what God has done, is doing, and will do for the salvation of the world'.[1]

The truth of the Bible implies its canonical, 'polyphonic' unity. Hence we treat the biblical canon and its authority before considering the truth of the Scriptures, following the order adopted by the Biblical Commission's *The Inspiration and Truth of Sacred Scripture.*[2]

Unfortunately, however, the Commission opened by endorsing a defective analogy between the way books become authoritative classics in various cultures and the way texts were received into the biblical canon.[3] Years ago Francis Schüssler Fiorenza drew attention

[1] K. J. Vanhoozer, 'Scripture and Tradition', in K. J. Vanhoozer (ed.), *The Cambridge Companion to Postmodern Theology* (Cambridge: Cambridge University Press, 2003), 140–69, at 167; italics mine.

[2] Pontifical Biblical Commission, *The Inspiration and Truth of Sacred Scripture*, trans. T. Esposito and S. Gregg (Collegeville, Minn.: Liturgical Press, 2014), 60–8 (on 'Toward a Two-Testament Canon') and then 69–121 (on 'The Testimony of the Biblical Writings to their Truth').

[3] Ibid. 62–3. David Tracy, e.g., interpreted at length the Scriptures as 'classics': *The Analogical Imagination* (New York: Crossroad, 1981).

to a basic flaw in this 'classic' interpretation of scriptural authority, which insufficiently distinguishes the Bible from 'inspired' and 'inspiring' classic works of literature (and art). The classics exemplify the deepest realities of human existence; in such books (and works of art), generations of readers have recognized 'the truth of their own identity'. But it is 'the identity of Jesus' that is the basis for scriptural authority rather than the power of Scriptures to elicit from one generation to the next compelling truths about the human condition. Schüssler Fiorenza recalled Krister Stendahl's observation: 'it is because of their authority as scripture that the Scriptures have become classics', and it is not that 'they have authority because they are classics'.[4]

One should add to Schüssler Fiorenza's argument by pointing out that classics, like Homer's two epic poems and Dante's *Divine Comedy*, may feature at the birth of a culture's literature, but not necessarily so. The dialogues of Plato and the works of Goethe, for instance, came long after Greek and German literature, respectively, was established. No 'canon' of literary classics can be declared to be closed. Outstanding writers may turn up today and in the future; their works will merit 'canonization' and inclusion among a people's classic texts. The inspired Scriptures, however, were completed in the foundational period of Christianity. The biblical canon, as we shall see, is closed and cannot be enlarged.

Thirdly, we should not forget what was pointed out in the previous chapter: some inspired books (e.g. the Epistle of Jude, apart from its closing doxology in vv. 24–5) and whole sections in other books (e.g. 1 Chron. 1–9) do not display the literary quality one expects from a literary classic. The Holy Spirit inspired the composition of all the books of the Bible, but such inspiration did not guarantee a 'high', classical standard of human writing.

In short, the particular kind of authority enjoyed by the Sacred Scriptures, their historical provenance, and the 'failure' of some biblical books to reach a 'classical' level disqualifies any easy comparison between these scriptures and the classical literature of various cultures around the world.

[4] F. Schüssler Fiorenza, 'The Crisis of Biblical Authority: Interpretation and Reception', *Interpretation* 44 (1990), 353–68, at 360–1.

THE CANON OF SCRIPTURES

We need to engage with three questions about the canon: (1) the formation of the canon; (2) the closed nature of the canon; and (3) the authority that belongs to the divinely authorized canon.

One might describe the canon as a closed list of sacred books, acknowledged by the Church as divinely inspired, and enjoying a normative value for Christian belief and practice.[5] 'Canonization' presupposed and went beyond biblical inspiration or the special guidance of the Holy Spirit in composing the Scriptures. In the Old Testament period, inspired texts came into existence before the *tripartite canon* of the law (the Torah or Pentateuch), the prophets (including the historical books Joshua to 2 Kings, sometimes called 'the former prophets'), and 'the writings' (mainly wisdom books) began to form in the seventh century BC. This canon gradually emerged after the return from the Babylonian exile, and seemingly became definitive only in the second century AD. The process was similar with the twenty-seven books of the New Testament. They were written under inspiration, and then sooner or later recognized as such by the post-apostolic Church.

Roman Catholics acknowledge in a decree from the Council of Trent (DzH 1502–4; ND 211–12) a definitive act of recognition which firmly established a clear canon of inspired writings. When making this solemn definition of the canon, Trent confirmed the doctrine of

[5] On the canon, see J.-M. Auwers and H. J. de Jonge (eds.), *The Biblical Canons* (Leuven: Leuven University Press, 2003); R. T. Beckwith, *The Old Testament Canon of the New Testament Church and its Background in Early Judaism* (London: SPCK, 1985); R. F. Collins, 'Canonicity', in R. E. Brown, J. A. Fitzmyer, and R. L. Murphy (eds.), *The New Jerome Biblical Commentary* (London: Geoffrey Chapman, 1989), 1034–54; H. Y. Gamble, *The New Testament Canon: Its Making and Meaning* (Philadelphia: Fortress Press, 1985); M. Hengel, *Die vier Evangelien und das Evangelium von Jesus Christus: Studien zu ihrer Sammlung und Entstehung* (Tübingen: Mohr Siebeck, 2008); M. W. Holmes, 'The Biblical Canon', in S. A. Harvey and D. G. Hunger (eds.), *The Oxford Handbook of Early Christian Studies* (Oxford: Oxford University Press, 2008), 406–26; L. M. McDonald, *The Biblical Canon: Its Origin, Transmission, and Authority* (Peabody, Mass.: Hendrickson, 2002); B. M. Metzger, *The Canon of the New Testament: Its Origin, Development, and Significance* (Oxford: Clarendon, 1987); A. C. Sundberg, 'The Bible Canon and the Christian Doctrine of Inspiration', *Interpretation* 29 (1975), 352–71; J. Trebolle, 'Canon of the Old Testament', in K. D. Sakenfeld (ed.), *The New Interpreter's Dictionary of the Bible*, i (Nashville: Abingdon, 2006), 548–63; R. Wall, 'Canon', in S. E. Balentine (ed.), *The Oxford Encyclopedia of Bible and Theology* (New York: Oxford University Press, 2015), 111–21.

the Council of Florence (DzH 1334–5; ND 208), which in its turn was based on teaching coming from local councils and Church fathers in the fourth and early fifth centuries.[6]

We cannot be expected to trace the ins and outs of the history of (a) particular books which were initially favoured but came to be excluded from the canon (e.g. the Epistle of Barnabas and *The Shepherd of Hermas*) or (b) those that came to be included after serious doubts (e.g. the Letter to the Hebrews, the Book of Revelation, and the deuterocanonical books of the Old Testament). Yet we should recall the three criteria used in acknowledging canonical books. But before spelling out these criteria, we need to clarify the terms: protocanonical, deuterocanonical, and apocrypha.

The term 'protocanonical' (or 'first-time members of the canon') applies to the thirty-nine books of the Old Testament which are universally accepted as inspired and canonical and correspond to the twenty-two books of the Hebrew Bible. The term 'deuterocanonical' (or 'second-time members of the canon') is a name for those seven books (plus further portions of other books) found in the Greek (Septuagint) version of the Old Testament (but not in the Hebrew Bible) and printed in Catholic Bibles. The seven books are Judith, 1 and 2 Maccabees, Sirach, Baruch, Tobit, and Wisdom. Some of these works (Judith, 2 Maccabees, and Wisdom) were written in Greek, while 1 Maccabees, Sirach, and much of Baruch were composed originally in Hebrew. Written in Hebrew before 180 BC, Sirach was translated into Greek fifty years later; since 1900 two-thirds of the original Hebrew text has been recovered. Tobit was originally written in either Hebrew or Aramaic, but, apart from some fragments in those languages, only the Greek version remains.

Some Protestant and all ecumenical Bibles include the deuterocanonical books, but normally call them 'Apocrypha'—to be distinguished,

[6] In his 39th festal letter (for Easter 367), St Athanasius of Alexandria listed the 27 books of the New Testament; the Muratorian Canon, generally dated to the late second century (see Bettenson, 31–2), included all the books of the New Testament, except Hebrews, James, and 1 and 2 Peter. As regards the Old Testament canon, Athanasius recognized the 22 books of the Hebrew Bible, which corresponded to the 39 protocanonical books of the Christian Bible. From the late second century Melito of Sardis provided the earliest Christian list of Old Testament books; it was much the same as the 22 books of the Hebrew Bible. See D. Brakke, 'A New Fragment of Athanasius' Thirty-Ninth *Festal Letter*: Heresy, Apocrypha, and the Canon', *Harvard Theological Review* 103 (2010), 47–66.

however, from the Apocryphal Gospels (e.g. 'The Gospel of the Hebrews', 'The Gospel of Mary', 'The Gospel of Peter', and 'The Gospel of Thomas'), works from the second or third centuries that no mainline Bibles include. For Catholic scholars and such Protestant scholars as Hans Hübner, who recognize the authority of some or all of the deuterocanonical books, being 'second-time members of the canon' refers to their being written in the second or first century BC (and hence *after* the protocanonical books) and their being accepted into the canon of Christian Scriptures *after* a certain hesitation (coming from some Church fathers such as St Jerome, who expressed doubt about the full canonical status of the deuterocanonical books). Hence the term 'deuterocanonical' is not intended to belittle their authority for Christians. The New Testament contains numerous allusions and verbal parallels to the deuterocanonical books of the Old Testament. In any case, around the Mediterranean world, Jews who became Christians brought with them the Septuagint, the Greek version of the Bible that included the deuterocanonical books and had fed their spiritual lives. When citing what came to be called the protocanonical books of the Old Testament, the New Testament authors often followed the Septuagint rather than the Hebrew original.

Formation of the Canon

What then of the criteria for receiving books into the canon and thus accepting them as the Sacred Scriptures in and for the Church? Surprisingly perhaps, inspiration itself did not directly function as a criterion for early Christians when they recognized or rejected sacred books. They understood the inspiration of the Holy Spirit to be widely present in the Church both during the apostolic era and later. Granted such a broad recognition of inspiration, an appeal to inspiration could not easily establish the canon. Moreover, both at the time of their writing and even more after the death of their authors, a claim to be inspired could not be readily verified. How were other Christians to know that *this* writer had been specially guided by the Holy Spirit unless they referred to other, public criteria? Such public criteria were needed, not least to counter the claims to have received revelation and inspiration made by the Gnostics in the second and third centuries. Three such criteria shaped the early Church's recognition of sacred or God-inspired writings: (a) *apostolic writings* (or apostolicity), (b) *orthodox teaching* (or 'the rule of faith'), and (c) *wide* and *consistent usage*, particularly in the Church's liturgy and catechesis (an appeal to catholicity).

(a) First, there was the historical criterion of apostolic origin. The Christian writings that complemented the scriptural books inherited by Jesus and his followers and were to constitute the canonical New Testament came from the period of foundational revelation, which climaxed when the apostles proclaimed the resurrection (and the outpouring of the Holy Spirit) and completed the foundation of the Church.

To be sure, apostolic origin was often taken narrowly, so that the books which would make up the New Testament were all understood to be written by the apostles themselves or one of their close associates: Mark (connected with Peter) as author of the Second Gospel and Luke (connected with Paul) as author of the Third Gospel and the Book of Acts. In such a view, apostles gave their authority both to the Jewish Scriptures (which they inherited) and to the new sacred books which they or their associates composed for Christian communities. Such a strict version of apostolic origin no longer works. Very few scholars agree, for example, that Paul wrote Hebrews or that Peter wrote 2 Peter. Hesitations about the strict 'apostolic origin' of Hebrews and 2 Peter, as well as the Book of Revelation, were expressed in early Christianity before Athanasius and others accepted these works into the canon of sacred texts.

Nevertheless, in a broader sense the criterion of apostolic origin still carries weight in sorting out canonical from non-canonical writings. Only those works which witnessed to Christ prophetically (the Jewish Scriptures) or apostolically (the Christian Scriptures) could enter and remain in the Scriptures. Those works constituted the inspired witness coming from believers who had experienced the *foundational* self-revelation of God that ended with the apostolic age. Only persons who shared in the events that climaxed with the crucifixion, resurrection, sending of the Holy Spirit, and full foundation of the Church were in a position to express through inspired Scriptures their testimony to those experiences. Later writings, even of such importance as the Nicene-Constantinopolitan Creed of 381 and the Chalcedonian Definition of 451, came from the period of *dependent* revelation. They could not as such directly witness to the experience of foundational revelation, and were composed at a time when the charism of biblical inspiration had ceased. Seen in this way, the criterion of apostolic origin still works to accredit canonical writing. Canonicity implies apostolicity.

(b) Secondly, there was the *theological criterion* of conformity to the essential message, 'the rule of faith (*regula fidei*)' highlighted by St Irenaeus, or, what was later called, 'the Catholic faith that comes to us from the apostles' (the Roman Canon). For a text to be recognized as canonical, it needed to be consonant with the orthodox tradition transmitted by the bishops. In particular it would be excluded if it contradicted the apostolic rule of faith expressed in various Christological affirmations (Irenaeus, *Adversus Haereses*, 3. 4. 2). Because it failed to meet clearly the test of orthodoxy, *The Shepherd of Hermas*, which was written perhaps in the very early second century and so might have made the grade in terms of time, was excluded from the canon. Other writings, like the Book of Revelation, were eventually included when their orthodox content was sufficiently recognized.

Of course, there was a certain circularity in applying 'the rule of faith'. Since they fitted their understanding of Christianity, the faithful and their leaders judged certain writings (e.g. the four Gospels and the letters of St Paul) to be orthodox, built the canon around them, and then used them to test orthodoxy. At the same time, these Scriptures, inasmuch as they were written under the special guidance of the Holy Spirit, never simply mirrored what the Christian community was but challenged Christians by picturing what they should be and should believe. In leading them to a fully transformed life, the canonical Scriptures proved themselves in practice. We might express the circularity this way. Just as Christian community shaped the canon, so the community and its basic identity were shaped by the canon.

(c) Thirdly, constant and wide use, above all in the context of public worship, also secured for inspired writings their place in the canon of the Christian Bible. We can spot this happening in the case of Paul: when various communities received his letters, they treasured, copied, and read them at liturgical assemblies. These texts shared the apostolic authority of Paul's oral witness and teaching. By the time of the composition of 2 Peter, the letters of Paul seemed to have been already collected (and misinterpreted by some on the issue of the final judgement being delayed) (2 Pet. 3: 15–16).

When treating this third (liturgical) criterion, we should recall the case of 1 Clement. Around AD 170 it was still being read in the church of Corinth, along with Scriptures that were to belong definitively to the canon.[7] But this letter never entered the canon of New Testament Scriptures, later attested by Athanasius and others, since it failed to win lasting and widespread liturgical acceptance. That counted against its canonical status, even if it might have been acceptable on the basis of the first (historical) criterion and the second (theological) criterion.

The Closed Nature of the Canon

In previous section we spoke of the canon as a closed collection of sacred writings. Several reasons justify the closed nature of the canon. First, since the charism of biblical inspiration ended with the apostolic age, there could be no later instances of inspired writings. Being a possible candidate for the canon closed when a particular epoch of history—in this case the foundational period of revelation and salvation—ended.

Secondly, without it being closed and so immune to modifications, the canon cannot function as canon: that is, as truly normative rule for Christian belief and practice from which the Church receives her identity. The canonical books are acknowledged as forming together an adequate version of Christianity. If they did not sufficiently reflect the basic Christian experience and identity which responds to the divine self-revelation through Christ and his Spirit, they could not serve as an authoritative norm for Christian faith and life.

Thirdly, the closed nature of the canon belongs to the closed and normative nature of the apostolic age. Just as the members of the apostolic Church shared in the unique, once-and-for-all character of the Christ event, so too did their sacred writings—both those they produced and those that they took over from their Jewish heritage. The composition of the inspired books shared thus in the unrepeatable role of the apostles and their associates.

The consequences of this argument for the closed canon are clear. On the one hand, to exclude some writings and thus *reduce* the canon (as Marcion did in the second century[8] and others later have done) tampers with the richness of the Church's foundational witness to the

[7] See L. L. Welborn, 'Clement, First Epistle of', *ABD* i, 1055–60.

[8] See J. J. Clabeaux, 'Marcion', *ABD* iv, 514–16; R. M. Grant, 'Marcion, Gospel of', ibid. 516–20.

divine self-communication, minimizes the diversity of the apostolic experience, and, ultimately, challenges the divine fullness of Christ's person and work (see Col. 1: 19–20). On the other hand, enlarging the canon by adding such later writings as the Gnostic 'scriptures' also calls into question the fullness of what Christ did and revealed through the apostolic generation.

In the second century we find Irenaeus of Lyons battling on two fronts in support of the emerging Christian canon. On the one front, he defended the enduring authority of the Old Testament Scriptures against Marcion's total rejection of them. On the other front, he upheld the unique value of the New Testament Scriptures, especially the one, fourfold 'Gospel' according to Matthew, Mark, Luke, and John, against Gnostic attempts to add further 'gospels' and other texts.

The Authority of the Canon

Like some others, but unlike the Biblical Commission in its latest document,[9] I have spoken above of the normative *authority* of the canonical Scriptures.[10] Can we explain more fully the nature of this authority as recognized by Christians and justify its binding quality?

Believers give permanent allegiance to the authoritative biblical texts as promising to preserve the Church's self-identity by constantly

[9] The Commission's *Inspiration and Truth of Sacred Scripture* does not introduce the language of biblical 'authority', but repeatedly speaks of the 'truth' of the Scriptures. Biblical truth implies authority. It would have been good to have, at least, sketched the links between such truth and divine authority.

[10] See W. P. Brown (ed.), *Engaging Biblical Authority* (Louisville, Ky.: Westminster John Knox, 2007); R. L. Culbertson, 'Known, Knower, and Knowing. The Authority of Scripture in the Episcopal Church', *Anglican Theological Review* 74 (1992), 144–74; T. E. Fretheim and K. Froehlich (eds.), *The Bible as Word of God in a Postmodern Age* (Minneapolis: Fortress, 1998); J. Goldingay, 'Scripture', in *Oxford Encyclopedia of Bible and Theology*, 267–79, esp. 270–2; M. Goshen-Goldstein et al., 'Scriptural Authority', *ABD* v, 1017–56; J. A. Keller, 'Accepting the Authority of the Bible: Is it Rationally Justified', *Faith and Philosophy* 6 (1989), 378–89; W. Pannenberg and T. Schneider (eds.), *Verbindliches Zeugnis*, i (Göttingen: Vandenhoeck & Ruprecht, 1992); H. Graf Reventlow, *The Authority of the Bible and the Rise of the Modern World* (London: SCM Press, 1984); id.,'Theology (Biblical), History of', *ABD* vi, 483–505; S. M. Schneiders, 'Scripture as the Word of God', *Princeton Seminary Bulletin* 14 (1992), 348–61, 478–89.

illuminating and enlivening her faith and practice. They read and hear the Bible as the rule of life for their community. They acknowledge the authority of the Bible because it shares in the authority of Christ and his Holy Spirit, a life-giving authority that builds them up and lets them grow. Here etymology proves suggestive. The Latin nouns 'auctor (author)' and 'auctoritas (authority)' are connected with 'augeo' ('cause to grow' and 'increase in value').[11] The 'authority' exercised by Christ and the Spirit through the Scriptures and in other ways does just that.

In other words, the Church's fidelity to the Scriptures rests on her fidelity to Jesus Christ as *the* Revealer and Saviour and on her faith that the Holy Spirit provided special guidance to those involved in producing the Scriptures. Apart from that fidelity and faith, the Scriptures cannot credibly claim any normative value, and become little else than 'mere' historical sources, the records of Israel's story and Christianity's origins, and an anthology of more or less edifying religious texts from the ancient Middle East. Through faith in Christ and his Spirit, however, believers acknowledge the Scriptures as sacred and embodying divine authority,[12] and accept them as the authoritative account and interpretation of Israel's history and the formation of Christianity through Jesus Christ and his first followers. As the official collection of foundational books, the canonical Bible witnesses to the history of revelation and salvation that climaxed with Christ and remains the decisive point of orientation for all subsequent believers and theologians.

The authority at stake is the *de iure* authority of the Scriptures: the canonical Bible in and of itself constitutes the primary norm for determining the Church's faith and practice. Such authority in principle goes beyond mere *de facto* authority, or the way in which the Scriptures as a matter of fact affect the life, worship, and doctrines of

[11] See P. G. W. Glare (ed.), *Oxford Latin Dictionary* (Oxford: Oxford University Press, 1982), 204–7, 212–13.

[12] Their faith in Jesus Christ *underpinned* the New Testament authors' sense of the authority of the Old Testament Scriptures, identified by them as the authority of God. They disclosed the heart of their theological convictions by citing the inherited Jewish Scriptures; see H. Hübner, 'New Testament, OT Quotations in the', *ABD* iv, 1096–104. The Letter to the Hebrews illustrates how Christians understood the Jewish Scriptures as divinely inspired and authoritative. Citing these Scriptures 37 times, Hebrews attribute all the passages to God, Christ, or the Holy Spirit, mentioning only two human authors—Moses (Heb. 8: 5; 12: 21) and David (Heb. 4: 7)—and even then referring twice to the divine 'author' (Heb. 4: 7; 8: 5).

Christians. Such *de facto* authority functions insofar as the Scriptures 'work' for us but does not allow them an independent authority to challenge and judge us and our society. To accept their *de iure* authority, however, involves acknowledging that they legitimately invite an obedient hearing because they derive from a foundational and authoritative past rooted in the missions of the Son of God, the Holy Spirit, and (by participation) the apostles.

This *de iure* authority of the Bible derives from its historical origins in the mission of the Holy Spirit, a mission invisible in itself but visible in its effects, and the visible mission of Christ (with the passage of authority from him to his apostolic collaborators). In short, the authority of the Scriptures is Pneumatological, Christological, and apostolic. It derives from persons: the Holy Spirit and Christ with his apostles. Through the Scriptures, as well as in other ways, Christ, the Spirit, and the apostles remain powerfully and authoritatively present.

THE SAVING TRUTH OF THE BIBLE

Before examining the saving truth of the Bible,[13] we need to take a stand on (a) terminology and (b) set aside a common but misleading view.

(a) Many Christians continue to speak of biblical 'inerrancy' or freedom from error. However, it is preferable to use a positive and more scriptural term, 'truth'. Biblical truth not only aims positively at saving human beings integrally (and not merely at keeping them free from error). It is also identified with the persons of the Trinity, as we shall see. It would be strange to characterize Father, Son, or Holy Spirit as 'Inerrancy itself', but we can and should call each of them 'Truth itself' or 'Truth in person'.

[13] See O. Loretz, *The Truth of the Bible*, trans. D. J. Bourke (London: Burns & Oates, 1968), J. van Oorschot et al. 'Wahrheit/Wahrhaftigkeit', *TRE* xxxv, 337–78, at 337–45; A. E. Padgett and P. R. Keifert (eds.), *But Is It All True? The Bible and the Question of Truth* (Grand Rapids, Mich.: Eerdmans, 2006); G. L. Parsenios, 'Truth', in *Oxford Encyclopedia of Bible and Theology*, 394–7; I. de la Potterie, *Vérité dans Saint Jean*, 2 vols. (Rome: Biblicum Press, 1977); G. Quell et al., '*alētheia*', in *TDNT* i, 232–51; M. Theobald and J.-Y. Lacoste, 'Truth', in J.-Y. Lacoste (ed.), *Encyclopedia of Christian Theology*, iii (New York: Routledge, 2004), 1632–9.

(b) Along with this issue of terminology, one should notice the frequent and misleading tendency to identify biblical inspiration with the truth (or inerrancy) of the Bible. Rather than being identical with inspiration, biblical truth (to be described below) is a major result or consequence of inspiration. The Bible was written under a special impulse of the Holy Spirit and, therefore, is true. Biblical inspiration enjoyed other results and consequences: for instance, it produced texts that over thousands of years have nourished personal prayer and public worship for Jews and Christians. Expressing and encouraging truth was a major consequence of inspiration.

In *The Inspiration and Truth of Sacred Scripture*, the Biblical Commission, while not identifying them, tied biblical truth more closely to inspiration by calling it a 'fundamental' and 'divine' *quality* (rather than result) of inspired Scripture.

> Since it originates in God, Scripture has divine qualities. Among these is the fundamental one of attesting the truth, understood . . . as a revelation of God himself and his salvific plan. The Bible, in fact, makes known the mystery of the Father's love, manifested in the Word made flesh, who, through the Spirit, leads to a perfect communion of human beings with God.[14]

This was to link the Bible's (testimony to the) truth with the *self-revelation* of the tripersonal God and its (inseparable) salvific purpose. This essentially personal account of biblical truth will now be developed under seven headings.

(1) First, the central purpose of the inspired Scriptures could be called *attesting the truth* about God and attesting the truth about ourselves which leads to salvation. But that truth is not necessarily and always derived straight from events in which God is revealed: for instance, the incarnation, life, death, and resurrection of the Son of God. As we saw in the last chapter, the Bible *also records faithfully* (under inspiration) matters that do not seem closely connected with God's self-manifestation. Some of what we read in Leviticus, for example, comes from human customs rather than any special divine disclosure. To use the language of the Biblical Commission, rather than all such passages being 'perennially valid', they may merely reflect 'a culture, a civilization, or even the mentality of a specific period of time'.[15]

[14] Biblical Commission, *Inspiration and Truth*, 162. [15] Ibid. 150.

(2) A second limit to be respected when reflecting on the biblical truth derives from the nature of language used in the Scriptures and beyond. Language may express a true judgement made by our intellect about the way things are. If what the intellect judges about reality (and hence causes us to say and write) actually conforms to reality (*adequatio intellectus et rei*), then we are in touch with truth.[16] This way of understanding truth highlights the individual person's intellect, emphasizing the mind and judgement of the thinking subject.[17] It may reduce 'truth' to that of propositions which represent reality and conform to the 'facts'.

This way of interpreting 'truth' risks reducing the biblical texts to a set of informative propositions, whose function is to make factual claims and state true judgements. The Bible, however, forms no such catalogue of propositions which are to be tested (solely by the correspondence theory of truth) for their truth or error. Unquestionably, the Scriptures do contain some true propositions: for instance, 'Christ died for our sins, was buried, has been raised, and appeared to Cephas and then to the Twelve' (1 Cor. 15: 3–5). But the Scriptures also use language in other ways by raising questions, issuing exhortations, conveying commands, and so forth.

Questions asked by God (e.g. Gen. 3: 9), Jesus (e.g. John 1: 38), Paul (e.g. Gal. 3: 1), and others in the biblical stories may be, as is the case elsewhere, clear, pertinent, and meaningful. But as such, questions do not aim at describing reality and may not be classified under the headings of truth or falsity. To ask a question does not amount to saying anything true or false. Furthermore, *exhortations* delivered by the prophets, the apostle Paul, and others abound in the Bible. These exhortations may be called for, may change attitudes, and may bring about right behaviour. But in and of themselves exhortations should not be called 'true' or 'false'; that would be a category mistake.

It is the same with *commands* and *laws*, like the two Decalogues of Exodus 20: 2–17 and Deuteronomy 5: 6–21. The first 'develops mainly a theology of creation', and the second 'insists mostly on the theology of salvation'. They summarize the Torah, and aim at constructing 'a true' or faithful community.[18] But it can be misleading to

[16] See R. L. Kirkham, 'Truth, Correspondence Theory of', in E. Craig (ed.), *Routledge Encyclopedia of Philosophy*, ix (London: Routledge, 1998), 472–5.

[17] But, as we shall see later in this section, biblical truth calls for much more than intellectual activity and invites human beings to 'do the truth' and 'follow' the personal Truth that is the Son of God incarnate.

[18] Biblical Commission, *Inspiration and Truth of Sacred Scripture*, 75–6.

say that 'the Decalogues combine the attestation of a truth concerning God (he is the *Creator* and *Saviour*) with a truth regarding the manner of a just and upright life'.[19] Other biblical passages directly attest these two truths, respectively: 'I am the Lord your Holy One, the Creator of Israel, your King' (Isa. 43: 15); 'happy are those' whose 'delight is the law of the Lord' (Ps. 1: 1–2). Such passages might be questioned in the light of the correspondence theory of truth: is it true that the YHWH is the Lord and Creator of Israel? Is it true that those who delight in the law of the Lord are happy and blessed people? But as such, the Decalogues are not precisely in the business of making such truth claims about the way things are, and should not be scrutinized as to whether such judgements correspond to the facts. Rather they enjoin a way of living and relating to other human beings and to God.

(3) We need to insist on the biblical notions of truth, which, while not always proving foreign to the pervasive correspondence view of truth,[20] have their particular accents as *interpersonal* and less one-sidedly intellectual. In the Old Testament the Hebrew term *emet*, generally translated by the (Greek) Septuagint as *alētheia*, bespeaks the consistent faithfulness and firm reliability of God, revealed in word and deed. The biblical history 'seeks to show that God is faithful in his relationship with humanity . . . God leads his people to salvation, in and with him, through the events of history'. God is totally reliable (Deut. 32: 4), so that 'the truth of the Lord is comparable to that of a rock (Isa. 26: 4)'.[21] God's 'truth' merges with the 'steadfast love' or *hesed* that secures his covenant with people. Numerous Old Testament texts catch the reciprocal, interpersonal nature of biblical 'truth': 'The Lord your God . . . is the faithful God; with those who love him and keep his commandments he keeps covenant and faith for ever' (Deut. 7: 9). By their fidelity to the covenant, the people should prove themselves to be loyally conformed to the divine reality and hence persons of 'truth'.

[19] Ibid. 77.

[20] Most post-modernists seem to oppose the idea of language as 'referential' and so dismiss the correspondence theory of truth. Hard-core common sense, however, constantly implies this theory in assessing what witnesses in court swear to, what professors of medicine propose to their classes, what people maintain in filling in forms for government agencies, and in a host of other ways.

[21] Biblical Commission, *Inspiration and Truth of Sacred Scripture*, 78, 79.

In the New Testament 'truth' features strongly in the Pauline and Johannine corpus: *alētheia* turns up forty-seven times in the letters attributed to Paul and forty-four times in the Gospel and letters of John. Paul links 'truth' to personal knowledge of God (Rom. 1: 18–19). Remaining faithful and reliable, God is 'proved true' (Rom. 3: 1–7) and is fully revealed through the person of his Son: 'the truth is in Jesus' (Eph. 4: 21).[22]

The witness of Jesus is 'true' (John 8: 14), because he has 'come from heaven' and provides testimony to what he has seen (John 3: 31–6). It is through Jesus that 'grace and truth' have come (John 1: 17).[23] We can sum up the divine self-revelation as the truth of salvation manifested in Christ. He himself is 'the true bread' (John 6: 32) and 'the true vine' (John 15: 1). In fact, he is the Truth (John 14: 6) who reveals the Father (John 1: 18; see 14: 7) and who will send the Spirit of truth (John 16: 7, 13).

The powerful presence of Christ and the Holy Spirit enables believers to 'do the truth' (John 3: 21) and to 'belong to the truth' (John 18: 37). The truth that 'sets them free' (John 8: 32) does much more than conform their minds to reality. It transforms their entire existence by bringing them into a personal relationship with God who is Father, Son, and Holy Spirit.

(4) Fourthly, a personal notion of biblical truth recognizes how it was *progressive*, a truth not communicated once and for all at the start. Earlier biblical authors faithfully recorded some unsatisfactory and even downright erroneous views of God: for instance, the idea that God could order the total destruction of all the Amalecites (e.g. Deut. 25: 19). Under the impulse of the Holy Spirit, the biblical authors recorded this and other instances of *herem*. It was an image of God that the Israelites genuinely entertained but it needed to be radically purified if they were to grow towards the true image of God who loves and cherishes all peoples, an image which we find in Second and Third Isaiah (Isa. 40–55 and Isa. 56–66, respectively), Jonah, and other later books and traditions.[24]

[22] The Book of Revelation calls Jesus 'the true one' (Rev. 3: 7); he is 'faithful and true' (Rev. 19: 11).

[23] Here the Scriptures prefigure the philosophical notion of truth developed by Martin Heidegger (1889–1976), according to whom something is true when it ceases to be hidden (*a-lethēs*) and discloses itself. In this sense truth is the unveiling or throwing open of being.

[24] See G. O'Collins, *Salvation for All: God's Other Peoples* (Oxford: Oxford University Press, 2008), 64–78.

Unless we recognize the progressive nature of biblical truth, we may find ourselves in the company of many people and even a few scholars who attempt to justify genocidal practices by arguing that God is the Lord of life and death.[25] What the biblical authors recall at times is nothing less than an horrendous (if, historically speaking, not a truly accurate) story: for instance, 'doing the divine will' by killing all the inhabitants of town after town as the Israelites took possession of the promised land (Deut. 2: 31–3: 7); God killing 70,000 people by sending a pestilence after David ordered a national census (2 Sam. 24: 1–16; 1 Chron. 21: 1–14); the sacrifice of a daughter in thanksgiving to God for a military victory (Judg. 11: 29–40). There is a sad truth in what these and other passages record under the impulse of divine inspiration: namely, a picture of what (at least many) Israelites thought at the time about God and about what God wanted from them. Their image of God called for massive purification; there was progress towards a fuller and more accurate truth about God reflected in later books that were also to be composed under the inspiration of the Holy Spirit.

(5) Fifthly, the progressive understanding of biblical truth leads naturally to acknowledging how biblical truth *is found in the whole Bible*. It is 'canonical truth', as the Biblical Commission puts it.[26] We cannot properly speak of the truth of the Bible until all the scriptural texts have been composed and then recognized as belonging to the canon. Hence we should not look for the truth of the Scriptures primarily in one passage, in one book, or even in one Testament. The truth is in the whole.[27]

An ancient Christian conviction, still reflected in a liturgical introduction 'The Gospel according to Matthew' (or 'according to Mark, Luke, or John'), conveys a sense of the (full) truth being found in the whole. There is only one Gospel of Jesus Christ, attested by the witness of four evangelists. The truth is found in the one, four-fold Gospel.

(6) We can, sixthly, state this unity more precisely and personally: the truth of the Bible is found primarily in the person of Jesus Christ.

[25] But see J. S. Kaminsky, 'Did Election Imply the Mistreatment of Non-Israelites', *Harvard Theological Review* 96 (2003), 387–425.

[26] Biblical Commission, *Inspiration and Truth*, 119–21, 163.

[27] This is not to play down the challenge involved in *interpreting* many individual passages of the Bible; see ibid. 123–56; G. O'Collins, *Rethinking Fundamental Theology* (Oxford: Oxford University Press, 2011), 235–9, 253–64.

He is the truth attested prophetically in the Old Testament and apostolically in the New Testament. Ultimately the Bible does not convey a set of distinct truths but has only one truth to proclaim and practice: the personal disclosure of the tripersonal God in Jesus. 'Other' biblical truths or 'mysteries' with their distinct contents do nothing else than articulate this one primordial Mystery, which the apostolic generation of believers experienced and transmitted to later generations. Likewise, just as Christ is the one Truth, so also there is the one Logos or Meaning.

(7) Seventhly and finally, the Scriptures create the conditions by which God speaks to us and enables us to acknowledge and practise the truth. In the last resort, the truth of the Bible is something to be lived. This truth is known by living in it and living by it. Biblical truth is to be experienced and expressed in action as much (or even more than) it is to be seen and affirmed in intellectual judgements. Through doing and 'speaking the truth in love' (Eph. 4: 15), we will know and understand, at least partly and provisionally, what this truth is.

12

The Divine Revelation Reaching the 'Others'

So far this book has attended to the divine self-revelation that has given rise to Jewish and Christian faith. What of the situation of those who accept and follow 'other' religious faiths or none at all? Does God's self-revelation reach them? If so, how might that happen?

Normally those who write about the followers of other faiths raise the question of their salvation.[1] The ancient adage, 'outside the Church no salvation (*extra ecclesiam nulla salus*)', casts a long shadow and inhibited reflection on the distinguishable but inseparable questions: should we exclude revelation outside the Church ('*extra ecclesiam nulla revelatio*')? But if we accept revelation 'outside' the story of Judaism and Christianity, how does such revelation happen and how is it connected with Christ?

The Biblical Commission document cited in the last chapter wrote of 'the spiritual treasures of other religions'. But it did not take a stand on the source of those treasures: divine revelation or human discovery? It went on at once, however, to recall Balaam in Numbers 22: 1–24: 25, and highlighted 'how (inspired) prophecy is not the exclusive prerogative of the people of God'.[2] The case of Balaam, a diviner from Mesopotamia and no Israelite, certainly illustrates how God can communicate oracles and blessings through 'outsiders'. But Balaam's prophecies did not enrich his own faith and that of those who shared his religion. What he said impinged rather on the history of the

[1] See G. O'Collins, 'The Faith of Others: A Biblical Possibility', *Irish Theological Quarterly*, 80 (2015), 313–26.

[2] *The Inspiration and Truth of the Sacred Scripture*, trans. E. Esposito and S. Gregg (Collegeville, Minn.: Liturgical Press, 2014), 166.

people of God, their victory over the Moabites, and fails to shed light on the issue of 'revelation for the others'.

Nevertheless, here and there the Bible does yield some help towards appreciating how the divine self-revelation reaches the 'others'. This is not to deny the frequently negative judgements coming, for instance, from the Old Testament oracles against the nations. Yet, as we shall see, that is not the whole story; there are positive pointers to be recalled. Let us begin with Genesis 1–11, chapters which focus not on Israel but on primeval human beings and their world—from creation to the new beginning after the flood.

ADAM, EVE, AND NOAH

The Book of Genesis deploys traditional figures and stories that symbolize the unity of humankind and God's concern to communicate with them and care for them. Thus ancient legends about Adam, Eve, Noah, and his family look back to the 'parents' of the human race and a mythical time when God related to humanity as one.[3]

The story of the creation and subsequent sin of 'the man' and 'the woman' (e.g. Gen. 3: 2, 6, 12–13) depicts symbolically the origin and sin of everyman and everywoman. The figures of 'Adam' and 'Eve' portray the whole human community and its life in the presence of God. Human existence, according to Genesis, consists in relationships—between human beings and nature, among human beings, and between human beings and God. Communication is both vertical (between God and humanity) and horizontal (among human beings themselves). It is to humanity as a whole that God speaks and delivers the injunction: 'be fruitful and multiply; fill the earth and subdue it' (Gen. 1: 28).

God conveys to humanity as such the task of presiding in the divine name over the rest of creation. In particular, God assigns three activities to 'the man': to cultivate the earth, to 'keep' or guard the Garden, and to name the animals (Gen. 2: 15, 19–20). A psalm echoes

[3] See A. Lacocque, *The Trial of Innocence: Adam, Eve and the Yahwist* (Eugene, Oreg.: Cascade Books, 2006); S. Schellenberg, 'Adam (Primeval History)', in S. E. Balentine (ed.), *The Oxford Encyclopedia of the Bible and Theology*, i (New York: Oxford University Press, 2015), 4–11; H. N. Wallace, 'Adam', *ADB* i, 62–4.

the Genesis account and celebrates what God has done by communicating to human beings an authority over the rest of creation: 'You have given them dominion over the works of your hands; you have put all things under their feet, all sheep and oxen, and also the beasts of the field, the birds of the air, and the fish of the sea' (Ps. 8: 6–8). This vocation is not created by human beings for themselves, but revealed to them by God.

Collectively humanity not only receives a favoured status vis-à-vis the rest of creation but also should obey commands coming from God—in particular, the command not to eat any fruit 'of the tree of the knowledge of good and evil' (Gen. 2: 16–17). 'The man' and 'the woman' eat the forbidden fruit, and lose both their innocent relationship with one another and their trusting relationship with God. Nevertheless, even if sin has disrupted this situation, God remains in contact with them and they can speak to God. Their instinct, of course, is to put the blame on someone else. 'The man' blames 'the woman' and even God: 'the woman whom you gave to be with me, she gave me fruit from the tree' (Gen. 3: 11). When speaking with God, 'the woman' blames the crafty serpent who has tempted her: 'the serpent tricked me, and I ate' (Gen. 3: 13).

The Genesis story picturesquely tells the story of what follows for everyman and everywoman when they deliberately disobey the divine command. Their sin does not terminate God's active relationship with Adam and Eve. God continues to speak with them (Gen. 3: 16–19) and do things for them (Gen. 3: 21). The astounding closeness of God to human beings does not end with their fall into sin. To use 'second-order' terminology that goes beyond the vivid, 'first-order' language of Genesis 1–11, revelation and salvation continue.

In particular, despite the presence of sin, human beings remain created in the image of God. The divine 'likeness' and 'image' are transmitted to the descendants of Adam and Eve: 'When God created humankind, he made them in his likeness. Male and female he created them and he blessed them.' When Adam begets Seth, he 'becomes the father of a son his likeness [in the likeness of God] and according to his image' (Gen. 5: 1–3). A sense of revelation and salvation shapes the vision of all humanity with which the Bible opens. Even after they fall into sin, human beings continue to manifest the divine image and likeness and to experience the loving concern of God.

The Genesis myths see the disobedience of Adam and Eve as initiating an avalanche of sin. Evil decisions coalesce and shape a 'world' situation which needs cleansing to allow for a new beginning (Gen. 9: 1–2). The biblical authors draw on Babylonian traditions of prehistoric floods. The divine judgement takes the form of a catastrophic flood, but the merciful love of God still operates, and rescues Noah and a remnant of human beings and animals. Before the flood, God speaks twice to Noah (Gen 6: 13–21; 7: 1–4), who hears and obeys the divine instructions. After the flood subsides, Noah, again instructed by God, is saved with his entire entourage of human beings, animals, birds, and 'creeping things' (Gen. 8: 15–19).

In the post-flood situation (Gen. 8: 20–9: 17), God communicates various regulations and promises to Noah 'and his sons'. Remaining amazingly close to them, God even reveals what he 'says in his heart' when reacting to a sacrifice Noah spontaneously offers (Gen. 8: 21–2). In particular, this closeness leads God to make known a covenant that will guarantee the preservation of the natural order against the powers of chaos: 'never again shall all flesh be cut off by the waters of a flood, and never again shall there be a flood to destroy the earth' (Gen. 9: 11).[4] Unlike the later covenants to be established with Abraham and Sarah (Gen. 17) and the people of Israel at Mount Sinai (Exod. 24), the covenant with Noah is not only 'everlasting' (Gen. 9:16) but also *universal* in its scope. As we shall see, the three sons of Noah are regarded as the ancestors of all peoples. The covenant is also made with every living creature and with the earth itself. The permanent symbol of this cosmic covenant with God will be the rainbow that in the sky unites heaven and earth (Gen. 9: 8–17). God discloses his desire to sustain faithfully the whole world and care for the well-being of all creatures.

The meaning given to the rainbow seems a striking innovation, since many peoples in ancient times regarded the rainbow as a weapon of the Divine Warrior who used it to shoot the arrows of lightning.[5] Such symbolism turns up in the Old Testament itself

[4] Even before Genesis recalls the covenant with Noah, God has already spoken and promised to maintain the stable course of nature: 'as long as the earth continues, seedtime and harvest, cold and heat, summer and winter, day and night shall not cease' (Gen. 8: 22). On the Noahic and other covenants, see S. Hahn and J. Bergsma, 'Covenant', in *The Oxford Encyclopedia of the Bible*, i, 151–66.

[5] See P. J. Kissling, 'Rainbow', in K. D. Sakenfeld (ed.), *The New Interpreter's Dictionary of the Bible*, iv (Nashville: Abingdon Press, 2009), 729.

(e.g. Ps. 7: 12–13; Hab. 3: 9–11). In Genesis 9, however, the sign of the rainbow ceases to manifest the divine anger. God says: 'the bow in the clouds' is 'the sign of the covenant that I have established between me and all flesh that is on the earth' (Gen. 9: 12–17). This meaning is more in line with the 'natural' symbolism of the rainbow, in that rainbows signify the *end* of a rain storm.

The universality of this covenant is also signified by Shem, Ham, and Japheth: 'these three were the sons of Noah, and from these the whole earth was peopled' (Gen. 9: 18). To drive home the universal relevance of Noah, his family, and the covenant God made with him, Genesis provides a table of the nations (Gen. 10: 1–32), and so uses ancient traditions to illustrate how all humankind originated from Noah and his family.[6] This means that the entire human race has inherited the divine blessings of the new age that follows the flood, and shares in the covenant God made with Noah. As Claus Westermann puts it, 'the whole of humankind in all its members is created, preserved, and blessed by God'.[7]

The Noahic covenant involves a divine blessing that is everlasting. It remains firmly in place in the list of seven covenants that ends with that made with King David (Sir. 44–7). Through Noah, God gives human history a fresh beginning and makes a covenant with all peoples and with the earth itself. Through a cosmic covenant all human beings (along with all non-human creatures) form a single family, share the same blessings from God, and know (or should know) these blessings revealed and activated by God.

Although, unlike its salvific aspect, its revelatory aspect is often neglected, the relationship of God with Adam, Eve, Noah, and his family is nothing if not a known relationship, manifested by God, initiating a *universal and everlasting* covenant, and inviting all human beings to participate consciously and faithfully in that relationship. The primordial figures who feature in Genesis 1–11 are also prototypical figures, who prefigure how all human beings should open themselves to God's astonishing and revealed closeness and read the rainbow as symbolizing God's cosmic covenant.

[6] H. D. Preuss observes: 'According to the Table of the Nations in Genesis 10, a type of literary document that is without analogy in the ancient Middle East, Israel enjoys vis-à-vis the nations no pre-eminence due to creation, mythology, or prehistory': *Old Testament Theology*, trans. L. G. Perdue, ii (Edinburgh: T. & T. Clark, 1996), 285.

[7] On 'The Table of the Nations', see C. Westermann,*Genesis 1–11: A Commentary*, trans. J. J. Scullion (London: SPCK, 1984), 495–530, at 526.

Without invoking the Noahic covenant and its sign of the rainbow, some biblical passages celebrate the universal revelation of God communicated through the created world: 'The heavens are telling the glory of God, and the firmament proclaims his handiwork. Day to day pours forth speech, and night to night declares knowledge. There is no speech, nor are there words; their voice is not heard. Yet their voice goes out through all the earth, and their words to the end of the world' (Ps. 19: 1–4). Even if the heavens cannot literally speak words, nevertheless, 'their voice goes out through all the earth' to reveal the glory of God and his handiwork. In the Middle Ages and later, Christians would talk about 'the book of nature', which was to be read alongside the Sacred Scriptures and which would also reveal God. In Psalm 19, however, nature is not a book to be read but a voice to be heard as it proclaims the glory of the Creator.

SOME PROPHETS ON GOD AS KNOWN BY 'THE OTHERS'

Here and there the prophetic books of the Old Testament, despite their vigorous oracles against the nations (e.g. Isa. 13: 1–23: 18), express or at least imply a saving knowledge of God that reaches the non-Israelites, even though it does not involve their accepting the divine self-revelation that came through the special history of Israel that unfolded from the time of Abraham and Sarah. Let us see three examples: from Jonah, Isaiah, and Malachi.

(1) The Book of Jonah, in an extended parable or piece of didactic fiction, pictures the hated Ninevites knowing the merciful love of God.[8] When Jonah preaches to them, they 'turn from their evil ways' (Jonah 3: 1–10) in a moral conversion rather than a religious conversion that would lead them to embrace the divine revelation made to Israel. Thus the section of Jonah dealing with the preaching to the Ninevites and their conversion uses the generic name of *Elohim* when

[8] See J. E. Fretheim, *The Message of Jonah* (Minneapolis: Augsburg, 1977); J. Magonet, *Form and Meaning: Studies in Literary Techniques in the Book of Jonah* (Sheffield: Almond Press, 1983); J. M. Sasson, *Jonah* (New York: Doubleday, 1990); U. Simon, *The JPS Bible Commentary: Jonah* (Philadelphia: Jewish Publication Society, 1999).

referring to God (Jonah 3: 5, 8, 9, and twice in 10). To be sure, when switching between *Elohim* (the universal God or God of the universe) and YHWH (who has entered a particular relationship with Israel),[9] the *whole* book of Jonah shows no 'overall pattern'.[10] Nevertheless, within Jonah 3: 4–10, the section that describes the Ninevites and their reaction to the prophet's preaching, significantly only *Elohim* is used. A shift to belief in and worship of YHWH as such, along with the adoption of the Mosaic law and practice, is not the issue. God remains content to let the Ninevites continue with their (limited) knowledge of the divine self-revelation, provided they undergo a moral conversion 'from their evil ways'. What God expects of the Ninevites is such a conversion and not that they take part in any great procession to Jerusalem which Third Isaiah depicts (Isa. 66: 18–23).

(2) Apropos of what 'others' experience of God's revelation and salvation, the Book of Isaiah wedges into some predominantly negative chapters several verses that foretell a coming relationship of Egypt and Assyria with YHWH. Isaiah proclaims the day when 'there will be five cities in the land of Egypt that speak the language of Canaan [= of the Jewish settlements] and swear allegiance to the Lord of hosts. One of these will be called the City of the Sun [probably Heliopolis]' (Isa. 19: 19).[11] The prophet announces that 'on that day there will be an altar to the Lord in the centre of the land of Egypt, and a pillar to the Lord at its border'. Blenkinsopp explains: 'the prohibition of regional sanctuaries in Deuteronomy may not have been thought to apply outside the land of Israel, or it may simply have been disregarded'.[12] Through the power of God, the Egyptians will experience deliverance from oppression just as Israel did (Isa. 19: 20). Without going to Jerusalem, 'the Egyptians will know the Lord on

[9] According to the Priestly tradition, the name YHWH was revealed to Moses (Exod. 6: 2–8). According to the Yahwist tradition, however, that sacred name was invoked by all humanity from the time of a grandson of Adam and Eve (Gen. 4: 16); this tradition would exclude in advance any particularism. Here we should, of course, add that some scholars doubt the distinct existence of the Priestly and Yahwist traditions; see E. Zenger, *Einleitung in das AlteTestament*, 5th edn. (Stuttgart: Kohlhammer, 2004), 90–123.

[10] Sasson, *Jonah*, 18 n. 15.

[11] This 'alludes to the spread . . . in Egypt of the Yahveh cult involving the use, at least for liturgical purposes of Hebrew and of the name of Yahveh in forensic affairs and in sealing contracts—a situation amply illustrated in the Elephantine papyri': J. Blenkinsopp, *Isaiah 1–39* (New York: Doubleday, 2000), 318.

[12] Ibid. 319.

that day, and will worship with sacrifice and burnt offering, and they will make vows to the Lord and perform them' (Isa. 19: 21). At that time 'the Egyptians will worship with the Assyrians' and Israel will be a blessing to the nations. 'Israel will be third with Egypt and Assyria, a blessing in the midst of the earth, whom the Lord of hosts has blessed, saying, "Blessed be Egypt my people, and Assyria the work of my hands, and Israel my heritage"' (Isa. 19: 24–5).

The last two verses constitute a remarkable statement of divine benevolence towards 'others' who already 'know' God through some form of divine self-revelation and so are in a position to worship God. These verses put Egypt and even Assyria (both denounced elsewhere in Isaiah for cruelly oppressing God's chosen people) on a par with Israel, as 'my people' and 'the work of my hands'. Such descriptions are normally reserved for Israel itself (e.g. Isa. 60: 21; 64: 8). Yet there is no question here of Egypt and Assyria accepting the covenant revealed at Sinai and joining themselves to the religious life of Israel.

(3) Malachi remains shrouded in much mystery; at best we can say that this prophet probably lived some time after 500 BC. His emphasis on fidelity to the covenant and high view of the Jewish priesthood led him to condemn strongly the priests for failing in their vocation, misleading the people, and corrupting the worship of God (1: 6–2: 9; 3: 3–4).

This involved a sharp contrast with the pure worship of God offered by the Gentiles. So far from being a threat to Malachi, diversity (here diversity in actual practices of cult) offered the prophet a source for criticizing the situation in Israel. Malachi did *not* ask about the 'nations': are they (totally) reliable guides in their version of God? What form of revelation brought them to know and believe in God? But he admired the 'way' they 'reverenced' and worshipped God, finding in their practice a standard to imitate.

The famous statement about worship offered by Gentiles comes as an 'oracle' from 'the Lord of hosts': 'from the rising of the sun to its setting my name is great among the nations and in every place incense is offered to my name, and a pure offering; for my name is great among the nations' (Mal. 1: 11). This oracle seemingly describes what is happening among the Gentiles around the world who pay homage to YHWH everywhere from East to West ('from the rising of the sun to its setting'), without a hint of this worship being centralized or needing to be centralized in Jerusalem. Hence this description differs from a psalm which announces the future glory of Jerusalem, where 'the nations will fear the name of the Lord, and all the kings of the earth' the divine glory (Ps. 103: 15). A few verses further on, Malachi reiterates this very positive description of the Gentiles, when 'the Lord of hosts' says: 'my name is reverenced among the nations' (Mal. 1: 14).

While treasuring the covenant through which God is revealed in a special way to the chosen people, Malachi looks at 'the nations' around the world ('in every place') and sees them enjoying some true knowledge of God, which leads them to reverence the name of YHWH and make pure offerings to him in their worship. It is hard to imagine a more positive view of the cultic practices of 'others', built on the religious faith by which they have responded to divine revelation. One should add, however, that, given the eschatological emphasis of the Book of Malachi as a whole, the prophet may intend 'the future establishment of the kingship of God over all the earth'.[13] Zephaniah, a prophet who was active around 630 BC and so earlier than Malachi, announces the *future* conversion of the nations and does so in terms of cultic worship: 'from beyond the rivers of Ethiopia my suppliants, my scattered ones, shall bring my offering' (Zeph. 3: 10).

Christians were to *apply* Malachi 1: 11 to the Eucharist, its sacrificial dimension, and its celebration by various communities of believers meeting from East to West.[14] Eventually, in its teaching on the Eucharist in 1562, the Council of Trent referred to our text from Malachi, understanding it to prefigure 'the clean oblation/offering of the Eucharist'. Then Trent spoke of the Eucharistic offering being 'prefigured by various types of sacrifices under *the regime of nature* and *of the law*. For it includes all the good that was signified by these former sacrifices: it is their fulfilment and perfection' (DzH 1742; ND 1547). This was a generous evaluation not only of the Jewish sacrifices ('under the law') but also of sacrifices offered in other religions ('under the regime of nature'). Presumably, just as the Jewish sacrificial system was believed to be prescribed by God, so the latter sacrifices were understood to be in some sense derived from God (and not, for example, from the forces of evil). Otherwise, how could they signify something good and in the divine plan reach their 'fulfilment and perfection' in the Eucharist?

[13] A. E. Hill, *Malachi* (New York: Doubleday, 1998), 219.

[14] See e.g. the late first-century *Didache*, 14; and in the second century Irenaeus, *Adversus Haereses*, 4. 17. 4.

Both in itself and in its later 'reception' by Christian teaching, our passage from Malachi evaluated positively the worth of sacrifices offered by 'the nations'. This presupposed that *in some sense* their sacrificial system was derived from God and appropriate for worshipping God.

WISDOM LITERATURE AND DIVINE REVELATION

The wisdom literature of the Old Testament has much to say about the divine revelation being available universally and not limited to the members of the chosen people.[15] Let us begin with the story of God's self-disclosure reaching the holy 'outsider' par excellence, Job.

(1) Written perhaps in the sixth century BC, the Book of Job draws on an ancient folktale about a saintly person called Job (Ezek. 14: 14, 20), a blameless man from Uz (somewhere in north-west Arabia, connected either with Aram or Edom[16]), who is terribly tested by unexpected and unmerited suffering. This holy non-Israelite loses his wealth, posterity, and health, and becomes an outcast from society and despised by other outcasts (Job 30: 1–8). While remaining totally committed to God, he is torn between feelings of despair and faith. This dramatic book, which features Job's long discussions with three friends (3: 1–31: 40), reaches what looks like a later insertion, four discourses by Elihu the Buzite (32: 1–37: 24). Finally, the Lord speaks out of a whirlwind (one of the settings in the Bible for divine appearances), puts 'impossible' questions to Job, and draws him deeper into the divine mystery (38: 1–41: 34), until Job experiences an intimate communion with God: 'now my eye sees you' (42: 5).

In the dramatic testing of Job, a non-Israelite, God reveals himself in his cosmic power: he is the God who 'brings rain on a land where no one lives' (38: 26) and is not revealed here as the God of the exodus

[15] See J. L. Crenshaw, *Old Testament Wisdom: An Introduction* (London: SCM Press, 1982); D. E Morgan, *Wisdom in Old Testament Traditions* (Oxford: Blackwell, 1987); R. E. Murphy, 'Wisdom in the OT', *ABD* vi, 920–31; id., *The Tree of Life: An Exploration of Biblical Wisdom Literature*, 3rd edn. (New York: Doubleday, 2002). D. Penchansky, 'Wisdom', *Oxford Encyclopedia of Bible*, ii, 418–27.

[16] See E. A. Knauf, 'Uz', *ABD* vi, 770–1.

from Egypt (or of any other key episode in Israel's history). Yet this God of cosmic majesty discloses himself as personally involved in the life and destiny of human beings. God wants the obedience of human beings but respects their freedom, without which there could be no real obedience. Under a terrible testing, Job perseveres and the restoration of his life and family matches his integrity and discloses the divine generosity (42: 7–17).

In an awesome dialogue with Job, God is disclosed to him as both majestically transcendent and caringly close. God is revealed as mysteriously involved in the whole of creation (38: 1–40: 2), the maker and conserver of all things who eludes the imagination of Job. Yet this same God speaks to and cherishes the one whom he calls 'my servant Job' (42: 7–8).

The drama of the Book of Job, like that of Noah and his family, would be impossible without God's self-revelation to them. Noah lives before the special history of divine revelation to the chosen people begins with the call of Abraham and Sarah. Job lives at the time of the ongoing Jewish history but, as a non-Israelite, does not share in it. Both cases drive home the lesson: God reveals himself to 'predecessors' and 'outsiders': there is revelation before and outside the people of God ('*revelatio ante et extra populum Dei*'). The figures of Noah and Job challenge any small, closed version of where divine revelation and responding human faith can be found. Job deserves a place alongside Noah in the roll call of heroes and heroines who respond in faith to the revelation of God (see Heb. 11: 7).

The Old Testament understood Wisdom, along with Word and Spirit, to serve as personified agents of God's self-revelation and other activity. Not yet recognized as persons, they operated with personal characteristics, and this was particularly so in the case of Wisdom. Our interest here focuses on Wisdom.

Hokmah or wisdom and its Greek equivalent, *Sophia*, occur over three hundred times in the Old Testament. Nearly 75 per cent of these occurrences turn up in Job, Proverbs, wisdom Psalms,[17] Ecclesiastes (Qoheleth), Sirach, and Wisdom. Wise counsels are found elsewhere: for instance, Tobit 4: 3–21; 12: 6–13; and Baruch 3: 9–4: 4. Personified Wisdom or Sophia becomes increasingly related to the divine work of

[17] See D. Jacobsen, 'Wisdom Language in the Psalms', in W. P. Brown (ed.), *The Oxford Handbook of the Psalms* (Oxford: Oxford University Press, 2014), 147–57.

creation, revelation, and salvation, and this in relation not only to the chosen people of God but also to all peoples.

The Book of Job abruptly introduces Wisdom at the end of a long dialogue between Job and his friends—in a poem that scholars have variously called an interlude, a bridge, or a later insertion (28: 1–28). The poem stresses the mysterious inaccessibility of divine Wisdom (28: 12–14; 28: 23–7). Although many of the subsequent features of Wisdom do not show up in this poem from Job, one feature appears: her mysterious inaccessibility. Wisdom will be seen constantly as divine gift rather than primarily human achievement. The books of Proverbs, Sirach, and Wisdom may represent the availability of Sophia, who invites all to her feast, dwells in Jerusalem, and graciously presents herself to those who love her. Yet the initiative remains hers.

What the presence of that chapter in Job celebrating Wisdom signals is her role in the religious life of 'outsiders'. Some sapiential literature (e.g. Sirach) clearly emerges from the history of the Jewish people. The presence of Wisdom in the Book of Job, a long work concerned with a non-Israelite and his non-Israelite friends, demonstrates that the same divine Wisdom also illuminates their lives. Wisdom and her teaching are shared by the people of God *and* 'others'.

(2) Such sharing in revealed divine Wisdom also emerges from Proverbs, a book which consists of several collections of proverbs attributed to 'Solomon, son of David, king of Israel' (Prov. 1: 1).[18] One section proves particularly relevant for the theme of Wisdom and 'outsiders'. Most scholars agree, as we noted in Chapter 10, that Proverbs 22: 17–24: 34 depend in some way on an Egyptian sage, Amen-em-ope. Entitled 'The Words of the Wise' (Prov. 22: 17), this collection in Proverbs includes many parallels to the work of that famous sage. The 'others' not only receive Wisdom from God but can also prove a source of revealed Wisdom teaching for Israel itself.

(3) Among the earliest deuterocanonical books (see Chapter 11) and longest books of the Bible, Sirach contains the most extensive example of Jewish wisdom literature we have.[19] It was originally

[18] See R. J. Clifford, *Proverbs: A Commentary* (Louisville, Ky.: Westminster John Knox, 1999); B. K. Waltke, *The Book of Proverbs*, 2 vols. (Grand Rapids, Mich.: Eerdmans, 2004–5).

[19] See P. W. Skehan and A. Di Lella, *The Wisdom of Ben Sira* (New York: Doubleday, 1987).

written in Hebrew before 180 BC and two generations later translated into Greek. Around two-thirds of the original Hebrew text have now been recovered from finds in Cairo, Qumran, and Masada. Wisdom appears at the beginning of Sirach (1: 1–30), at the halfway mark (24: 1–34), and at the end (51: 1–27).

Two aspects of the presentation of Wisdom concern us: Wisdom is present 'in every people and nation' (Sir. 24: 6); yet by the divine choice she dwells in Israel and finds her home in Jerusalem (Sir. 24: 8–11). On the one hand, a universal presence does not preclude a special dwelling place for Wisdom being chosen by God. On the other hand, such a particular divine choice does *not* mean that Wisdom is absent elsewhere in the world and hence unavailable for the whole human race.

(4) Probably written shortly before the birth of Jesus and, in any case, the last of the Old Testament books, the Wisdom of Solomon yields much for the theme of God and 'the others'.[20] The second section from the first half of Wisdom describes how Sophia is to be found (Wisd. 6:1–11: 4). Although closely and remarkably identified with God, she makes herself accessible: 'One who rises early to seek her will have no difficulty, for she will be found sitting at the gate' (Wisd. 6: 14). Indeed, she herself 'goes about seeking those worthy of her, and she graciously appears to them in their paths, and meets them in every thought' (Wisd. 6: 16). The speaker, supposedly Solomon, addresses the Jewish community in an exhortation to seek Wisdom. Yet no restrictions are placed on the general accessibility of Wisdom (Wisd. 6: 1–25). She will come to all who are 'worthy of her'.

Being present everywhere and 'the fashioner of all things', Wisdom is not limited to Israel. 'All-powerful' and 'overseeing all', she 'penetrates all things', and 'penetrates through all spirits that are intelligent'. This vision of Wisdom closes by declaring: 'she reaches mightily from one end of the earth to the other and she orders all things well' (Wisd. 7: 22–8: 1).

Identified with the divine 'spirit', Wisdom proves to be a saving power for 'those on earth', a guide to God for all humanity: as one might say, she is the universal self-revelation of God that brings true, spiritual life. A prayer for the gift of wisdom says this to God: 'Who

[20] See H. Hübner, *Die Weisheit Salomons: Liber Sapientiae Salomonis* (Göttingen: Vandenhoeck & Ruprecht, 1999); C. Larcher, *Le Livre de la Sagesse ou la Sagesse de Salomon*, 3 vols. (Paris: Librairie Lecoffre, 1983–5).

has learned your counsel, unless you have given wisdom and sent your holy spirit from on high? And thus the paths of those on earth were set right, and people were taught what pleases you, and were saved by wisdom' (Wisd. 9: 17–18).

The involvement of Wisdom in the particular history of Israel (Wisd. 10: 15–18) does not exclude her role in the lives of all 'those on earth', human beings at large who can receive the light and saving power of Wisdom. She pervades all creation and the whole human story. Not surprisingly a list of seven stories (Wisd. 10: 1–11: 4) opens with two universal figures, Adam and Noah. Like Sirach, the Book of Wisdom respects both the universal revealing and saving function of Wisdom and her specific role in the history of Israel.

Before leaving the Old Testament, we need to face the question: to what extent could the Book of Wisdom encourage us to interpret world religions as being, at least in part, the fruit of the activity of Wisdom? Yet the long closing meditation on history (Wisd 11: 5–19: 22) dismisses the cult of the stars and of other beautiful things in nature (Wisd. 13: 1–9), indulges in strong polemic against the folly of worshipping idols (Wisd. 13: 10–19), and singles out for ridicule the folly of those who trust in a wooden image on the ship's prow when they put to sea (Wisd. 14: 1–14). Idolatry not only entails ignorance of God but also proves 'the beginning, cause, and end of every evil': a section on the bad results of idolatry spells out in detail this argument (Wisd. 14: 22–31). The writer contrasts the folly and wickedness of worshipping idols with the positive results of worshipping the true God: essentially, 'complete righteousness' here and now and 'immortality' to come (Wisd. 15: 1–17).

Thus, after some luminous chapters on the universal accessibility of Wisdom, the later chapters of the book pass a sombre judgement on what happens widely among non-Israelites: the worship of idols and the evil results of this. Nevertheless, a partial exception is made in the case of those who worship the forces of nature, the least culpable form of false worship (Wisd. 13: 1–9). Such idolatry can arise from an honest search for God: 'these people are little to be blamed, for perhaps they go astray while seeking God and desiring to find him' (Wisd. 13: 6–7). Even so, such a gentler judgement highlights the human search for God rather than the primary divine 'search' for human beings, which has been indicated by the universal activity of Lady Wisdom. Thus the teaching of the Book of Wisdom leaves us with some unresolved tension.

Nevertheless, the Book of Wisdom, we might argue, would not pass a negative judgement on (later) religions such as Islam, where idolatry is not the issue. A full length study of what that book brings to the study of world religions would need to raise this issue.

JESUS, PAUL, LUKE, AND HEBREWS

Moving to the New Testament, we can only sample the biblical witness that, while accepting Christ as the prime mediator of revelation and salvation (1 Tim. 2: 5), sheds light on the issue of the divine self-revelation reaching 'the others'. A full treatment would call for at least a book.[21] Let us look at some items: from the preaching of Jesus, the letters of Paul, the Book of Acts, and Hebrews.

(1) The Gospels record episodes in which Jesus responded to the needs of non-Jews, both specific individuals and groups. In Capernaum, for instance, a non-Jewish military officer appealed to Jesus for help when his son (or servant) fell desperately ill (Matt. 8: 5–13). Apparently the centurion knew that, as a Jew, Jesus should not enter the house of a Gentile. But (through some kind of divine revelation) he was convinced that a word of command would be enough, since diseases obeyed Jesus just as soldiers obeyed their officers. Jesus was astonished at the way the centurion trusted his (Jesus') power to work a cure: 'Truly I tell you, in no one in Israel have I found such faith'. The faith of this outsider put Israel to shame, in the sense that his faith went beyond anything Jesus had so far experienced in his ministry to Jews, those who enjoyed the special revelation of God given through Abraham and Moses.

We are left in the dark about the religious practice of the centurion,[22] and how God had become known to him. Whatever his state, Jesus did not invite him to join the ranks of the disciples, but healed the boy with a simple word of command. Before doing so, he

[21] It took me a book to deal, even then incompletely, with the biblical witness that sheds light on salvation 'for the others': *Salvation for All: God's Other Peoples* (Oxford: Oxford University Press, 2008).

[22] In Luke's version of the story, leaders of the Jewish community plead on behalf of the centurion: 'he loves our nation, and it is he who built our synagogue for us' (Luke 7: 1–10).

introduced the image of God's final banquet to warn what would happen at the end. Many 'outsiders' will enter the kingdom while many Israelites will be excluded: 'I tell you, many will come from the east and west and will eat with Abraham, Isaac, and Jacob in the kingdom of heaven, while the heirs of the kingdom will be thrown into the outer darkness'. This is a 'pointed threat rather than something irrevocable. It may well go back to Jesus.'[23] Ulrich Luz comments on how the faith of the centurion 'the first member of the gentile church',[24] signalled that the final gathering of the nations had already begun in the ministry of Jesus. Instead of streaming to Mount Zion and joining themselves to Jewish faith and life (as Third Isaiah and other prophets had foretold), the Gentiles will find the goal of their pilgrimage in 'the kingdom of heaven'.

We may be asking for too much precision from Matthew's Gospel and, ultimately, from what the historical Jesus said. But should we characterize the centurion as 'the first member of the gentile church'? He was not invited to become a disciple, and for the moment simply returned home. Did he continue to live by the knowledge of God that had already been given to him, like the Ninevites after their encounter with Jonah? What happened to the centurion historically may not have corresponded to what he could symbolize as 'the first member of the gentile church'.

(2) In his masterpiece, St Paul takes up the teaching of Wisdom 13: 1–9 about God being made known to human beings everywhere, even if they have widely failed to accept this revelation: 'What can be known about God is plain to them, because God has shown it to them. Ever since the creation of the world his eternal power and divine nature, invisible though they are, have been understood and seen through the things he has made' (Rom. 1: 19–20). We deal here with God's initiative in revealing himself ('God has shown it to them'), and not primarily with a human search for God. The apostle then spells out in detail the evil results that come from failing to accept this divine revelation (communicated through the created world) and lapsing into idolatry (Rom 1: 21–32). But then Paul acknowledges that, despite the terrible sins Gentiles commit, there are also morally sensitive and responsible Gentiles: 'when Gentiles who do not possess the law [of Moses], do by nature what the law

[23] U. Luz, *Matthew 8–20*, trans. J. E. Crouch (Minneapolis: Fortress, 2001), 9.
[24] Ibid. 11.

requires, these, though not having [received] the law, are their own law' (Rom. 2: 14). Their praiseworthy conduct prompts Paul to draw the conclusion: 'they show that what the law requires is written on their hearts, to which their own conscience bears witness'. These honourable Gentiles will not be condemned at God's final judgement, they will be justified by 'the law' which 'has been written on their hearts'—with 'heart' understood biblically as the personal centre that receives knowledge and revelation and is the seat of the emotions and the will (Rom. 2: 15).[25]

The language of Paul extends to the Gentiles some prophetic promises (Jer. 31: 33; Ezek. 11: 19–20; 36: 26–7) about the divine law and what it requires being written on the hearts of Israelites and enabling them to know, instinctively, what to do. The metaphor of writing implies a writer. In Romans 2, Paul presumably has in mind a divine 'Writer' as the One who writes on the hearts of Gentiles. We may unpack Paul's explicit statements and recognize the Holy Spirit at work within honourable Gentiles, writing the law on their hearts, supporting the 'witness of their conscience', and enabling them to practise the essential requirements of the divine law.

What Paul said about divine revelation being communicated universally through the created universe and the witness of conscience would be echoed many centuries later, as we saw in Chapter 5, by Immanuel Kant (1724–1804), who remarked that two things reveal God to human beings: '*the starry heavens above me and the moral law within me*'.[26] Two basic features of the universe, 'out there' in visible, created reality and 'in here' within the moral conscience of human beings, disclose something of God and the divine nature, character, and purposes.

In its Pastoral Constitution on the Church in the Modern World (*Gaudium et Spes*), the Second Vatican Council (1962–65) cited Romans 2: 15–16 when teaching that the voice of God is heard in the human conscience and that the eternal, natural law is written by God on human hearts (*GS* 16). This was to imply some form of divine self-revelation which reaches every human heart and every human being.

[25] See J. D. G. Dunn, *Romans 1–8* (Dallas: Word Books, 1988), 98–9; J. A. Fitzmyer, *Romans* (New York: Doubleday, 1993), 128–9, 305–12.

[26] I. Kant, *Critique of Practical Reason*, trans. M. J. Gregor, rev. edn. (Cambridge: Cambridge University Press, 2015), 129; emphasis his.

(3) Through Paul's sermon in Athens, Luke depicts the major Christian missionary in the second half of Acts confronting and being confronted by the Graeco-Roman culture for the first time (Acts 17: 16–34).[27] There is much in Paul's words that continues to touch the issue of revelation for those who have never heard of Christ or have not (yet) accepted the message about him. Let me mention just one point: the way in which the apostle engages the Athenians' desire for *knowledge* of God (Acts 17: 19–20), a basic human orientation to which divine revelation has responded. Anticipated by Plato (d. 347 BC) and Aristotle (d. 322 BC), many Christian thinkers, ancient and modern, have expressed this orientation. Thus Karl Rahner (1904–84) understood the human person to be dynamically open to the fullness of being. The human spirit is born with a primordial desire to know the Infinite One, who is disclosed in the universal as well as the special history of revelation.[28]

(4) Our final sampling of the New Testament turns to the Letter to the Hebrews and a classic passage on faith (11: 1–12: 2). On the one hand, Hebrews teaches that 'without faith it is impossible to please God' (Heb. 11: 6). This is tantamount to saying that 'without receiving in faith the divine revelation, it is impossible to please God'. (As we pointed out in Chapter 6 above, without human faith divine revelation does not occur, and vice versa: without divine revelation human faith is impossible.) On the other hand, Hebrews offers a generously 'open' version that fits the faith that can be embraced and lived by those who remain 'outside' the particular history of Judaism and Christianity: 'Faith is the assurance of things hoped for, the proof of things not seen. By this [faith] the elders [our ancestors who include Noah] received approval [from God]. By faith we understand that the universe was fashioned by the word of God, so that from what cannot be seen that which is seen has come into being' (Heb. 11: 1–3).[29] A further verse clarifies the notion of faith envisaged: 'whoever would

[27] See J. A. Fitzmyer, *The Acts of the Apostles* (New York: Doubleday, 1998), 599–617; and R. W. Wall, *The Acts of the Apostles*, in *The New Interpreter's Bible*, x (Nashville: Abingdon, 2002), 241–50.

[28] K. Rahner, *Foundations on Christian Faith*, trans. W. V. Dych (New York: Seabury Press, 1978), 51–71, 138–75, 311–21.

[29] On faith in Hebrews, see C. R. Koester, *Hebrews* (New York: Doubleday, 2003), 468–553; on applying to the 'others' what Hebrews says about faith, see O'Collins, 'The Faith of Others: A Biblical Possibility', *passim*.

approach him [God] must believe that he exists and that he rewards those who seek him' (Heb. 11: 6).

This description of faith involves a view of the past—understanding the world to have been 'fashioned by the word of God'. Faith also relies on the divine promise when considering the goal of the world (the things 'hoped for' and 'the rewards of those who seek him'). Both in their view of the past and hope for the future, the lives of those who have faith are entwined with the invisible God. As such, this account of faith makes no mention of Christ, who appears only later (Heb. 12: 2). The opening verses of Hebrews 11 offer examples of those who have lived on the basis of faith: some (Abel, Enoch, and Noah) who existed before Abraham, Sarah, and the formation of the chosen people. One figure of faith is 'Rahab the prostitute' (Heb. 11: 31), an outsider who belonged to the story of the conquest of the promised land. All in all, Hebrews 11 lets us glimpse the possibilities for those called to faith by divine revelation in the universal history of human kind.

In its Pastoral Constitution on the Church in the Modern World (*Gaudium et Spes*, *GS*), the Second Vatican Council could have cited Hebrews 11 (or, for that matter, Rom. 1: 19–20) but, in fact, cited the wisdom teaching of Sirach when it said: 'by the gift of the Holy Spirit and through faith, human beings come to contemplate and savour the mystery of the divine plan' in the visible works of creation (*GS* 15). This unqualified statement was tantamount to saying that, through the work of the Holy Spirit, all human beings can, in some real sense, receive the gift of faith.

JUSTIN, IRENAEUS, AND VATICAN II

In developing the Johannine theme of the pre-existent Logos as universal mediator of creation *and revelation*, St Justin Martyr (d. around AD 165) wrote of 'the seeds of the Word' that have been dropped everywhere and, at least to some extent, in every person (*Second Apology*, 8, 10, 13). He argued that, in one way or another, the whole human race shares in the Logos (*First Apology*, 46). Many people live only 'according to a fragment of the Logos'. Christians live 'according to the knowledge and contemplation of the whole Logos, who is Christ' (*Second Apology*, 8). This amounts to recognizing how, in one form or another, the divine revelation, through the Word of God, reaches everyone.

A younger contemporary of Justin, St Irenaeus of Lyons (d. around 200), maintained the universal role of the Word in the work of revelation: 'The Word of God, present with his handiwork from the beginning, reveals (*revelat*) the Father to all, to whom he wills, when he wills, and how the Father wills' (*Adversus Haereses*, 4. 6. 7). A little later Irenaeus added: 'Through the Word all his creatures learn that there is one God, the Father, who controls all things, and gives existence to all. . . . The Son makes the Father known from the beginning' (ibid. 4. 20. 6–7).

A fuller study of what the Fathers of the Church taught about revelation being, in some sense, available universally would include Clement of Alexandria, Origen, Athanasius, Augustine, and others. Some of their teaching was to be cited in the opening chapter of the Second Vatican Council's Decree on the Missionary Activity of the Church (*Ad Gentes*), a chapter drafted by Yves Congar. Vatican II, particularly through the Dogmatic Constitution on the Church (*Lumen Gentium, LG*) and the Declaration on the Church's Relation to Non-Christian Religions (*Nostra Aetate, NA*), recognized elements of revealed 'truth' accepted by the religious 'others'.

Specifically, *Nostra Aetate* followed the Fathers in valuing the prologue of John's Gospel on the Light that enlightens everyone (John 1: 4, 9). The declaration observes that 'the Catholic Church rejects nothing of those things which are *true* and *holy* in these [other] religions'. Rather, 'it is with sincere respect that she considers those ways of acting and living, those precepts and doctrines, which, although they differ in many [aspects] from what she herself holds and proposes, nevertheless, often reflect a ray of *that Truth* [upper case], *who illuminates all human beings*' (*NA* 2; italics mine; see *GS* 57). Here Vatican II respected the universal scope of John 1: 9, and the way revelation (light and truth) and, by association, salvation (life and holiness) reach all peoples.

Like Clement of Alexandria, whose reflections on the religious situation of 'the others' took him beyond generalities to some specific comments on Buddhism and Hinduism,[30] Vatican II went into some details about Judaism, Buddhism, Hinduism, and Islam with a view to having at least a platform for dialogue (*LG* 16; *NA* 2–4). But it did not consider the sacred literature of other religions. Many scholars have, of course, done so. Thus R. C. Zaehner put the question apropos of the

[30] See G. O'Collins, *The Second Vatican Council on Other Religions* (Oxford: Oxford University Press, 2013), 18–19.

Hindu *Bhagavad-Gitā*: 'In non-Christian theistic religions, how can anyone who accepts Christian revelation be certain [that] no revelation is captured in Krishna's declaration of "the unheard of secret of God's love for men"?'[31] W. M. Watt examined the Qur'an and judged it to be in some sense the result of a divine initiative and therefore revelation, or the word of God addressed by God to human beings.[32]

Here two closely related questions bulk large: did, first, the Word 'who illuminates all human beings' in some sense enlighten those responsible for composing the sacred scriptures of 'other' religions? Secondly, to what extent have these scriptures subsequently become the means of divine revelation for their readers and hearers? As Geoffrey Parrinder remarked, 'a book is the word of God in the abstract, but it becomes such a word when it reveals God to men at particular times and in different ways'.[33] Here Parrinder carefully avoided the kind of mistake made by many when they simply identify revelation with Scriptures they accept as inspired (see Chapter 10). Scriptures can and do become *means* for communicating the divine self-revelation, but as such are texts and not living events of revelation.

UNIVERSAL PRESENCE OF CHRIST AND HIS SPIRIT

To conclude, we return to Irenaeus (d. around 200) who acknowledged the universal presence not only of revelation (see the previous

[31] R. C. Zaehner, *At Sundry Times: An Essay in the Comparison of Religions* (London: Faber & Faber, 1958), 213.

[32] W. M. Watt, *Islamic Revelation in the Modern World* (Edinburgh: Edinburgh University Press, 1969). See also, A. J. Arberry, *The Koran Interpreted* (London: Allen & Unwin, 1955), and id., *Revelation and Reason in Islam* (London Allen & Unwin, 1957); G. D'Costa, 'Revelation and Revelations: Beyond a static valuation of other religions', *Modern Theology* 10 (1994), 164–84; J. Dupuis, *Christianity and the Religions: From Confrontation to Dialogue*, trans. P. Berryman (Maryknoll, NY: Orbis, 2002), 125–37; id., *Toward a Christian Theology of Religious Pluralism* (Maryknoll, NY: Orbis, 1997), 244–53; A. N. Moreland, 'The Qur'an and the Doctrine of Private Revelation: A Theological Proposal', *Theological Studies* 76 (2015), 531–49.

[33] G. Parrinder, 'Revelation in Christianity and Other Religions', in M. Dhavamony et al. (eds.), *Revelation in Christianity and Other Religions: Studia Missionalia* (Rome: Gregorian University Press, 1971), 101–13, at 107; see also I. Vempeny, *Inspiration in Non-biblical Scriptures* (Bangalore: Theological Publications in India, 1971).

section) but also of divine action for human salvation: 'the Word of the all-powerful God . . . on the invisible plane is co-extensive with the whole of creation', 'rules the universe', and as the Son of God 'has traced the sign of the cross on everything' (*Demonstratio*, 34). A little later Origen (d. around 254) also underlined this universal presence: 'Christ is so powerful that, although invisible because of his divinity, he is *present to every person* and extends over the universe' (*In Ioannem*, 6. 15; italics mine). This was not to deny that Christ was present in a special, fuller way in the lives of the baptized. But that fuller presence did not mean an absence elsewhere.

A proper treatment of the divine self-revelation that is offered to all human beings would entail exploring at length the universal presence of Christ and his Spirit. Here one should not so emphasize Christ as to bypass the revealing (and life-giving) power of the Spirit, or vice versa. There is no revelation outside Christ *and* the Spirit ('*nulla revelatio extra Christum et Spiritum*'). But one should add at once: Christ and his Spirit are present everywhere and to everyone.[34] Despite all the historical, cultural, and religious differences in the world, Christ's revelation and salvation do reach everyone. 'Other' religions can, to a greater or lesser extent, prove revelatory and, therefore, means of salvation. This effect depends always on the work of Christ and his Spirit.

[34] See O'Collins, *Salvation for All*, 207–47.

Epilogue

This book has aimed in twelve chapters to clarify the major characteristics of the divine self-revelation that attained its decisive highpoint with Jesus Christ. I hope it has proved sufficiently Christological, Pneumatological, and Trinitarian and done justice to faith in Jesus Christ, the Holy Spirit, and God the Father. It set itself to account satisfactorily for the saving revelation that, through the missions of the Son and the Spirit, will bring the final return to God of humanity and the world.

One could press on and raise further issues. Should the book have also aimed to illuminate much more fully God's self-revelation in the functioning of the Christian Church, her sacramental life, and service of the world? How much light has it shone on the spiritual state of those who follow 'other' faiths or none at all?

Furthermore, some secular critics, alarmed by the violent irrationality of religious fundamentalists, charge commitment to revelation with suffocating the life of reason and even worse. Should this book have put the case that faith in genuine divine revelation nourishes and expands the life of reason, as well as respecting human dignity, rights, and responsibilities?

I finish this book recognizing the value of these and further such questions, and also more convinced than ever that 'outside Christ and the Spirit there is no saving revelation (*extra Christum et Spiritum nulla revelatio salvifica*)'. To that statement one must always add at once: no one and no created reality is 'outside' Christ and the Spirit. Inseparably they form a universal, revealing, and saving presence.

APPENDIX

The Inspiring Power of Scripture

When interpreting biblical inspiration, some scholars, as well as acknowledging its role for the biblical authors themselves, hold that the charism of inspiration *also* includes an inspiring impact on those who read or hear Sacred Scripture.[1] What might such a *theory* of biblical inspiration look like in *practice*?

In the case of St Antony of Egypt (d. 356), St Augustine of Hippo (d. 430), and Girolamo Savonarola (d. 1498), specific biblical texts 'inspired' dramatic changes in their lives. St Athanasius of Alexandria (d. 373) recorded the occasion when Matthew 19: 21 turned around the existence of Antony and led him to found the eremitic monasticism of solitary hermits.[2] Augustine and Savonarola left their own accounts of how Romans 13: 13–14 and Genesis 12: 1, respectively, influenced the course of their lives. Without being the founder of collective or cenobitic monasticism—for which St Pachomius (d. 346) takes the credit—Augustine and St Benedict (d. around 550) promoted it widely in Western Christianity. Savonarola's heroic attempt to reform the Catholic Church in the heartland of Italy was brutally terminated by his execution. Let us glean the ways in which scriptural texts shaped the story of these three figures.[3]

Antony of Egypt

Born into a wealthy family, Antony was about nineteen years of age when his parents died and left him to care for his younger sister. Less than six months later, on the way to church he recalled how the apostles gave up everything

[1] See H. Gabel, *Inspiriert und Inspirierend: Die Bibel* (Würzburg: Echter Verlag, 2011); U. H. J. Körtner, *Der inspirierter Leser. Zentrale Aspekte biblischer Hermeneutik* (Göttingen: Vandenhoeck & Ruprecht, 1994).

[2] Athanasius of Alexandria, *The Life of Antony: The Coptic Life and the Greek Life*, trans. T. Vivian and A. N. Athanassakis (Kalamazoo, Mich.: Cistercian Publications, 2003). The traditional attribution to Athanasius of this life of Antony should be accepted; see D. M. Gwynn, *Athanasius of Alexandria: Bishop, Theologian, Ascetic, Father* (Oxford: Oxford University Press, 2012), 15.

[3] For the basic data and bibliographies, see F. L. Cross and E. A. Livingstone (eds.), *The Oxford Dictionary of the Christian Church*, 3rd edn. rev. (Oxford: Oxford University Press, 2005), 81 (St Antony), 129–32 (St Augustine), and Savonarola (1468–9).

and followed Jesus (see Matt. 4: 20; 19: 27) and how early Christians sold their possessions and laid the proceeds at the feet of the apostles for distribution to the needy (see Acts 4: 34–5). When he arrived and went into church, the Gospel was being read and he heard the Lord saying to the rich man: 'If you want to be perfect, go, sell all your possessions and give them to the poor, and come follow me, and you will have treasure in heaven' (Matt. 19: 21). Antony took to heart that passage, realizing how 'it had been read for his sake'. He distributed to people of his village the three hundred 'fertile and very prosperous acres' he had inherited. Then, by selling his possessions, he raised much money and distributed it among the poor, keeping only a little for the needs of his sister.

A second text from Matthew touched Antony when he returned to the church and heard the Lord saying in the Gospel: 'Do not be concerned about tomorrow' (Matt. 6: 34). Antony then distributed anything he still owned to the poor, and began an ascetical life close to his own village. First he sought the guidance of an old hermit who lived in a neighbouring village. Whenever he heard of anyone else practising serious asceticism elsewhere, he would go like 'the wise honey bee' (see Prov. 6: 8) to meet and learn from that person. Since the New Testament disapproved of lazy people (2 Thess. 3: 10), he worked with his hands, spent part of what he earned for his own food, and gave the rest to those in need. Obeying strictly another New Testament injunction, he prayed without ceasing (1 Thess. 5: 17). He followed so closely what was read in church that nothing in the Scriptures escaped his attention; his memory became a kind of biblical library. Eventually he was led to initiate a new form of asceticism: life in the distant desert.

For the details of Antony's life, we rely almost entirely on what Athanasius wrote. His *Life of Antony* presented someone who was both a model of ascetic life and a champion of orthodox faith against the inroads of Arian heresy. Accepting these reservations, what can we say about the impact of Matthew 19: 21 on the spiritual journey of Antony?

First of all, in the history of Christianity Antony became the first person to practise literally the invitation of Matthew 19: 21. Other Christians were to do so later. But Antony led the way in divesting himself of his wealth and giving it to the poor and needy. In summarizing the history of interpretation of this verse, Ulrich Luz recalls Antony as someone who completely rejected possessions but fails to mention that he was the first known case of someone accepting Jesus' radical invitation.[4] When Antony sensed that Matthew 19: 21 had been 'read for his sake' and let the verse inspire his immediate action, he broke new ground in the 'practical' interpretation of the Scriptures.

[4] U. Luz, *Matthew 8–20*, trans. J. E. Crouch (Minneapolis: Augsburg Fortress, 2001), 518–23, at 519.

Secondly, Antony was around nineteen years of age when this verse decisively influenced him. To judge from *The Life of Antony*, he had enjoyed a devout, sheltered upbringing and proved himself a 'good', undemanding, and not very intellectual son.[5] All this set him apart from his fellow African, Augustine.

Thirdly, unlike Augustine, from his youth Antony 'listened attentively to the readings from the Scripture, and kept in his heart what was profitable from them'.[6] Making his way to church on the day when Matthew 19: 21 made its demanding claim on him, he was already mulling over other New Testament passages concerned with divesting oneself of possessions. The lifelong biblical orientation of the young Antony set him apart from Augustine. In his first contacts with the Scriptures, Augustine found them barbarous in comparison with the works of classical culture (*Confessions*, 3. 5).

Fourthly, in mediating the dramatic call to Antony, Matthew 19: 21 did not stand alone. As we saw above, hearing on another day in church another text, Matthew 6: 34, clinched matters by prompting Antony into totally divesting himself of worldly goods. After setting himself to pursue a thoroughly ascetical life, Antony, as we also saw, drew guidance from two of Paul's letters. He continued to take to heart the Scriptures he heard read in church, until, as Athanasius expressed it, his memory became a biblical library. Matthew 19: 21 provided the peak, inspiring experience in Antony's story. But right from his youth the Scriptures had nourished his existence, and continued to do so in fresh and lasting ways.

Fifthly, a church setting provided the context in which one and then another text from Matthew's Gospel affected Antony. He did not read these texts at home, but heard them proclaimed in church.

Sixthly, the text from Matthew inspired Antony to divest himself of all his possessions. In and through his poverty and prayer, he became a rich blessing to his own village and later to many more people—not least to those who followed him by embracing a monastic existence.[7] As David Gwynn says, Antony 'engaged with the world around him', and his 'pastoral achievements' proved 'greater than those of many bishops and represented Athanasius' ideal model, inspiring through spiritual leadership those who could not reach the same degree of perfection'.[8] By the time he died in 356, Antony's influence already reached as far as Spain and Gaul. Written after his death, *The Life of Antony* was translated into Latin. In 386 it would affect Augustine when he stayed in Milan, becoming a key element in his conversion.[9]

[5] *Life*, 56–7. [6] Ibid. 57. [7] *Life*, 65, 91–5.
[8] Gwynn, *Athanasius of Alexandria*, 119. [9] Ibid. 130.

Augustine of Hippo

Augustine had almost turned thirty-two when two verses from Paul helped change his life and opened the way for his being baptized by St Ambrose of Milan. On the very day that Augustine was deeply affected by Romans 13: 13–14, the *Life of Antony* prepared him for that experience. A fellow African, Ponticianus, visited the house in Milan where Augustine was staying and told him about the holy life of Antony, the miracles he had worked, and his continuing impact in attracting Christians to an ascetic and monastic life (*Confessions*, 8. 6–8).

After Ponticianus left, Augustine went out into the garden attached to his residence. His *Confessions* describe the tumult of memories, questions, and emotions that welled up inside him. He was weeping his heart out when he heard the voice of a child coming from a nearby house and repeating over and over again 'take and read'. Recalling what he had heard earlier that day about the 'revelation' which came to Antony' by hearing Matthew 19: 21, Augustine hurried to the place where he had left a copy of Paul's letters, opened it, and read in silence the first passage his eye fell upon: '[let us live honourably as in the day], not in revelling and drunkenness, not in debauchery and licentiousness, not in quarrelling and jealousy. Instead, put on the Lord Jesus Christ, and make no provision for the flesh, to gratify its desires' (Rom. 13: 13–14). As soon as Augustine had read these words, 'all the darknesses of doubt were dispersed, as if by a light of peace flooding' into his heart. Augustine went inside and told his mother Monica what had happened. For years she had prayed for her wayward son, and now she blessed God, 'who can accomplish far more than we ask or understand' (Eph. 3: 20) (*Confessions*, 8. 8–12).[10]

As Augustine told the story of his conversion, Antony played a significant part in what happened and, not least, through Augustine's expectation that some biblical passage might solve his problems and bring him peace. Yet the two stories differ markedly. (1) Antony was about nineteen and already baptized, when he reacted generously to a verse from Matthew. Augustine was more than ten years older and not yet baptized, when two verses from Romans opened the way to a new future. (2) Unlike Antony who grew up with the Scriptures, Augustine did not accept them easily. Earlier in life he had dismissed the Christian Bible as unworthy of comparison with Cicero and other classical authors (*Confessions*, 3. 5).[11] (3) In terms of a cultured education and public standing as a scholar, he stood apart from Antony who

[10] For more detail about the conversion of Augustine, see P. Brown, *Augustine in Hippo: A Biography*, new edn. (Berkeley and Los Angeles: University of California Press, 2000), 69–107.

[11] Debates between Manichees and Elpidius, an otherwise unknown Christian, helped open Augustine up to the Scriptures (*Confessions*, 5. 11).

was brought up in a sheltered fashion at home. (4) The decisive moment came for Antony when both his parents had died and he heard a passage from Matthew read in church. In the case of Augustine, his mother was still very much alive and shared immediately in his moment of conversion. That change came, not in church and hearing a Gospel proclaimed, but in a garden where he heard a child's voice directing him to read.

Perhaps the most startling difference (5) concerns the way in which Augustine described his struggle with fleshly desires and worldly aspirations. Abruptly two verses from Paul dispelled the darkness and gave Augustine instant peace. We find nothing like that in *The Life of Antony*, which remains silent about his spiritual and psychological state when he heard the words from Matthew that transformed his life. *The Life of Antony* describes at length something similar but it came later: the spiritual struggles when he was assaulted by demonic powers.[12]

It is Augustine himself who tells the story of how his life was transformed by reading a passage from Paul. Interestingly, in a letter (*Epistola*, 55. 37), written around 400 and so shortly after writing the *Confessions*, Augustine disapproves of seeking guidance for worldly affairs by consulting the Gospels at random.[13] Of course, what motivated the random consultation of Paul's epistles that confronted him with Romans 13: 13–14 was the desire to be liberated from a spiritual crisis and not a desire to be guided in some worldly affair.

One curious 'omission' brings Antony and Augustine together. *The Life of Antony* quotes or, much more often, echoes passages from the Old and New Testament. But the key verse that triggered the revolutionary change in the saint's life, Matthew 19: 21, appears (as a quotation) only once, when in church he heard it 'read for his sake'.[14] Since this verse enjoyed such a deep impact, one might have expected it to recur, even frequently, in the story that followed. But it is acknowledged only as the point of departure for a life that shaped eremitic monasticism. When Antony was around nineteen years of age, the text did its job and that was it.

In the case of Augustine, one might have expected him to return to Romans and the specific passage that had brought him light and peace. Instead, his major biblical commentaries and sermons took up Genesis, the Psalms, the Gospel of John, and the other Gospels. He composed two minor works on Romans: *Expositio Quarumdam Propositionum ex Epistola*

[12] *Life*, 64–91; see also 106–51, 168–71, 190–3.

[13] In this letter to Januarius, a Catholic layman, Augustine wrote: 'As for those who read their fortunes in the pages of the gospels, though it is preferable that they do this rather than run to consult the demons, I still do not like the custom of wanting to use for worldly affairs and for the vanity of this life the words of God that speak of the next life'; *Letters 1–99*, II/1, trans R. Teske (Hyde Park, NY: New City Press, 2001), 235.

[14] See the scripture index in *Life*, 273–9.

ad Romanos (which made only a passing mention of Romans 13: 14) and *Epistolae ad Romanos Inchoata Expositio* (which referred neither to Rom. 13: 13 nor to 13: 14).[15] The sermons of Augustine mentioned incidentally Romans 13: 13–14: for instance, sermons on Christmas Day, Easter Sunday, and at the start of Lent. But he did not dwell on these verses, let alone connect them with his personal history.[16] Nor did he do that, when he made a passing reference to these verses in two other sermons.[17]

After a passage from Matthew inspired a new existence for Antony, he left behind only seven letters, increasingly acknowledged as authentic.[18] Augustine left behind not only his *Confessions* and numerous writings (e.g. his letters) that give us historical access to his story but also a huge legacy of theological and biblical works. Both of them lived on for many years, Antony as a hermit until his death in 356 and Augustine as a priest (from 391) and bishop (from 395) until his death in 430. Their long lives stand in tragic contrast with Savonarola who was not yet fifty when a brutal martyrdom ended his life.

Girolamo Savonarola

Born in Ferrara in 1452, Savonarola grew up shaped, both intellectually and spiritually, by his grandfather.[19] By the age of eighteen he had memorized the entire Bible. He had also become disgusted with the decadence of morals and religious practice in Italy. He was on holiday in Faenza on 1 May 1474 when he entered the church of San Agostino. An Augustinian friar was preaching, but it was a word from God (to Abraham) that suddenly struck Savonarola: 'go forth from your country and your kindred and your father's house (*egredere de terra tua*)' (Gen. 12: 1). The call of '*egredere de terra tua*' gave him no rest: 'he heard it everywhere; it cast its shadow over family affections; it woke him from his sleep. The conflict within him raged, but only for a short time. Before a year had passed, the young man, his mind finally made up by a dream, set out to follow his call.'[20] Without saying anything to his

[15] In PL 35, these works run to col. 2063–88 and 2087–2106, respectively; the reference to Rom. 13: 14 comes at col. 2085.

[16] See *Sermons* III/6 (184–229Z) on the Liturgical Season, 190. 1; 205. 1; and 229B. 1; trans. E. Hill (Hyde Park, NY: New City Press, 1993), 38, 104, and 273.

[17] See *Sermons* III/2 (20–50), 49. 3, trans. E. Hill (Hyde Park, NY: New City Press, 1990), 335; and *Sermons* III/8 (273–305A), 293A. 6 (on the birth of John the Baptist), trans. E. Hill (Hyde Park, NY: New City Press,1994), 162.

[18] See Gwynn, *Athanasius of Alexandria*, 107–8.

[19] For further biographical details, see R. Ridolfi, *The Life of Girolamo Savonarola*, trans. C. Grayson (London: Routledge and Kegan Paul, 1959), 1–12. I wish to thank Fr Robert Ombres, O.P., for drawing my attention to the story of Savonarola.

[20] Ibid. 7.

parents, on 24 April 1475 he slipped out of Ferrara and walked to Bologna where he joined the Dominicans.

We can compare and contrast Antony, Augustine, and Savonarola. Like Antony, Savonarola was changed by a biblical passage that, seemingly by accident, he heard in church. Unlike Antony and Augustine, the scriptural verse that inspired Savonarola's change of life not only took time to produce its impact but also remained with him for ever. In several sermons preached late in his life, he referred to the way in which in a church in Faenza he heard the verse from Genesis that came to haunt and change him.[21]

Unlike Augustine, who was struggling with his secular ambitions and sex drives when two verses of Romans brought him light and peace, Savonarola's turmoil was prompted by the dreadful state of the society and church around him. Like Augustine, Savonarola became a powerful preacher, albeit one who practised an apocalyptic style that prophesied impending divine punishment and drew on special revelations which he claimed to receive.

Unlike Antony and Augustine, Savonarola came into lethal conflict with civil authorities (in Florence) and with the scandalously corrupt Bishop of Rome (Alexander VI). He was not yet fifty when he was hanged and burned. Some honour him as a prophet and martyr; others dismiss him as fanatical and misguided.

Conclusions

The biblical texts from Genesis, Matthew, and Romans that changed Savonarola, Antony, and Augustine, respectively, did so because they provided not some merely speculative insight but a source for radical action. All three were ready to let the Scriptures come home to them in ways that led them at once (Antony and Augustine) or within a year (Savanorola) to surrender possessions (Antony), plans for his personal and professional future (Augustine), and life at home with his parents (Savonarola), and to embrace a new way of life as a hermit (Antony), as a baptized Christian and within ten years a bishop (Augustine), and as a Dominican teacher and preacher (Savonarola).

In two of the cases (Augustine and Savonarola) we know how powerful emotions made them 'hearers of the word'. Painful and confused feelings over his past conduct and future course of action were disturbing Augustine

[21] In a sermon preached on 21 December 1494, for instance, he quotes the verse from Genesis 12. 1 and refers to its impact on him: *Prediche sopra Aggeo*, Luigi Firpo (ed.) (Rome: Belardetti, 1965), 324. In a sermon preached on 28 February 1497, he refers to what happened in the church of Faenza but without quoting the words of Genesis; *Prediche sopra Ezechiele*, vol. 1, Roberto Ridolfi (ed.) (Rome: Belardetti, 1955), 374.

when enlightenment and peace suddenly came from two verses in Romans. Disgust and anger at the dismal religious state of church and society provided the matrix in which Savonarola heard the words of Genesis, 'go forth from your country'. In the case of Antony, the death of both his parents might have fashioned the mood in which Matthew 19: 21 led him to divest himself of his home and all his possessions.

This appendix has illustrated the inspiring influence of Scripture on three great figures from the history of Christianity. Antony, Augustine, and Savonarola write large what happens in the lives of innumerable others: the charism of inspiration affects the readers and hearers, as well as the writers, of biblical texts. Detailed surveys would, I am sure, confirm that conviction, as well as showing the richly diverse ways in which the inspired Scriptures change the lives of those who attentively hear and read them.

[This appendix originally appeared as 'The Inspiring Power of Scripture: Three Case Studies', *Irish Theological Quarterly* 79 (2014), 265–73. It is reprinted with permission.]

Select Bibliography

Abraham, W. J., *Crossing the Threshold of Divine Revelation* (Grand Rapids, MI: Eerdmans, 2006).

Avis, P. D. L. (ed.), *Revelation* (London: Darton, Longman and Todd, 1997).

Brown, D., *Tradition and Imagination: Revelation and Change* (Oxford: Clarendon, 1999).

Bultmann, R., 'The Concept of Revelation in the New Testament', *Existence and Faith*, trans. S. M. Ogden (London: Hodder and Stoughton, 1961), 58–91.

Caldwell, P., *Liturgy as Revelation* (Minneapolis: Fortress, 2014).

Dale, P., *The Rhetoric of Revelation in the Hebrew Bible* (Minneapolis: Augsburg Fortress, 1999).

Dalferth, I. U. and Rodgers, M. Ch. (eds.), *Revelation: Claremont Studies in the Philosophy of Religion. Conference 2012* (Tübingen: Mohr Siebeck, 2014).

Donovan, D., 'Faith and Revelation', in D. Marmion and M. F. Himes (eds.), *The Cambridge Companion to Karl Rahner* (Cambridge: Cambridge University Press, 2003), 83–99.

Dulles, A., *Models of Revelation* (New York: Doubleday, 1983).

Grey, M., *The Wisdom of Fools: Seeking Revelation for Today* (London: SPCK, 1993).

Haught, J. F., *Mystery and Promise: A Theology of Revelation* (Collegeville, MN: Liturgical Press, 1993).

Hoping, H., 'Theologischer Kommentar zur dogmatischen Konstitution über die göttlichen Offenbarung', in P. Hünermann and B. J. Hilberath (eds.), *Herders Theologischer Kommentar zum Zweiten Vatikanischen Konzil*, iii (Freiburg im Breisgau: Herder, 2005), 695–831.

Lacoste, J.-Y., 'Revelation', in Lacoste (ed.), *Encyclopedia of Christian Theology*, iii (New York: Routledge, 2004), 1383–91.

Latourelle, R. and Fisichella, R. (eds.), *Dictionary of Fundamental Theology* (New York: Crossroad, 1994).

Levering, M., *Engaging the Doctrine of Revelation: The Mediation of the Gospel through Church and Scripture* (Grand Rapids, MI: Baker Academic, 2014).

Mavrodes, G., *Revelation in Religious Belief* (Philadelphia: Temple University Press, 1988).

Menssen, S. L. and Sullivan, T. D., *The Agnostic Inquirer: Revelation from a Philosophical Standpoint* (Grand Rapids, MI: Eerdmans, 2007).

Niebuhr, H. R., *The Meaning of Revelation* (New York: Macmillan, 1941).
O'Collins, G., *Rethinking Fundamental Theology* (Oxford: Oxford University Press, 2011).
O'Collins, G., *The Second Vatican Council on Other Religions* (Oxford: Oxford University Press, 2013).
O'Collins, G., 'The Faith of Others: A Biblical Possibility', *Irish Theological Quarterly* 80 (2015), 313–26.
O'Collins, G., 'The Theology of Religions Revisited', *Pacifica* 28 (2015), 54–67.
Pannenberg, W., 'The Revelation of God', in *Systematic Theology*, trans. G. W. Bromiley, i (Grand Rapids, MI: Eerdmans, 1991), 189–257.
Quash, B., 'Revelation', in J. Webster, K. Tanner, and I. Torrance (eds.), *The Oxford Handbook of Systematic Theology* (Oxford: Oxford University Press, 2007), 325–44.
Rahner, K., *Foundations of Christian Faith: An Introduction to the Idea of Christianity*, trans. W. V. Dych (New York: Seabury Press, 1978).
Rahner, K. and Ratzinger, J., *Revelation and Tradition*, trans. W. J. O'Hara (London: Burns & Oates, 1966).
Ratzinger, J., 'Dogmatic Constitution on Divine Revelation', trans. W. Glen-Doepel, in H. Vorgrimler (ed.), *Commentary on the Documents of Vatican II*, iii (London: Burns & Oates, 1969), 155–98.
Ricoeur, P., 'Toward a Hermeneutic of the Idea of Revelation', *Harvard Theological Review* 70 (1977), 1–37.
Swinburne, R., *Revelation: From Analogy to Metaphor*, 2nd edn. (Oxford: Oxford University Press, 2007).
Tillich, P., *Systematic Theology*, i (Chicago: University of Chicago Press, 1951).
Wahlberg, M., *Revelation as Testimony: A Philosophical-Theological Study* (Grand Rapids, Mich.: Eerdmans, 2015).
Ward, K., *Religion and Revelation: A Theology of Revelation in the World's Religions* (Oxford: Clarendon Press, 1994).
Wiesner, G. et al., 'Offenbarung', *TRE* xxv, 109–210.
Wolterstorff, N., *Divine Discourse: Philosophical Reflections on the Claim that God Speaks* (Cambridge: Cambridge University Press, 1995).

Index of Names

Biblical Index